BLOOD BROTHERS

Michael Weisskopf

BLOOD BROTHERS

Among the Soldiers of Ward 57

HENRY HOLT AND COMPANY ★ New York

Henry Holt and Company, LLC
Publishers since 1866
175 Fifth Avenue
New York, New York 10010
www.henryholt.com

Henry Holt® and are registered trademarks of
Henry Holt and Company, LLC.

Library of Congress Cataloging-in-Publication Data

Weisskopf, Michael.
Blood brothers : among the soldiers of Ward 57 / Michael Weisskopf.
    p.   cm.
ISBN-13: 978-0-8050-7860-2
ISBN-10: 0-8050-7860-6
    1. Iraq War, 2003– —Personal narratives, American.   2. Weisskopf,
Michael.   3. Embedded war correspondents—Wounds and injuries—
United States.   4. Walter Reed Army Hospital (Washington, D.C.).
I. Title.
DS79.76.W45   2006
956.7044'3092—dc22
[B]   2006043382

Henry Holt books are available for special promotions and premiums.
For details contact: Director, Special Markets.

First Edition 2006

Designed by Meryl Sussman Levavi
Printed in the United States of America
1 2 3 4 5 6 7 8 9 10

For Rebekah

Some of them died.
Some of them were not allowed to.

—"Elegy" by Bruce Weigl

CONTENTS

BLOOD BROTHERS

PROLOGUE

The National Cemetery was cast in an amber light, as lonely as an old battlefield on this rainy Memorial Day morning. We walked down a narrow path, stopping at a simple headstone. My pal Pete fixed his gaze on the date of death, etched in black. His eyes closed for several minutes, then opened as he bent down and reached with his silver hook for four little American flags strewn on the ground. Pete carefully picked up each one and replanted it at the foot of the grave.

We were an odd couple of mourners, Pete and I, with just a single hand between us to dab the tears. The Iraq war had taken the other three, still leaving us better off than the nineteen-year-old buried beneath our feet in the red earth of Mobile, Alabama.

A young soldier and a weathered journalist, we certainly had our own wounds to lick, but we had lived. Living exacted a daily price in pain and angst, the dull ache of knowing how a few seconds or inches created the difference between us and the young man in the ground. Pete Damon was a thirty-one-year-old National Guard sergeant, fixing helicopters in Balad, Iraq, when a tire exploded in October 2003 and took his arms. In December 2003, I was riding through Baghdad as an embedded reporter in an army Humvee when a grenade landed, blew up, and tore off my right hand.

As Pete plunged the four flags into the wet ground, I thought of another pair of combat amputees, both living within a thousand-mile arc of Mobile. They too were spending this Memorial Day mourning comrades who fell in the killing fields of Iraq. The flags that Pete righted struck me as powerful symbols of survival, one for him, one for me, and one for each of the others.

★

In the little town of Asheboro, North Carolina, Corporal Bobby Isaacs hobbled onto the pulpit of the Bailey's Grove Baptist Church. Nearly eighteen months earlier, he'd been given up for dead after a roadside bomb exploded during his patrol in the northern Iraq city of Mosul. The fundamentalist congregation had invited Bobby to a special Memorial Day service that Sunday to give testimony on the loss of his two legs. But he focused instead on a higher cost of the December

2003 blast: the death of his squad leader, who had been sitting in the passenger seat of the Humvee.

"I was standing behind him," Bobby said, in a soft Carolina drawl. "If I'd been sitting, it would have killed me, too."

He stood uneasily on a pair of artificial legs, a departure from the wheelchair he usually got around in. No way he'd let a little pain keep him from honoring his squad leader's sacrifice. A patriotic southerner from a religious home, Bobby had found an ideal blend of duty and adventure in the army. Now, at twenty-four, the same age his buddy was when he died, he had literally to regain his footing. Bobby knew he had gotten the better end of the deal and wore a black metal bracelet to remind him of it. The dead man's name was engraved on it in silver.

★

Five hundred miles due west, Master Sergeant Luis Rodriguez brought his own Memorial Day presentation to church in Clarksville, Tennessee. He had downloaded from the Internet photos of soldiers at nearby Fort Campbell who had been killed in Iraq and burned them onto a CD. The thirty-five-year-old medic had come close to having his own picture displayed at a commemorative event like this one when his right leg was blown off in Mosul by a remote-controlled bomb in November 2003.

Rodriguez studied the photos projected on a large screen in the front of the chapel. He kept his composure until the pictures of men he recognized appeared. Then he rose from his seat and strode to the back of the room, taking wide swings with his prosthetic leg. He stood in the dark, covered his face, and wept.

★

The three soldiers had very different backgrounds, but I was the oddest of the lot—a fifty-eight-year-old Washington reporter who hated guns, scrutinized authority for a living, and avoided the draft during the Vietnam War. Yet fate had erased our differences. Over a fifty-day period in late 2003, all of us were seriously wounded in Iraq and sent to a place the world came to know as Amputee Alley: Ward 57 of Walter Reed Army Medical Center in Washington, D.C. No rank was recognized on the alley—not social class, wealth, age, religion, or race. We were all just gimps, fighting pain and fear.

For the public, the long corridor of our darkest days assumed an iconic status. Few news stories on the wounded missed Ward 57. Doonesbury moved in. So did politicians on the prowl for a sound bite. It became a Rorschach test of public opinion—to supporters of the war, the young amputees represented the price of freedom; to critics, they were the sacrificial lambs of misguided policy.

For me, Ward 57 was life at its lowest ebb. But it was also a place of renewal, a refuge where my three friends and I picked up what remained of our lives, never forgetting the alternative.

I.
TOY SOLDIER

The army convoy rattled through Al-Adhamiya like a carnival roller coaster, each turn as blind as the next. Not that the soldiers could see much anyway. Night had fallen on the old Baghdad quarter, a byzantine maze lit only by kerosene lamps flickering from rugged stone houses. We moved warily in the darkness, patrolling for insurgents in blind alleys custom-made for ambushes and narrow passages perfect for concealing roadside bombs. Only the piercing wail of a minaret's call to prayer broke the silence. It was anyone's bet who faced a more dire risk, the hunted in terrorist cells or the hunters in Humvees, along with whom I was riding under a half moon this December 10, 2003.

I was in Iraq to profile the American soldier as "Person of

the Year" for *Time* magazine. It was a dream assignment, a chance to escape Washington and work in exotic environs on a big story. I had teamed up with another reporter, Romesh Ratnesar, and set out three weeks earlier to find a unit representative of the 120,000 U.S. troops then in Iraq. We had chosen a platoon of the First Armored Division that operated in a district of northwest Baghdad considered crucial to any hope of securing Iraq. Al-Adhamiya was nestled in a bend of the Tigris River, a historic crossroads for the Sunni Muslims who dominated political life in the days of Saddam Hussein. Sunnis actively fueled the anti-U.S. resistance after he fled: insurgents launched rockets from its alleyways, hid weapons in houses, and seeded the roads with booby-trapped bombs concealed in everything from trash to dead cats.

The platoon's commander had been killed by a roadside device in late October. I was reminded of his death every time I strapped on body armor—a sixteen-pound Kevlar vest with super-hard ceramic inserts—as I did this chilly night before climbing into the cab of one of three Humvees lined up for the patrol. The sergeant had a different plan. "No, you're going in the high-back," he said, directing me to an open-air vehicle usually used to transport equipment or troops. "Okay, let's go out there and be targets," he barked as our convoy pulled out for the 8 P.M. patrol.

The soldiers played a daring game of chicken, cruising the streets to draw fire and lure resisters. But tonight there seemed to be no takers. We emerged an hour later into Al-Adhamiya's main marketplace, a large treeless square that was host to what looked like a block party in full swing. Old men, rocking back and forth on tiny stools, shuffled dominoes. Boys volleyed soccer balls. Women veiled in black fed their children from stalls of roasted chickens and shashlik. No one seemed to notice the foreign invaders passing by. I was scribbling notes from the wooden bench of my Humvee, which was built like a large pickup truck. Across from me, *Time* photographer Jim Nachtwey was snapping pictures. Two young soldiers, Private Orion Jenks and Private First Class Jim Beverly, pointed M-16s out of the back of the vehicle and kibitzed about Baghdad's crazy drivers.

"I'd hate to have a nice car here," said Jenks, a lanky, twenty-two-year-old Californian who had joined the platoon a few days earlier.

"Yeah, someone would ding you, and you're in a country that has no gun control laws," Beverly joked back. At nineteen, he was even younger than Jenks, a baby-faced kid from Ohio who sketched fantasy figures in his spare time.

Sergeant Ron Buxton, a short and taut Missourian in his early thirties, was riding shotgun in the cab. He whipped around and yelled, "I don't care if you joke or smoke, but make sure you watch our back."

We turned onto Market Street a few minutes before nine and got stuck in traffic in front of the Abu Hanifa Mosque. Second in the line, our Humvee was idling near a clock tower of the sacred Sunni shrine that U.S. tanks had poked a hole in nine months earlier. Elaborate wooden scaffolding encircled the tower now. I wondered if the heart of this ancient capital would mend as easily.

At first I thought it was a rock, the specialty of street urchins—a harmless shot against an armored Humvee. But the clanking sound that interrupted my thoughts couldn't be ignored. Nothing in Baghdad was what it appeared to be. You survived by sensing danger in little unordinary things: overcoats on a hot day, shadows flitting across a rooftop. For me it was the sound of a projectile landing louder than any stone should have.

It bounced off the steel blast wall behind me. I gazed down, then to the right, and spotted an object on the wooden bench two feet away. The dark oval was as shiny and smooth as a tortoiseshell, roughly six inches long and four inches wide. None of my fellow passengers seemed to notice. Private Jenks, who sat closest to it, was facing the other way. I confronted the intruder alone, a journalist caught in a military moment. Something told me there was no time to consult the soldiers.

I rose halfway, leaned to the right, and cupped the object. I might as well have plucked volcanic lava from a crater. I could feel the flesh of my palm liquefying. Pain bolted up my arm like an electric current. In one fluid motion, I raised my right arm and started to throw the mass over the side of the vehicle, a short backhand toss. Then everything went dark.

★

The Humvee bed was cold and hard, an inhospitable place to awaken. I struggled to sit up and fell back. Over my left shoulder, I could see sparks and a bluish flame rising in smoke. I took stock in the flickering light. My right leg burned from knee to hip, as if pricked by hundreds of hot needles. Blood was oozing from it and forming a cold, wet layer over my pant leg; my right arm felt heavy and numb. Was I having a nightmare? The hollow, faraway sound of voices was dreamlike. So was the sepia hue of the winter sky. I shook my right arm, trying to wake it up. Still no response. I elevated it to see why.

My wrist looked like the neck of a decapitated chicken. The wound was jagged, the blood glistening in the light. My mouth was dry, my brow soaked in sweat; my heart beat quickly and weakly, little dings in my chest.

All sound and sight dimmed, as my thoughts turned inward. This is not how I pictured my life ending: futilely and unglamorously, on the frigid floor of a truck, thousands of miles away from anyone I loved.

Noises muffled just a few moments earlier suddenly became distinct: "Are there casualties?" I recognized Buxton's voice.

"Yes, we need to go now," Beverly answered tersely.

"How serious? Are you wounded?"

"We don't have time to answer these questions right now, Sergeant. We need to get back to the base. We need to go now."

"We're hit, we need help," screamed Nachtwey. "Get us out of here. Move it." I tried to join in but could barely muster a whisper. Jenks was no better. He was glassy-eyed and slumped in the corner, his automatic weapon dangling at his feet. He looked dead.

Buxton ordered the driver to move. He didn't see Specialist Billie Grimes, who had jumped out of the vehicle behind us and was sprinting toward us in a hail of enemy fire. "Stop. Stop," she yelled. We did so long enough for the slight, twenty-six-year-old medic from rural Indiana to leap in. She landed on a floor that was so slick from blood she slid over me, barely able to stay on her feet. The driver gunned it again, all but pulling her legs out from under her. She straddled my hips to maintain her balance and quickly took inventory. Jenks was stunned, but breathing. Beverly, bleeding from his knees and mouth, was strong enough to hold up his weapon and guard the rear. Nachtwey was wounded in his knees and abdomen. Instinctively, he reached for his camera to document the scene. He leaned forward and focused the camera on me. The flash startled Grimes.

"Put down the camera, Jim," she yelled and flipped him a roll of gauze battle dressing to press on his wounds. Nachtwey ignored her and shakily snapped another frame. Then he passed out, camera in hand.

I became the priority the moment Grimes saw my arm: protruding, ivory-white wristbones in a bed of severed tendons and blood vessels. Moving quickly, she tossed aside her medic bag and pulled an elastic cord from her left belt loop. The band was usually used to pop up veins before drawing blood. Now Grimes contained my blood with it, an impromptu tourniquet she wound tightly around my stump. For good measure, she ripped open a roll of gauze with her teeth and wrapped it around the cord. It stanched the flow, freeing Grimes to take command of what was now essentially an emergency room on wheels.

Her voice carried over the open speaker of the cab's field radio as she shouted instructions to Buxton through an open panel separating the cab from cargo section. "Take the fastest route you can get to. I have four people injured. One amputation . . ."

Minutes later, the vehicle crashed through concertina

wire blocking the back gate of the base, a shelled-out Saddam fleshpot renamed Gunner Palace after the artillery brigade occupied it. We hurtled toward the aid station so fast I thought we'd knock it down. The driver screeched to a halt a yard from the door. "Bring the litters, bring the litters," ordered Grimes. Four medics and a physician's assistant deposited Nachtwey and me on stretchers and brought us into an L-shaped clinic big enough for two gurneys. The place was roiling, medics scurrying in all directions. Nachtwey was begging for more painkillers. I had lost so much blood it took three soldiers to locate a vein. Within seconds, the morphine's warming, relaxing effect set in. I needed it for what came next: a wooden stick was tied between two pieces of cloth wrapped around my right arm, then turned like a tire wrench. Medics twisted the tourniquet tighter and tighter on my numbed limb, as if I had no bones left to worry about.

Grimes was so thoroughly soaked in my blood that the other medics assumed she'd been wounded. Throwing off her body armor, she jumped into the fray, moving as nimbly as a point guard—prospecting for a vein here, securing the tourniquet there. I was leaking blood, and no one could determine the source. Grimes snipped off my clothes and found it. "Why did you have to wear so much? It's not that cold out," she complained good-naturedly. The back of my upper-right thigh had been peppered by shrapnel, dozens of tiny metal shards. Medics swaddled it in a broad abdominal dressing.

I was naked and cold in the unheated aid station. Everything was playing in slow motion and elongated sound. The medics strapped me in the stretcher and drove me to the base's helipad. The only protection I had against the freezing night was a "shock blanket," a piece of aluminum foil that lined the gurney and folded over my feet. Grimes tried to tuck in the flimsy cover, but it kept blowing off and finally flew away in the gale of the Black Hawk's landing. I was loaded into the chopper, its door wide open and propellers slicing the air. Shivering uncontrollably, my teeth slammed like pistons; every muscle seemed to have gone into spasm. It occurred to me that I might be going into shock.

Loading the other three casualties seemed to take forever. As I lay there, I realized I was missing something: the makeshift photo album I always carried in my vest pocket. My eight-year-old daughter, Olivia, had crafted the wallet-sized trinket out of tiger-striped fleece and taped pictures of herself and her older brother, Skyler, inside. Olivia had presented the treasure to me the night I left for Iraq. I had taken to rubbing it for good luck in moments of danger. This seemed precisely such a moment, and I felt the talisman's absence keenly.

We finally took off. A medic placed his jacket over me and, when that didn't stop my shaking, lay on top of and warmed me with his body heat.

★

Raising my head a few inches, I wondered if I was having a religious vision. On the wall across from me was an image of the Virgin Mary holding Christ's body after his death. An odd way to greet a Jew in a Muslim country: if this was heaven, I must have gotten off on the wrong floor. Actually, it was the intensive care unit of the 28th Combat Support Hospital (CSH, pronounced "cash") in Baghdad, where I had been deposited by the medevac helicopter about ten o'clock and rushed to surgery. I had awakened in an alcove of the ICU, an austere room enlivened by a local artist's copy of Michelangelo's *Pietà*.

My right side was on fire. The surgeon had not only cleaned the open wound and cut off the surrounding dead tissue, but filleted my forearm to relieve pressure from swelling. The process had taken a little over two hours. Now I was crisscrossed in tubes discharging fluids and delivering narcotic relief, my stump wrapped in gauze as thick as a Thanksgiving drumstick.

It was a busy night at the CSH, which the army had built from the bombed-out remains of a hospital in Saddam's presidential compound, renamed the "Green Zone" by U.S. occupiers. The other casualties from what was confirmed to be a grenade attack were recovering in rooms down the hall. Jim Nachtwey had had surgery to remove shrapnel from his knees. Private First Class Jim Beverly and Private Orion Jenks lay next to jars of metal fragments pulled from their bodies. The brightly lit ICU occupied by two other patients—a Pakistani contractor with a bad heart and a Syrian insurgent shot in the head by American soldiers—churned all night. Only the medical staff clad in desert mufti changed when the desert sun broke through a small, yellow-curtained window. A middle-aged nurse with blond highlights approached my bed.

"You're a hero," she said. "You lost a hand and saved lives."

Hero? I was feeling anything but valiant. Mangled. Pitiful. Disoriented. Scared. I was anxious about my ability to work again with one hand and to parent my children, who lived with me half-time in Washington. Skyler was eleven years old, the same age I had been when my father, a workaholic community newspaper publisher, dropped dead of a heart attack. Olivia was roughly as old as my sister had been. I couldn't bear to think I might let such wrenching family history repeat itself.

Mostly, however, I was angry at myself for getting in the wrong Humvee, releasing the grenade too slowly, even grabbing it in the first place. Nothing would have happened if I hadn't picked it up. Why had I been acting like a cowboy? Why hadn't I just left the damn thing alone?

"It was an impulsive act," I told the nurse. "If I hadn't picked it up, I'd still have a hand."

"You probably wouldn't have had a life," she retorted. "You and everyone else in the vehicle would have died. It wasn't an impulse; it was an instinct to survive."

I still didn't buy the idea that getting in the way of danger was heroic. But her words got me to think beyond my pain. For the next two days, I studied computer printouts of bionic hands brought by another nurse. I received visitors, including the platoon I had shadowed for the previous three weeks and my *Time* coauthor, Romesh Ratnesar. My reporting partner from a previous trip to Iraq, Brian Bennett, watched over everything from the anesthesia to the guest list.

The Iraqi employees of the magazine's bureau visited and expressed their remorse. Driver Sami al-Hillali, a doe-eyed man with a salt-and-pepper beard, understood my pain all too well. A land mine had blown off his right foot in the Iran-Iraq war in 1983. I knew he wore a wooden foot but had never before heard the backstory. Standing at my bedside, Sami recalled how he'd gone more than a day without painkillers and antibiotics; he finally reached a surgeon in Baghdad who wanted to amputate at the knee and, when Sami balked, kicked him out of the hospital. Sami went home and spent a year in bed, nursing the open ankle wound by himself.

If he told the story to give me courage, it worked. I had every benefit that he had gone without—quick first aid and evacuation and the world's best medicine. If Sami could fight another day, so could I.

But I would have to get out of Iraq first. The air force was the only thing flying, a tough ticket for a civilian. My army buddies pushed, as did my *Time* colleagues. After another surgery to clean my wounds, doctors cleared me to go. I arrived at the Baghdad airport in a pool of my own urine and came close to being hit by mortars in a holding tent before I was finally loaded on to a transport plane. We took off just after 3 A.M., December 13.

The German countryside was waking up as we landed near Frankfurt and rode to the Landstuhl Regional Medical Center. Only a five-hour flight from Baghdad, LRMC is a sprawling, world-class trauma center and the first stop for those seriously wounded in the Iraq war.

It was almost my last. Not long after arrival, I was taken for a routine surgery to clean my wounds. In the recovery room my heart rate spiked dangerously. The arrhythmia corrected itself before doctors could treat it, and tests for a heart attack proved negative. But the spike represented my second brush with family legacy in four days. My father had died of a heart attack at age thirty-six; his father at forty. Since my preteens, I had religiously followed all the rules of diet and exercise, determined to break the chain. And yet here I was, having tempted fate with an assignment I could have avoided.

The scare landed me in the ICU. I slept all day, awakening to news from Iraq on December 14: the arrest of Saddam Hussein. I felt the pull of a big story, but all I could do was pass on the TV report to *Time* news director Howard Chua-Eoan, who had come to Germany to escort me home. He awakened New York editors in time to change the magazine's cover for half the run: "Weisskopf is on duty from his hospital bed," Howard quipped over the phone.

He brought me a dozen e-mails and notes sent to the magazine. Most of them mentioned my supposed heroism, a notion I once again batted away. But an e-mail from the mother of Private Jenks cast the episode in different light: "I would like to get in touch with Mr. Weisskopf to thank him for saving my son's life."

I had bumped into Jenks in a surgical waiting room the previous day. "Hey, thanks," he said as our gurneys passed. The significance of my actions hadn't sunk in until I pictured Jenks as someone's son.

I had reason to think of my own son later that same day. I was walking the corridor for exercise with the help of nurse Nina McCoy, a thirty-one-year-old army captain. We were talking about loss and my good fortune to have suffered it in middle age. I already had a full life, Nina reminded me, complete with professional achievements, world travel, and a chance to play catch with Skyler. Most war amputees hadn't had that opportunity. They were half my age and just starting to get a taste of life. A soldier who had lost both hands in Iraq recently confided in one of McCoy's colleagues that he had planned to get married when he got home. "How am I going to wear the ring?" he had asked angrily.

The nurse told him to put it on a chain around his neck where it would hang even closer to his heart.

I was moved by the story and asked for details. The soldier's name was Sergeant Pete Damon. An aviation mechanic in the Massachusetts National Guard, he had lost his hands in a freak accident while servicing a Black Hawk chopper on October 21.

★

The day my sister, Leslie Flesch, learned of my injury, she vowed to find me the world's best doctor. Starting her search almost immediately from her small study in her Beverly Hills home, she placed a call to a well-connected Los Angeles doctor and asked him to recommend the top surgeon, regardless of location and cost. He polled a couple of experts. Everyone had agreed on a man named Andrew C. Friedman, who had the rare combination of board certification in highly specialized hand work and experience in traumatic injury. He also happened to work out of Washington. Leslie got his phone number and dialed it.

Friedman took the call right away and said he'd be happy to take the case, except for one problem: I wasn't in the military.

Leslie had failed to run down a critical part of Friedman's résumé. He was a lieutenant colonel in the U.S. Army, based at the Walter Reed Army Medical Center, which treated only soldiers. I already had run into red tape as a civilian in a military world when I sought an airlift from Baghdad.

"Don't you have a private practice, too?" asked Leslie incredulously.

"You don't understand," said Friedman. "I'm in the military. I don't just come in and work here." He could treat me only if I obtained a special waiver from the secretary of the army. "Don't count on it," Friedman warned. "It's almost impossible. I never knew of it actually happening."

Of course, the way to make things happen in Washington is to leverage personal connections. My colleagues at *Time* asked their Pentagon contacts to get word to acting Secretary of the Army Les Brownlee. A childhood friend and Washington radio commentator who was savvy in local politics enlisted our D.C. congresswoman, Eleanor Holmes Norton. She personally called Brownlee, a decorated Vietnam veteran, and requested the exception.

The waiver was granted as I was leaving Baghdad for LRMC. I would be treated at Walter Reed, the first reporter wounded in a war ever to receive that privilege.

★

The bus arrived at Ramstein Air Base on the evening of December 16 and drove on to the lantern-jaw ramp of a C-141 Starlifter, the army's behemoth troop and cargo transport plane. The twenty-six of us numbered enough men for a platoon, yet another wave in the sea of Iraq war casualties airlifted from Landstuhl every Monday, Wednesday, and Saturday night.

I was placed on a litter, a rack where soldiers were stacked four-high in the center of the aircraft. It wasn't first-class seating. I could barely move, with the next litter lying six inches above my nose and the aisles so narrow I was constantly being bumped by passing medical aides. The cabin resembled a tunnel: poorly lit, stuffy, and more than half a football field long. Everyone was issued ear plugs to muffle the industrial roar of four huge turbofan engines. The stench of urine and blood permeated. The temperature continuously fluctuated from steamy to frigid. *Time* editor Chua-Eoan looked after me from a bench along the side of the plane; a Critical Care Air Transport Team—the fully-equipped airborne ICUs deployed for the first time in war to keep soldiers alive until they reached hospitals—stood by to monitor my heart rate.

The CCATT also kept a close watch on the patient lying to my right. Corporal Bobby Isaacs had occupied the room next to mine at the Landstuhl ICU; I had overheard the nurses describing him as "questionable," uncertain to make it.

On the afternoon of December 10, a few hours before I was hit in Baghdad, the twenty-two-year-old member of the 101st Airborne had been standing guard in the open cargo section of a Humvee when insurgents detonated two 155mm mortar rounds buried in a curb. The explosion ripped through the passenger side of his truck, knocking Bobby to the floor. Medics found his legs shattered and bleeding profusely; they had to resuscitate him twice. He had been given seventy-two hours to live, but hung on after heroic medical efforts and survived the trip to Germany.

Doctors sent Bobby on the plane covered in a maze of tubes so extensive that nurses had to rig up a cargo strap to hang the bags of fluid. His head was raised and turned to one side, eyes wide open and fixed. He was moaning incoherently. Halfway home, Bobby became nauseous from too much morphine. A colonel came by to check on him and, thinking

Bobby needed help to sit up, grabbed the air-sickness bag in Bobby's hand.

The vomit hit the senior officer square across his front. "Good job," a nurse joked.

The ride was an ordeal—a "nine-hour subway ride between stops," as Chua-Eoan put it. But the Starlifter performed its job. At 9:15 P.M. it landed safely at Andrews Air Force Base, ten miles southeast of Washington. We had completed the journey of every soldier wounded in Iraq, from the battlefield to a CSH, to Landstuhl, and finally to U.S. soil.

A bus was waiting to drive us to a new destination, where we would face our toughest test.

2.
WARD 57

The soldiers wounded in Iraq came home to a lonely tarmac; no fanfare, just a team of litter bearers to stack us in white shuttle buses. The procession was solemn and silent, except for a harrowing scream from Corporal Bobby Isaacs as his legs dropped to the floor from his gurney. Young men like Bobby had left their families swollen in pride and muscle, only to return broken and bewildered. I wondered as we drove in darkness if there was more dignity to dying, a nobler place for those sealed in body bags on other flights home. At least the Pentagon had announced their passing. The gravely injured and dismembered got no such mention. What they got was a berth at Walter Reed Army Medical Center, where my bus pulled in just after midnight, December 17.

Armed soldiers in combat gear met us at the front gate of a vast, fenced compound near Washington's northern border. The hospital was the color of sand, a squat concrete structure balanced on concrete pillars like a spacecraft ready for takeoff. It was set back from the street by a hundred yards of grass and short trees. Light radiated from rows of glass windows, a beacon from the Vatican of military medicine.

I was whisked through a flag-draped lobby and brought to the triage center for incoming war casualties, known as the "Body Shop." The long, narrow room contained six beds lined up in a row. As I was unloaded onto one, a man in a green, open-collar army shirt approached and introduced himself as Dr. Friedman. He examined my wounds, snipped off stitches in my right flank to permit drainage, and redressed them. An anesthesiologist prescribed painkillers. Noting the late hour, Friedman excused himself until the next day and released me for transport to a hospital room.

My gurney glided down the hall to the north side of the fifth floor and under an archway marked by my new address. I recognized the name Ward 57 from news stories as the grim destination of soldiers who bore the signature wounds of the Iraq conflict: limb loss. The little I had seen of the corridor didn't put me at ease. It was brightly lit and empty, like a bus station between runs. At 1:30 A.M., I was moved into Room 5735, the ward's fifty-sixth amputee since the Iraq war had begun.

The trip left me too wound up to sleep. I got up for a look, limping along with my IV pole. The ward was configured like an *H*, with a nurse's station connecting a pair of long, whitewashed corridors. Eight rooms occupied each side. A large whiteboard hanging near the entrance identified its eleven current patients by name and severity of injury, based on a numerical system; the highest number represented those who needed feeding and bathing.

Except for the camouflage uniforms and combat boots, I could have been in any hospital. The head nurse, a forty-year-old army major, accompanied me on my walk. Tammy LaFrançois was a thin, pretty brunette who in August 2002 had taken over a ward that traditionally housed orthopedic patients, mostly elderly retirees with bad hips and knees. But with the Iraq war looming, hospital commanders, anticipating an onslaught of amputees, had designated Ward 57 as the first stop in a comprehensive program of recovery and rehabilitation. LaFrançois was ordered to train her staff for a new breed of patient: young, in chronic pain, traumatized, and long-term.

Amputees began arriving in the early days of the U.S. invasion of Iraq, and by July 2003 filled the place that became popularly known by the shorthand "57." Nurses faced all of the anticipated issues, plus a few no one saw coming. The ward was overrun by bereaved families who traveled to Washington on government doles and often camped out in hospital rooms. LaFrançois found herself playing concierge, not to mention PR flack for reporters who came to interview the wounded and politicians eager for the spotlight. Army nurses had always received reports on "command-interest" patients, the handful of people considered important enough for generals to track them. Before long, Walter Reed's command was noting interest in every soldier on 57. Was he progressing fast enough? Was the family comfortable? The demand for VIP treatment required new rules for LaFrançois's staff, which wasn't used to bringing chocolate milk to injured grunts. She called everyone together after a few weeks of the war and ordered them to envision the ward as a hotel. "The Ritz-Carlton is where you'd want to go, not Motel 6," the major said. "That's how I want all my patients treated."

Walter Reed had a history of treating high-profile patients. Established in 1909, it was named for an army research scientist who discovered the agent (mosquitoes) for yellow fever—the signature casualty of that period's big conflict, the Spanish-American War. The hospital had occupied a place in Washington's political life ever since Calvin Coolidge's teenage son had surgery and died there of septic poisoning in 1924, an event covered by radio, hour by hour. World War I general John J. "Black Jack" Pershing had famously spent his last seven years in a three-room suite, playing host to the next great war's general George S. Patton. Before departing for North Africa in 1942, Patton got down on one knee in the sitting room and asked the legendary soldier for his blessing. President Dwight D. Eisenhower passed his final days in the VIP suite, as had Secretary of State John Foster Dulles and Generals Douglas MacArthur and George C. Marshall.

From its first patients to its frontline work with amputees nearly a century later, the hospital had provided top-notch medical care for hundreds of thousands of combat casualties. Every war of the twentieth century produced amputees, but Walter Reed began specializing in limb loss only during the Iraq conflict. In the Vietnam years, it was one of eight regional centers that treated amputees, along with Fitzsimmons Army Hospital in Denver, Philadelphia Naval Hospital,

and Brooke Army Medical Center in Texas. Lacking the outpatient facilities it has today, Walter Reed kept patients far
longer and didn't house families. Patients were segregated by
rank, enlisted men placed in a large, open orthopedic ward
and officers in smaller rooms, ranging from one to a dozen
men; the largest was called the "Snake Pit" because of a large
serpent mosaic inlaid on the tile floor, a symbol of the Greek
god of medicine. Among its graduates was Max Cleland, who
lost both legs and his right arm in 1968 and later became a
U.S. senator from Georgia.

My arrival at the latter-day Snake Pit presented nurse
LaFrançois with yet another new challenge. I was a journalist
paid to snoop. I had no military background, and I was older
and more independent than most soldiers. She kept a close
eye on me, riding the air base bus to fetch me and putting me
in the private room nearest to her office and farthest from the
busy entrance. She assigned a pair of her most seasoned and
skilled nurses to me full-time to avoid the potential confusion and mistakes of rotating caregivers.

★

A nurse flicked on the light at 5:30 A.M. My first day on Ward
57 had begun. "What's your pain on a scale of zero to ten,
with ten the worst pain you've ever had?" she asked. Pain
was apparently so endemic here it was charted on a meter.
"Five," I replied, testing the waters. Morning rounds immediately followed, a raucous rush hour of doctors consulting
with night nurses and checking on their patients. A pair of in-
terns entered in bright yellow smocks, face masks, and rubber
gloves—protection against a drug-resistant bacterial infection

common to Iraq, *Acinetobacter baumannii*, which is contracted through open wounds. The young doctors rebandaged my arm. They used tiny tweezers to pull out and replace pieces of cotton string in eight deep holes of my right thigh and buttocks. I screamed ten on the pain scale and received a shot of Demerol.

At 7 A.M., a caravan of gurneys arrived to transport soldiers to surgery. I was spared, left to the legions of specialists who proved the old adage about hospitals being the last place to get rest. I welcomed the anesthesiologists and their pain relievers. But the nonstop traffic was annoying. The social worker bumped into the dietitian, who passed the shrink. As the veterans' rep left, a candy striper arrived. So many clergymen popped in, from a Catholic priest to Episcopalian ministers to a rabbi, I could have chaired an ecumenical conference. The brass brought commemorative coins, the Red Cross socks, occupational therapists a mechanical reacher.

The onslaught of hospital pros had one saving grace: no one seemed fazed by my injury but me. Just the word *amputation* made me shudder. It conjured up a disjointed series of images: a childhood friend who had lost his leg in an auto accident; World War II veterans wheeled into ballparks for holiday games, their empty trousers or shirt sleeves pinned up. I had avoided mirrors all week. Now I feared seeing the startling reality in the faces of my family and friends who would be visiting later that day.

My fears turned out to be groundless. The one emotion everyone showed was happiness to see me alive, maimed or not. But two exchanges stood out. My sister surprised me with a gift: a 1900 silver dollar our gambler father had won in Las Vegas and given to her in 1956 when she was eight years old. Leslie figured if I ever needed a father, it was now.

I held my father's winnings and thought of the larger bet he lost. He deferred a family life to business success, and died before he had either. I had almost repeated the mistake. The realization put my father's death in a new light. I understood for the first time why he exited before getting to know me: he had gambled on a future that never materialized. It was a mistake I could begin to forgive.

I had gambled on a job assignment and had my own damage-control problems. Skyler had reacted angrily when he first heard of my injury from my old friend David Maraniss, who had broken the news to my children and estranged wife, Judith Katz. "He lied to me, he lied to me," Skyler shouted, referring to my parting words when I left for Iraq. "He promised me he wouldn't get hurt." According to Judith, Skyler had moped and cried every day until I came home.

He was the first one through the door when visiting hours began. He and Olivia bounded onto my bed, showering me with hugs and get-well posters. Dressed in camouflage pants, Skyler pointed out the intricate drawings of battle scenes in his artwork. Before long, he had grabbed a roll of gauze and wound it around his right hand. He was identifying with my loss, a gesture I saw as a sign of forgiveness. I had shaken his sense of safety, the security blanket only a father can provide. Skyler's act of generosity capped a day of pardons across three generations of Weisskopf males.

President George W. Bush visited the ward on December 18, my second day at Walter Reed. He moved from room to room, thanking soldiers for their sacrifice and consoling families. When he reached 5735, no one was home. I'd been taken to surgery hours earlier. In Washington, even hospitals have political agendas. Major LaFrançois was the president's advance man, and I had gotten in her way.

Actually, my job had. Up until that point, I was convinced that nothing mattered to me except the next shot of morphine. But LaFrançois had thrown me an ethical curveball. Midway through my first day, she asked to have a word alone. She told me that the White House was planning a visit and wanted to know if Bush would be welcome in my room. It didn't take long to decide. I knew the president would be on a well-publicized PR tour to strengthen support for his war. I had favored the invasion of Iraq, believing U.S. intelligence reports of unconventional weapons. But reporters had no business helping officeholders make their case even if they agreed with it.

I declined as diplomatically as I could. The president was coming to thank soldiers and shouldn't waste his time on a civilian who didn't fight. LaFrançois thought I was questioning not the appropriateness of a visit but my worthiness. "We feel you are as worthy as anyone else," she said. "You did so much for our troops to put your life on the line. You actually saved soldiers."

My story had gotten around. From NBC *Nightly News* to the *New York Times*, the media reported it widely, and soldiers added their own editorial flourishes as they passed it along. It occurred to me that people were exaggerating the valor of my actions to help me salve the loss. I had trouble processing the praise, especially from military men whose objectives contrasted so sharply with my own. I was ready to acknowledge that my actions had saved lives, though I was still a long way from understanding what motivated those actions. I did know one thing for certain: I didn't grab that grenade as a soldier fighting the president's war. His political aims were at issue now. I found myself having to straddle the chasm between military and journalistic cultures. LaFrançois didn't understand why any American would refuse a visit from the president. Nor did her bosses, who had also been contacted by Bush's advisers and took the time to weigh in. The hospital's commander, Major General Kevin Kiley, stopped by. "We all consider you a hero for what you did," said Kiley, a six-foot-six onetime collegiate wrestler. "The fact you grabbed that grenade and tried to get it out, you saved some lives doing that." We chatted for a while, and Kiley brought up the presidential visit. He said he heard that I wouldn't see Bush. "Are you sure?" the general asked. "He would really like to see you." I politely demurred again, moving up the chain of command.

I didn't realize how much trouble I was causing. The hospital had an open-door policy for presidential visits. It wouldn't have looked good on TV for a reporter to shut out the commander in chief. Kiley asked LaFrançois to persuade me to reconsider, questioning whether I had been clearheaded enough to make an informed decision. She took another crack at it, returning late that night. After I declined again, LaFrançois, like any good soldier, improvised. I was supposed to have my wounds surgically cleaned the next day. She made sure I ended up in the operating room while Bush made his rounds. The next morning, I was taken out before the dawn security sweep.

I was operated on from 9:00 to 10:40 A.M. and parked in the recovery room until the president left just after noon.

★

The staff of Ward 57 did its best to create a holiday spirit in the days leading up to Christmas. A tree decorated in colorful ornaments greeted visitors at the entrance. Nurses hung stockings and candy canes from the reception desk. The doors of each room were wrapped in bright red and green tinsel and bows.

But there was no dressing up the suffering of the patients inside. Young soldiers, carved up like sides of beef, lay in a narcotic haze amid the inevitable trappings of hospital life: get-well cards, family photos, children's drawings, comic strips, smiley faces, and wilted flowers. Some patients hung wall calendars with circles around the day their lives blew up in a single instant, cut down at the peak of their power and dreams.

For contradictory reasons—the deadly efficiency of insurgent bombs and the capability of U.S.-combat lifesavers—a staggering number of soldiers had been returning from Iraq without arms or legs. By the time I was hit, more than 3 percent of the 2,230 wounded in action had lost at least one limb, twice the rate of amputations in every war of the previous century, except Vietnam, for which there were no good statistics. Nearly all of the most recent war's casualties wound up on 57. I had landed in a monument to the human wreckage.

The toll was stupefying. My neighbor to the left was a twenty-six-year-old former all-state high school runner from

New Jersey whose left leg was amputated above the knee and his right knee connected to his hip by a titanium rod. Down the hall, a twenty-four-year-old Virginian who loved to drive fast cars was missing both legs above the knee. Across from him was a twenty-two-year-old expectant father from Pittsburgh, blinded and separated from both of his hands. To his right, a thirty-six-year-old Green Beret from Texas, three years short of retirement, had one arm removed above the elbow; the other was held together by skin and bone grafts. The litany of misery moved from bed to bed.

The ward's population mirrored American diversity: white, black, Hispanic, and Asian. Everyone had a different story, many of which I would learn in eighteen months as a patient and outpatient. But even in those first days, I recognized the common plight of men who'd come home with less than they had left with—the trajectory of a life stopped cold in a hospital bed.

Down the hall from me was a thirty-four-year-old soldier who had lost his leg and the only job he ever wanted. Sergeant First Class Luis Manuel Rodriguez had dreamed of being a combat medic since his first glimpse of Vietnam war movies as a young boy in a low-income suburb of San Juan. He wasn't just fascinated by the idea of saving lives; he wanted to do it in war, one hand holding a gun, the other a syringe. He joined the army in 1990, trained as a medic, and spent the next twelve years preparing for the inevitable. At five-foot-three and 145 pounds, with close-set black eyes, a patch of coarse black hair, and the thin black mustache of a 1930s lothario, he didn't look like a warrior. But Rodriguez was so fit he regularly scored near-perfect in army physical training tests.

As war with Iraq loomed, Rodriguez had been given his own infantry platoon of medics in the 101st Airborne Division, Third Battalion, 502nd Infantry Regiment, Headquarters Company. His men addressed him as Sergeant Rod, but privately they called him a "straight-up dick," a taskmaster who had no time for excuses or clingy children or weepy wives. No relationship mattered more than the mission. His soldiers would form an island of self-reliance, a mirror of their leader. He trained them eighteen hours a day, insisting that they sleep in their cars on the base so they could respond to drills that he might decide to call in the middle of the night. Sergeant Rod pressed no one harder than himself. When he ordered a four-mile run, he kept pace with the fastest man, even though he was at least ten years older and had to ice down afterward. He was a stickler for details, the little things that didn't seem to matter—until a life counted on them. Pity the soldier who forgot his ballpoint pen when Rod expected him to take notes. Rod would get right up to the culprit's nose and yell in his accented English, "How many times do I have to go over this?"

While other platoon sergeants waited for orders to pack up, Rod started collecting supplies five full months before the 101st shipped out. He squirreled away food, water, medicine, truck parts, batteries, blankets, gasoline, ammunition, and weapons. When the orders finally came, Rod's platoon was sitting pretty. Other sergeants were scrambling for provisions, but Rod had so much—fifteen extra cartons of Meals Ready to Eat alone—he ordered his men to stuff the surplus in vehicles headed for the Persian Gulf. He even obtained a rare second shipping container to transport medical supplies, ensuring that he'd have enough for the seven hundred soldiers in his battalion.

His fastidiousness paid off when the 101st spearheaded the invasion of Iraq, rolling up the desert in late March 2003. The medical supply unit that was assigned to back up his platoon had disappeared. Rod couldn't even reach it by radio. Yet his twenty-five medics had everything they needed to patch up their wounded in some of the heaviest and most sustained fighting of the war.

In late April, the 101st moved north to secure the town of Mosul, a hotbed of Sunni resistance. The invaders had become an occupying force, a mission with little relief from danger. Rod always put the morale of his soldiers first. A superior officer came into his platoon's barracks one day and ripped down magazine foldouts of nude women, contending they'd offend Iraqi culture. Rod stood by and watched. After the officer left, the sergeant slapped the pictures back on the wall. "We're not Muslims," he told his troops. "When do we stop being humans?"

By the fall of 2003, the insurgency had become more lethal. Rod brought so many injured soldiers to the 21st Combat Support Hospital that he became a familiar figure in its emergency room and a friend of its chief nurse, Lieutenant Colonel Mary R. Miles. She admired how Rod would linger awhile to check on a soldier's prognosis or to console him; he was a model of courage and calm. When a small uniformed figure was carried in on the afternoon of November 24 missing a leg and covered in dirt and blood, Miles didn't recognize him at first. Shrapnel cuts covered his face, and he was groggy. Realizing it was Rod, she tried to console him. "Hey, this is part of war," he responded. "My guys have to keep driving on. I'm going to be okay. I'll mend."

Like so many soldiers he had saved, Rod had been struck down by a booby-trapped bomb set off in a convoy of Humvees. The explosion lifted his vehicle onto its left wheels and flung it thirty feet, throwing Rod onto the radio mount in the front seat. He knew he was in bad shape from the taste of blood streaming down his face. With his thumb he rubbed the fingers of his left hand and felt protruding bone. Enemy gunfire was coming from nearby rooftops. He was trapped, unable to move or reach for his weapon. He worried he'd never see his two young daughters again. "Don't let me die here," he prayed.

When the medic arrived, Rod found himself on the other side of the tourniquet. "I can't feel my right leg," he yelled. It had been blown off at the knee. Nine months into his tour, Rod was thrown from the stage he had practiced so long to occupy. The bomb severed more than a limb. It dismantled Rod's identity.

★

At twenty-two, Robert Blan Isaacs III had found the army an escape from his devout and sheltered upbringing. Abandoned by his father three months after birth, Bobby grew up in a household of religious women—mother, aunt, and grandmother—whom he called his "three moms." They put down a double-wide trailer in the country town of Roxboro, North Carolina, and sent Bobby to a fundamentalist Christian church school about thirty miles away in Durham. He attended services three times a week, became best friends with the preacher's son, and learned about the evils of alcohol and dancing. But a pair of irreverent uncles introduced Bobby to more earthly interests. They took him deer hunting with six-packs of beer, a barrel full of stories, and a libertarian take on life. Some of it rubbed off on Bobby, who loved to soup up cars and dip Copenhagen, which he jokingly referred to as his favorite vegetable.

Bobby was bright and self-confident, a redhead with dimples rounding out a big smile that the girls seemed to love. But he didn't have money for college and went to work servicing cars. The army had always appealed to his sense of patriotism. It took the events of September 11, 2001, to provide impetus. Somebody had to stand up for the American way. He did so on September 17.

A few months later, Bobby boarded his first airplane, heading off to basic training and an utterly foreign lifestyle. He was assigned to the 101st Airborne Division, Third Battalion, 502nd Infantry Regiment, Charlie Company. His thirty-man platoon was filled with colorful characters boasting nicknames like Juicy, Junkie, and Loggerhead. For an only child, barracks life at Fort Campbell, Kentucky, was heaven. The soldiers wrestled nonstop, played practical jokes, and drank. No one in the battalion could match the alcohol consumption of his inner circle, which called itself the Borrachos—Spanish for drunks. They tore through the nightlife of nearby Nashville. Bobby shot pool, clowned around on the dance floor, and batted his steely blue eyes at the girls. He outdrank everyone and, after a few beers or rum-and-cokes, got into fights and got tossed out of bars. He punched in the glass window of one in retaliation. Another time, he was arrested after a 2:30 A.M. brawl and charged with disorderly conduct.

Everybody dried out during the 101st's march into Iraq. In the early April battle for Karbala, Bobby picked up and fired the machine gun of a wounded comrade, earning a promotion to gunner. Even in hot, tedious, and perilous Mosul, he thrived on the army life. He lifted weights, played gin rummy, and fantasized with guys like Specialist Tim McKinnis about buying an RV back home, visiting old buddies, drinking beer, and eating steaks. He hoped to join the elite Special Forces and make a career of it. The army was family.

When his brothers filed into the field hospital a couple of hours after Bobby was slammed by the roadside bomb in Mosul on December 10, he was unconscious and not expected to leave alive.

McKinnis grabbed his hand, talking to his friend for what he thought would be the last time. "Hey, Bobby, it's Tim. I'm here with you. Everyone loves you, man. We're pulling for you. You just got to hang in there. When we get back to the States, I'm going to visit you. We're going to do all the things we talked about doing. We're going to take our road trip and drink some beer and eat some steaks. You just gotta hang tough, man."

★

Peter John Damon exchanged a pair of roses in place of rings when he got married on December 20. But there were no substitutes for the hands that were so central to his being. He grew up in Brockton, Massachusetts, a depressed, crime-ridden city, where fists were a livelihood and passport to respect. He was profane and quick-tempered, with a voice heavily resonant of nearby Boston and a formidable bearing— broad-shouldered and strong-jawed. Pete was only part tough guy, however. He had a searching mind reflected in his warm brown eyes and expert pencil sketches of cartoon characters. He was a jokester with a laugh that crackled like machine-gun fire.

Wiring things interested him more than high school. He quit at fifteen to work as an electrician, though he never qualified for a union wage because he lacked the education for a license. By 1997, with the birth of a daughter, Allura, who lived with his on-again, off-again girlfriend, Jenn, he realized he had more than himself to support. But Pete wasn't ready to settle down. He had done "what you gotta do to keep the party going," as he used to say, drinking heavily and brawling. Many of his high school friends went to prison for drug-related crimes. Pete realized his life was spiraling downward. In 2000, he started looking for a way to get it under control and figured the military was his best shot.

He decided on the National Guard, which required only a weekend every month and two weeks a year of active duty. Everyone said he didn't have to worry about foreign conflicts. Even more intriguing was the prospect of learning a new trade. He considered the guard's military police, which might lead to a job as a cop. But the recruiter in Brockton recommended training as a helicopter mechanic. The idea appealed to Pete. He could work with his hands on something different every day. It was respectable. Not many people could say they maintained aircraft. Pete signed up, and after the September 11, 2001, terrorist attacks, was sent to Fort Bragg in North Carolina to work on Chinook helicopters before they were shipped to U.S. troops in Afghanistan.

The job engaged him more than anything else he'd done. He loved to break down and fix the big birds, and his bosses liked his work. He decided to make it a career. In January 2003, he went back home to Otis Air Force Base, which had a full-time shop, and took low-paying, temporary jobs to get his foot in the door. His big break came in March, when he was hired as a mechanic for $20 an hour—more than he'd ever earned—with good benefits and, most important, iron-clad security. After years of uncertain paychecks, his future looked brighter than it had at any time.

But Pete's prospects dimmed on March 17, when his unit got an order to send Chinook mechanics to Kuwait. He happened to be there when the directive arrived and quickly weighed his options. He wanted to have a role in the Iraq war and knew his skill was in such demand he was likely to be called up anyway. The risks seemed minimal for mechanics located far from the front. He saw financial advantages: base pay with no expenses and a fat allowance to cover his rent while he was gone. The extra money would come in handy. He had gotten back together with Jenn, who had given birth to their second child, Danny, in 2002. Pete figured the Otis job would be there when he returned from the war effort. "Put me right on that list," he told his sergeant.

He joined an Alabama aviation unit in Kuwait in June 2003, and three months later was sent to an air base in Balad,

Iraq, to service helicopters closer to the battlefield. At 9:20 A.M., October 21, Pete was inflating a tire on a Black Hawk when the metal rim around it exploded, disintegrating into chunks of steel that flew across the hangar like missiles. The boom bounced off the concrete walls and sounded like a mortar attack. Pete was knocked down on his left side. He tried to get up, but had nothing with which to push off. Both his hands were gone, sliced off by the projectiles.

"I can't feel my fucking arms," he screamed.

Other mechanics ran over to hold him down and stop the blood that was pumping from both of his arms. They pulled off their belts and tightened them like tourniquets and pressed rags against the open wounds—anything to keep him alive. His partner, Specialist Paul J. Bueche, couldn't be saved. The blast had thrown the nineteen-year-old Alabaman into a pile of boxes twenty-five feet from the tire, severing both arms and a leg and inflicting severe wounds to his head and pelvis. Metal piping and a nut and bolt had lodged in his midsection.

Medics arrived within ten minutes and loaded the two men into a Humvee. Pete's heart was beating so hard he feared it would burst. One of his buddies tried to keep him conscious by asking questions—How old are your kids? Do they play Little League? But all Pete could hear was an inner voice, telling him he was dying. He was fighting for his life and apparently losing the battle. Pictures of his two young children and Jenn flashed before him. "Oh my God, my God, don't let me die, please don't let me die," he blurted.

Field hospital surgeons closed his wounds and sent him

two days later to Landstuhl. Lying in the ICU, he decided he wanted to marry Jenn and live together as a family. But the hands that kept enemies at bay and earned him a dream job had disappeared.

★

The draft of *Time* magazine's "Person of the Year" story— "The American Soldier"—was spread out before me, forty-two pages, double-spaced. Washington bureau chief Michael Duffy had dropped off the copy on the night of December 18, after my first surgery. He also gave me a red pen for corrections and a deadline of forty-eight hours to use it.

I was hanging on to my career trajectory with one hand. The next morning, I asked a nurse to rummage through my luggage for the plastic bag that contained my reporter pads. A few hours before my accident, I had sat down at a laptop computer, typed out notes from the last of ten notebooks, and sent them to my writing partner. Romesh Ratnesar had been forced to compose a complex story in the emotional aftermath, shaken by both the injuries and feelings of guilt for missing the patrol that night. We had worried that the story lacked action scenes—a firefight or a terrorist bust—to fully portray the mission of U.S. troops. I realized from my hospital bed that photographer Jim Nachtwey and I had filled in the gap.

It was odd to see the chaos of that moment compressed into words. The story led off with a description of the grenade attack. I had accomplished a lot as a journalist but never before doubled as the lead of a story carrying my byline. A few details seemed off. I hunted for the eleventh notebook, the one I had with me the night of my injury. A soldier had discovered it in the demolished Humvee. I opened it warily. The pages contained the last words written by my right hand, a script that had evolved from the perfectionist penmanship of a schoolboy to the urgent scrawl of reporter on deadline. I had developed my own shorthand over the years—a Latin term here, a Chinese character there. My last entry was splattered in blood. It recorded details of that final patrol, but no sign of danger.

8:11 p.m., roadblock on River Road . . .

8:20, passing through narrow, twisting street with open produce stands, pomegranates, bananas and dates . . .

8:40, Lieutenant yells "go." Red BMW (thought to be involved in earlier attacks but is wrong vehicle). Sergeant yells "clear."

The notes sucked me back into the story. I turned my hospital bed into a desk, cluttered with notebooks, pens, and pages of the draft. It was a pleasant distraction, though the staff wasn't thrilled. Tammy LaFrançois feared I'd exhaust myself. She offered to cull notes or take dictation. But I jotted my own ideas in left-handed hieroglyphics and called Romesh at his desk in New York on December 20. I suggested a few changes and set a condition for the next time we worked together—he'd have to provide the dramatic detail.

3.
CUTTING TIME

By mid-2003, the media had cemented the popular image of Ward 57 as the human scrap heap of the Iraq war. But in the world of combat medicine, it was a showcase of progress. Most of the maimed soldiers wouldn't have come home alive in past wars. They were success symbols.

The survival rate in Iraq was eye-popping—only one of every ten soldiers hit was dying, compared to one of every four in Vietnam and one of every three in World War II. Deployment patterns in the novel Iraq theater accounted for much of the difference. Fighting a guerrilla war in a few miles of urban grid, U.S. soldiers bunched up in convoys to root out the enemy. Humvees created a large target, raising the odds of attack by the insurgents' favored weapon: a remote-controlled bomb concealed in the road. But the troop concentration also ensured quicker first aid. A medic had only to jump from one vehicle to another to care for the wounded, instead of traveling miles to reach a radio call for help. Knowing where the rebels operated made it possible for the army to maintain field hospitals a short distance from the war zone, improving chances of delivering advanced medical care to injured troops within the "golden hour" of a battle wound.

Ward 57 may have been predestined for most of the survivors. U.S. soldiers went to Iraq in new body armor reinforced with impenetrable plates to protect vital organs, new Kevlar helmets to reduce head injuries, and hard plastic glasses to shield eyes. But nothing guarded their arms and legs. More than half of the casualties evacuated from Iraq had wounds to their limbs. The same blast or piece of shrapnel would have penetrated the vitals in past conflicts, causing instant death.

Other advances in combat medicine contributed to the survival rate. In Vietnam a large number of troops—2,500 by one estimate—bled to death for lack of first aid. Today's army invested heavily in efforts to control bleeding, including super-clotting pellets made from volcanic ash, and bandages lined in shrimp shells. Newly designed tourniquets made them easier to ratchet up and apply with one hand—a boon to soldiers who had to wait their turn for a medic.

Four Combat Support Hospitals all but ensured survival for anyone who arrived alive. Larger, more stationary, and better supplied with surgeons and technology than their MASH predecessors, the CSHs racked up better success rates—only 2.7 percent of the soldiers who reached one died, compared to 3.6

percent at the most advanced units in Vietnam. The chances of getting to a CSH alive improved as a result of new high-tech life-support systems installed in medevac helicopters.

The rules of American military medicine were being rewritten in Iraq. Instead of a golden hour, the critical period for trauma accelerated to a "platinum ten minutes" after injury. Wounded soldiers who were stabilized in the first few minutes had significantly better fates. For all the advances in technology and gear, it was the oldest lifesaving asset—medics—that drove up survival rates. The beneficiaries on 57 owed their lives to people like their own Sergeant First Class Luis Rodriguez. As much as anyone, he set the standard for the new first-responders who got to the wounded faster by fighting alongside them. Rod considered himself a soldier first. He preached a philosophy that "fire superiority is the best medicine on the battlefield" and trained his medics' platoon to perform every infantry job better than the soldiers responsible for it. The bantam sergeant led by example. When the 101st Airborne marched on Baghdad, he shouldered an M-4 carbine and strapped a pistol on his hip. In an April ambush, he directed a rescue mission under heavy fire, shooting his automatic weapon for cover as he and his men loaded twenty-two casualties into field ambulances and treated them. Rod was personally credited with saving six critically wounded soldiers. He earned a Bronze Star for bravery, a medal rarely given to a medic.

Even when he was hit November 24, his first reaction was to command. "Take cover; fire back," he yelled, trying to extricate himself from pieces of twisted metal in the crushed Humvee. Dorian "Doc" Perez, riding in another truck, validated Rod's training. A baby-faced twenty-six-year-old private, Doc had practiced medicine in his native El Salvador before joining the U.S. Army and becoming one of Rod's medics. Now he raced toward Rod under enemy fire, briefly stopping to handcuff a suspected insurgent. "I can't feel my leg," said Rod, screaming instructions to him in Spanish. Doc ratcheted the tourniquet so tight, Rod yelled out, "I can't take it." But it stopped the bleeding, enabling Doc to pull him out of the truck and get him into a field ambulance.

Rod was treated at the 21st CSH and the army hospital in Germany, arriving at Ward 57 on December 3, the latest amputee to have a medic to thank for his life.

★

Doc Perez had another starring role sixteen days after rescuing Rod. He was the medic assigned to Bobby Isaac's platoon, and had been riding in the Humvee in front of Bobby's on the way to battalion headquarters in Mosul. The convoy pulled within two hundred yards of the gate about 2:30 P.M., Bobby standing guard in the rear truck with an M240 Bravo machine gun. The first two trucks rounded a final turn.

Doc heard the bomb explode behind him and waited for a break in gunfire before dashing the twenty-five yards to Bobby's vehicle. He saw Bobby stretched on the floor of the open cargo section. His right femoral artery was sliced by shrapnel and pumping out blood. Everything below his knees looked like raw hamburger: his legs had multiple fractures and penetration wounds; the tibias and shinbones were exposed. Doc and another soldier pulled Bobby to the ground behind the Humvee, safe from enemy fire.

The medic tied tourniquets above the wounds on both of Bobby's legs. Neither stanched the gushing blood—a bad sign. Failure of two tourniquets usually means a patient is doomed. Doc tied a third near the groin, and the hemorrhaging stopped. But so did Bobby's breathing. He was in shock from losing what Doc figured was half his blood, enough to kill most people. He had no pulse and was cold and pale. Doc figured he was dying. He leaned over Bobby, pinched his nose, and performed mouth-to-mouth resuscitation. Bobby began to breathe again, but couldn't sustain it. So Doc kept breathing for him until an ambulance arrived with oxygen a few minutes later.

By the time Bobby arrived at the 21st CSH, he had stopped breathing again. "Get the surgeon," yelled a nurse after putting her hand on his chest. A doctor stuck a tube down Bobby's throat and into his trachea to open an airway and rushed him to surgery.

Bobby was double-teamed by surgeons. One drove large pins into bones on both sides of his leg fractures, holding them together with horizontal bars called external fixators. Another harvested a superficial vein from Bobby's lower leg and used it to splice a two-inch segment missing from his femoral artery and vein. Midway through the six-hour operation, doctors decided they didn't like Bobby's chances and initiated his military retirement, a rare practice employed to boost government payments to survivors beyond what they would receive if the soldier had died in combat.

Bobby made it out of surgery alive, but had received so much borrowed blood—his entire supply had been transfused—that he lost his natural clotting factors. He needed coagulants to stop bleeding. The CSH had no plasma; the freezer necessary to preserve it had broken. Only a dramatic solution would keep the young corporal alive.

It arrived in the form of a command broadcast over the public address system that night: "Attention in the compound! Attention in the compound! Anyone with A-positive blood report immediately to the EMT." Less than two minutes later, nearly fifty hospital staffers had shown up to the Emergency Medicine and Trauma tent. Lieutenant Colonel Mary Miles ran to the front of the line. "Come on, blood, come on, blood, the guy's bleeding," she said to herself, pumping her fist to speed up the flow.

A technician rushed Miles's blood to the operating room's chief nurse. Borrowed blood is normally brought in frozen and allowed to thaw to room temperature before it is transfused. In her twenty-year career, this was the first time the nurse had received a bag of hot blood, one soldier directly passing her life force to another. Within minutes of it reaching Bobby's veins, he stopped bleeding. During his stay at the CSH, Bobby would receive enough blood to replace his natural volume twice over.

But a few hours after the transfusion, Bobby was back in surgery. Muscles swelling in his limbs threatened to cut off blood to nerves and arteries. Doctors sliced open both of his forearms, lower legs, hands, and feet, opening the tough connective tissue around the muscles for relief.

The surgeon followed Bobby to the ICU, staying up all night to watch his vitals. The vigil was intense; numbers on the monitors kept changing every five seconds. Running through the likely prognoses for his patient, the doctor

wistfully concluded that only a person with a strong w
live could make it.

★

I never gave much thought to how a hand worked until I
lost one. My fingers always flew into action without plan or
prompt: each function was hardwired in my brain, performed
efficiently and spontaneously. I knew instinctively everything my right hand could do, from throwing a punch to
threading a needle. But I had no more concept of *how* it performed than of what I needed to do to replace it, a dilemma I
faced first thing Monday morning, December 22.

Dr. Friedman had come to my room the previous night to
talk about sewing me up. In his early forties, dressed in jeans
and a plaid shirt, he was not as tall or elegant as I had imagined for a world-class surgeon. (Nor was he as elitist—lately
he had been spending less time in an operating room than on
a shooting range, trying like any soldier to pass qualifications
for an M-16 automatic weapon.) He wanted to discuss options for what he called the "definitive" cut of my forearm.
He explained that length was an issue in choosing a prosthesis and that he'd have to shorten my stump—he didn't say by
how much—if I hoped to take advantage of the latest technology. I didn't even know that length was open for discussion. I had assumed my wound would simply be closed like
any open laceration. Friedman couched the subject so aca-
demically that I didn't realize a major decision was upon me.

But when he returned twelve hours later with a group of
doctors, he left no doubt. Friedman said pointedly that if I
wanted the ability to rotate the wrist of an artificial hand, he

would have to take off another 3.3 inches. Otherwise, its move-
ment would be restricted to opening and closing. Friedman recommended the surgery as a way to achieve maximum function.

The possibility of a bionic hand had buoyed me since an
army nurse in Baghdad had shown me pictures of one. Now I
was getting the bill. I already had suffered an involuntary amputation; Friedman was now suggesting I volunteer for another.
I was in a double bind: more dismemberment or more disability. Wrist rotation sounded good. But I had a hard time pin-
pointing why I needed it, and whether it was worth the loss of
leverage from my arm. When I asked Friedman to break it down
in pluses and minuses, he motioned to another white coat.

John Zenie introduced himself as a prosthetist who specialized in fitting fake arms. He was an imposing figure—six-
foot-two and 240 pounds—with a booming voice and a simple
message: a battery-powered wrist rotator would give me
greater dexterity at negligible cost; I'd still have a relatively
long stump with no less lifting power. But when I questioned
why the length of my arm was relevant to the technology, the
answer he delivered was crammed with technical jargon. I
found myself befuddled, as much by Zenie's lecture as by almost two weeks of narcotics and sleeplessness. I had forgotten
what it took to lock a door, open a jar, or turn a page, and had
even less idea of how an electronic hand worked. I tried to dis-
till Zenie's explanations as if they were elements of a complex
news story. But I had stopped absorbing information. And I
felt pressured by the presence of a gurney outside. I turned to
Friedman. "Do I have to decide now?"

"No, take your time," he insisted. And while I did, Friedman said, he wanted to point out something that I might have

missed in the discussion. Even if I decided against the wrist gizmo, I was still facing an amputation. My wound was too extensive to simply sew closed. He needed loose skin to cover the wound and would have to remove at least another inch of bone to free it up.

I had thought the question was to cut or not to cut. In fact, the issue was how much—an inch for closure or just over three inches for better function. "We're arguing over two inches?" I asked.

Friedman nodded and led the group out of my room while I stewed. Faced with a choice between amputation or less dexterity, I probably would have elected surgery. But at least it would have been *my* choice. Over the course of the past twelve days, I had steadily lost control over my life. This would be yet another loss, though more palatable. If I had to be cut, why not benefit from it?

An hour later, the group reassembled, led by Zenie, who carried props to explain why the two inches mattered. He drew a sketch of the basic assembly for an artificial hand, a shell that fit over the stump. Then he held up an actual electric hand designed to screw into the end of the shell. Together, these two pieces enabled an amputee to electronically open and close the hand. With the addition of a computer module—Zenie pointed to a black, barrel-shaped component—the hand would also be able to turn. This lengthened the assembly by two inches. Unless I made room for it by shortening my stump, the prosthetic hand would drop below my natural one, dangling to the knees like an ape's. At last I understood. The length of my forearm had nothing to do with technology of the prosthesis; it had everything to do with body symmetry.

Zenie wasn't finished with his presentation. With a shorter stump, he explained, I'd be eligible for breakthroughs in prosthetic design that were already in the works. The Iraq war had expanded the population of upper-extremity amputees and government research to re-arm them. Everything new would require at least as much space as the rotator module. I'd have a mortgage on the future if I created room now. I was sold.

The operation began at 1 P.M. that day. Friedman pulled back a few inches of flesh and cut the bone with a handheld electric oscillating saw. He sliced at a slight angle to keep the bone smooth, rounding off the edges with a file—the stump had to be shaped like a cone to fit into a prosthetic shell. Nerves that no longer had a home in my hand were trimmed next. The final act was closing the wound, an art form requiring the surgeon's well-known attention to detail. Excess skin would be folded over the end of my stump. Friedman factored in inevitable shrinkage to determine the right size of the flap—not so short that it would become taut, not so long that it would become flabby. Only a precise estimate would prevent tissue from bulging at the sides. He took a couple of extra measures to ensure comfort in a rigid prosthesis: assembling soft tissue to cushion the end of my stump and stitching up the inside of my arm, which would have less contact with a shell than the top. Friedman completed the job in an hour and forty-five minutes.

I woke up in excruciating pain, far more than I had experienced from the grenade blast or past surgeries. My right forearm was throbbing and burning, as if a hot knife were slashing it, digging deeper with every sweep. I had never howled from pain before. But now I let out a bloodcurdling cry. I wanted whatever it took to stop the agony immediately—a megadose of morphine, a full arm amputation—anything. Nurses kept injecting clear liquids into my IV bag, but nothing made it through my veins fast enough. I screamed for more anesthesia. "You've had the max," a nurse said. I didn't care. I continued shrieking and cursing for the better part of an hour, at which point the pain finally, mercifully, began to ease, a slow descent into an unconscious state.

While I was in the recovery room, *Time* editor Michael Duffy dropped off a carton of magazines back at the ward. The "Person of the Year" edition had hit the streets, a seventeen-page spread bylined by me and Romesh Ratnesar and photographed by Jim Nachtwey. Nachtwey had recovered sufficiently to promote the package that morning on the *Today Show*. Asked about the grenade attack, he responded, "Michael's reaction wasn't something that was thought out. It was just based on the way the man is wired. And he made the move that would help save people rather than himself, and he paid for the lives of four people with his hand, a very high price."

I was in surgery and missed the show, but when I was told of his comment a few hours later, I thought to myself, only half-jokingly, that perhaps the price had been too high.

★

Sergeant First Class Luis Rodriguez had arrived at Ward 57 on December 3 minus the bottom half of his right leg and the tips of two fingers on his left hand. Four surgical cleanings earlier had failed to stave off infection, so Walter Reed surgeons were forced to cut an inch above his knee five days later. Sergeant Rod took it in stride, as he had other obstacles in his rise from a Puerto Rican private to the army's third-highest noncommissioned post. The day after surgery, he started a regimen of dips on his aluminum walker to build upper-body strength, as well as chin-ups on the trapeze, a metal triangle hung from a cable over the bed of leg amputees to help them move. To recover the weight he had lost since the accident, he munched Fruit Loops from a big box kept close by. Everyone who visited received the same message: "Don't worry about Sergeant Rod." He was fine, just eager to return home and "get back to business" at Fort Campbell.

On December 16, Rod had all but packed his bags. Antibiotic beads that surgeons had inserted in his wound had worked so well they were able to sew him up. It was a day to celebrate in Room 5741. He still had his full femur, the strongest and largest bone in the body—and a big asset in supporting and maneuvering an artificial leg. He had pushed the envelope yet again, eligible to be discharged in just two weeks and fit for a prosthesis a scant three weeks after losing his leg.

But winds shifted quickly on 57. A couple of days after his final surgery, the end of his stump darkened into crimson and reeked like rotten meat. His surgeon delivered the bad news on December 22: "Rod, you're not healing, we have to cut more." The infection had taken hold again.

Sergeant Rod was used to giving orders, not taking them. But he had to obey his body. He choked back tears. "God, you're kicking my ass," he muttered under his breath. He had reached the top of the hill, step by painful step, only to be pulled down to the bottom. It was like losing his leg again. He cleared the room of everyone but his wife, Lilliam. Rod's partner of fourteen years tried to comfort him, but he was inconsolable. "Why? Why? Why?" he screamed out. "When is it going to stop?" If they continued to slice away at him like salami, he'd have no leg left.

His despair hardened as other doctors gathered for a second opinion. One of them leaned down to remove the dressing. Anger and frustration palpable on his face, Rod pushed away the surgeon's hand and ripped off the bandage himself, in the process removing skin, loosening stitches, and exposing a bloody mess of nerves, tendons, and muscle.

On Christmas Eve, surgeons sawed off another three inches from Rod's femur. He awoke in agony. Pain riveted his right leg like a power drill, moving deeper and deeper. He held on to the rails of the gurney in the recovery room and begged for relief: "I'm dying here."

★

"You like chocolate milk shakes?" Sitting on the toilet in my room, I thought I was hearing voices. "Strawberry?" I looked up and saw a middle-aged man with brown hair and pasty complexion sticking his head into a partially open doorway. He introduced himself as Jim Mayer, better known as the "Milk Shake Man."

I had heard about Jim, who apparently delivered McDonald's shakes and burgers several times a week. He was one of the angels of Ward 57, a special breed of patrons who brightened up a day otherwise filled with surgery, needles, bad food, and pain. The angels usually arrived in the quiet times. Doctors weren't making the rounds. Metal meal wagons had stopped clanking, the traffic of institutional do-gooders from the Red Cross and veterans' groups temporarily halted.

As I would quickly learn, Jim had a feel for combat amputees no doctor could match. He was one of us, having lost both legs to a land mine in Vietnam. He had lived through every stage of recovery and knew what we were enduring beyond the pain: identity crises, loss of self-confidence, and fears about supporting ourselves and attracting the opposite sex. Jim passed along biofeedback tips—he called the process "mind fuck"—for combating the jumble of severed nerve endings called phantom pain. He coached families on the need to validate their loved ones' suffering, pulling them into the hallway for a piece of advice: never tell amputees they should feel lucky to be alive.

He believed in the curing power of humor, especially slapstick. One of his favorite routines was mimicking awkward hospital volunteers who invariably said the wrong thing. When a leg amputee was convulsing in so much pain he couldn't talk, Jim handed him a chocolate shake and a three-by-five-inch index card with a scribbled message: "That will be $5. Bless you." But he mainly used treats to break the ice. After a couple of shakes, amputees were asking questions of the man who walked on two fake legs and worked for the U.S. Department of Veteran Affairs. He was living proof there was life after Ward 57.

By the time I arrived, Jim was delivering a dozen shakes three times a week, a cost he absorbed for months until a group of VA colleagues chipped in for McDonald's gift certificates just before the holidays. About the same time, Jim had befriended a Vietnam vet and Washington restaurateur named

Hal Koster, who offered to host Walter Reed patients at his Fran O'Brien's Stadium Steakhouse, located in the basement of the downtown Capital Hilton. Jim rounded up transportation and circulated the invitation on 57. Before long, Friday nights at Fran's became a tradition. Koster drew a big enough crowd a few days before Christmas to fill up four tables, amputees wielding steak knives in their hooks and hobbling to the bar on prosthetic legs.

For visitors who were less familiar than Jim Mayer, the ward had a gatekeeper, an odd little man known as Mr. Nick. Sporting silver loops in both ears and wrapping his salt-and-pepper braids into a bun behind his head, fifty-six-year-old James Melvin Nicholas stood out in the crew cut, uniformed staff. The breast of his white lab coat was smothered in good-will medals given to him by VIP guests. His accent was effeminate and Mississippian. He held the lowly title of medical support technician. But from behind the nurse's station, where he worked, everyone knew who was in charge.

Mr. Nick's outpost bridged the H-shaped corridor at the ward's entrance. No one passed it without his review. He could serve as kindly crossing guard for those with appointments or as rough bouncer for those without. He transcribed the daily histories of 57 on patient charts and on the whiteboard out front. He knew the private numbers of every doctor and how to reach them quickly.

New arrivals often did a double take when the mustachioed African American sashayed in for the first time. But they quickly learned the benefits of staying on Mr. Nick's good side. He'd boycott the room of anyone who gave him lip. For those who didn't, such as a badly injured nineteen-year-old, there was nothing he wouldn't do. The soldier was so depressed he could barely speak, until Mr. Nick persuaded him to confess that he was homesick for his parents, who couldn't afford the trip to Washington. Mr. Nick immediately left the room, returning a few minutes later with a form for government assistance. He helped the patient fill it out and walked it back to the right office. "Let Uncle Sam deal with it," Mr. Nick advised. The parents arrived a few days later.

A sixteen-year veteran of the ward, Mr. Nick was its sage and institutional memory. Nurses came to rely on his judgment. Above all, he advised that they keep their emotions in check around patients. These days that was a particularly tall order. For all but the past nine months, the staff had worked primarily with retirees recovering from orthopedic problems; they rarely stayed more than a few days, and the pace had been relaxed. Only fourteen amputees had been treated at Walter Reed during the brief Gulf War of 1991, and they had been scattered around the hospital. Although nurses had been warned to expect a large influx of amputees from Iraq this time, no one was prepared psychologically for the relentless, wrenching sight. Bombs left the body looking very different than a surgical amputation. Blast wounds were dirty and gory, usually accompanied by the ravage of shrapnel—BBs, nails, and metal shards. Just six weeks into the war, the patriotism and professionalism that drove the ward's workers began to crumble. It wasn't just the carnage—the patients were difficult to comfort. The endless cycle of surgery led to endless pain, usually accompanied by anger, amplified by relatives who squatted like gypsies, and directed at those who were held responsible for easing it. Media and VIP visits made for a tense, fishbowl atmosphere.

Even head nurse Tammy LaFrançois, a fourteen-year veteran of army hospitals, wasn't immune to the strain. She went home many nights in tears, and was particularly struck by the plight of a twenty-six-year-old sergeant who had arrived in early August with both hands missing. Months later, his wounds had healed; his pain was managed. But he continued to live on 57 because he couldn't take care of himself. One autumn day he approached LaFrançois at the front desk. He seemed so normal to her until he asked her to tie his shoes. LaFrançois waited until that night before she broke down. "You can't believe the things we see," she told her husband.

When many of LaFrançois's twenty nurses complained of burnout and threatened to quit, she took the problem to hospital commanders, who called in the hospital psychiatry department. Already overburdened with patients, therapists let the nurses vent and recommended ways of coping. First lesson: Remember the patient has suffered a life-altering loss. Second: Don't personalize the emotional aftermath.

It took novel strategies to persevere. Mr. Nick swallowed the sadness until he left work, then unwound by listening to classical music at home or window-shopping at malls. My day nurse, Tami Barr, had her own game plan. One of the civilians hired to replace army nurses deployed to Iraq, Tami was overwhelmed her first day on the job: the responsibility of caring for young men who had fought for her principles was daunting. Pulling herself together, she decided that she would take it day by day, shift by shift, sizing up each patient's individual needs, then striving to meet each one of them. Armed with her checklist, she was careful not to remove the bedsheet of a soldier who was unusually self-conscious of his deformity or fail to administer anesthesia when changing the dressing of a patient in extreme pain.

Tami was a full-figured forty-year-old with blond hair, blue eyes, and a firm idea of what I and her other patients should be doing on her watch. Basically, she ran my life. The day after my final surgery, she decreed that I had lost too much sleep socializing, and blocked all visitors and calls to my room. She disciplined my rambunctious son, who ran down the halls demanding to see the gun of everyone in uniform. She helped me decide to euthanize my fifteen-year-old cat. I had been informed by the vet that he was dying of kidney trouble, and the question was whether to attempt a heroic procedure. "Putting a suffering animal to sleep is the last great act of love you can do for him," said Tami, who had a houseful of felines herself. I made the call and bawled in her arms.

Even Tami had her emotional limits, though. Down the hall, a twenty-two-year-old specialist named James Fair wouldn't accept the loss of his two hands. He had also lost both eyes when a bomb he tried to defuse exploded, and nerve sensations tricked him into thinking he still had hands. He kept asking Tami to pass him objects. "James, you don't have any hands," she'd reply. He'd refuse to believe her, demanding next that she hold one of his stumps.

Some caretakers intentionally kept their distance from the soldiers to maintain their morale. Captain Kathleen Yancosek couldn't get close enough. A rehabilitation specialist known by everyone simply as "Captain Katie," she was a razor-thin blonde who almost dissolved into tears when she visited her first patient on the ward, a teenage soldier who had lost a leg in Iraq. He was crying from the pain. His mother was hysterical. The twenty-seven-year-old therapist braced herself, realizing that she was supposed to be the one whom they had confidence in to help him get better.

The best way to toughen up, Katie decided, was to look past the grievous injuries and to treat her patients as friends, not as amputees. She got to know them as intimately as they would permit, moving quickly beyond their hobbies and children's names. With her soft touch and sisterly concern, she often picked up more information than the hospital psychologists. Captain Katie knew if a soldier was checking out Internet dating services, fighting with a spouse, fretting about bills, or struggling to knot a tie with one hand. She made a habit of staying up at night to acquaint herself with their personal stories and continuously updating them. In mid-November, she walked in on Sergeant Heath Calhoun on his first day on the ward. He was sobbing in the arms of his wife and questioning how he could survive after both of his legs had been blown off by a rocket-propelled grenade. Though uncomfortable at first, Katie stuck around to console the twenty-four-year-old Ranger and from that day on followed each phase of his recovery. When he was on furlough and had to bounce on his butt up a flight of stairs to check on his crying son, Katie commiserated. When his young wife seemed overcome by the burden of a handicapped husband, Katie fretted for their marriage. After he went snowboarding on an amputee outing to Colorado, Katie brimmed with compliments.

Aside from a limb, the biggest loss to patients was their dignity. We were half-naked, helpless, fed from tubes, drugged, and constantly poked and prodded. Tami and Katie specialized in personal care, hoping to remind the wounded they were more than medical specimens. Jim Mayer made milk shakes his calling card because they were the last thing you'd find in a hospital; they established a personal bond, like a pitcher of beer. Jim learned everyone's favorite flavor as if he were an old drinking buddy who had bought a round at the neighborhood tavern.

Most of 57's workers could have pulled up a stool. They treated us like family members, warm and sensitive. I never would have imagined such a focus on individual needs in an institution that emphasizes group uniformity. But in a season of giving, they held nothing back.

★

Christmas Eve was a day like any other on Ward 57, with one notable exception: at about noon, I noticed I was having trouble breathing. A nurse took my temperature and recorded 100 degrees. Minutes later, my breathing had become even more labored; when the thermometer registered 102, the nurse called for help. Technicians responded with a mobile chest X-ray, blood-sample cart, and electrocardiogram. They worked as urgently as an ER team. The temperature continued to rise, reaching 103.5. My blood wasn't absorbing enough oxygen. When the tests failed to uncover a cause, the attending doctor loaded me into a wheelchair and sent me for a CAT scan.

The X-ray found a pulmonary embolism in my right lung, which was blocking an artery in the right lobe. The blood clot threatened to cut off adequate blood flow and put a mortal strain on my heart. Prolonged immobility was the primary cause of PEs. Doctors blamed the fourteen hours of air travel from Baghdad and Germany and long periods under anesthesia. In April, NBC correspondent David Bloom had died of a PE while riding in a cramped army tank as it moved up the desert to Baghdad. The clot spotted by my radiologists was small. But there was a danger of other ones forming and blocking a bigger part of an artery to my lungs, causing instant cardiovascular collapse. I had a time bomb in my chest as deadly as the Iraqi grenade.

I was sent to the cardiac intensive care unit on the fourth floor, where nurses injected an anticoagulant drug into my stomach. The drug was supposed to prevent new PEs and give my body a chance to break down the existing one. A tube lowered down my throat pumped oxygen into my blood.

For the second time in two weeks, heart trouble had landed me in an ICU. The clot was more dangerous than the irregular heartbeat I had experienced after surgery in Landstuhl. Embolisms were silent killers. My father had been given little warning before a blood clot in a coronary artery felled him forty-six years earlier; the arrival now of his last living sibling, my aunt Julia, who had shown up unannounced for a visit on Christmas Eve, struck me as perhaps prophetic.

For all its difficulties and unpleasantness, Ward 57 represented a way station to recovery. The cardiac ICU was a last stop. I was so depressed I turned down Christmas dinner and all visitors except Julia. I snarled at nurses full of holiday cheer and a young resident who botched the replacement of a painkilling catheter. When a smiling Captain Katie hand-delivered a miniature bottle of champagne sent to each patient by the White House, I came close to targeting her with it.

"He's a very, very angry boy right now," Aunt Julia warned before Katie entered my room.

I had one moment of comic relief on Christmas night. Lieutenant General Kevin Kiley had spent the day escorting Deputy Secretary of Defense Paul Wolfowitz on visits to wounded soldiers. Earlier, Wolfowitz, a principal architect of the Iraq invasion, had directed his Secret Service detail to stop at a local drugstore and buy out its inventory of *Time* magazines. As he walked from room to room, he handed out copies to patients, signing them on the hospital commander's stooped back. Finally reaching me, Wolfowitz held up the cover photo of three soldiers and said he had one critical question: "Why didn't you include a woman?"

I chuckled. It was easy to mistake the most prominent figure in the photo. The specialist was dressed in full combat gear and had a male's name: Billie Grimes. You had to look hard to find the tapered nails on the hand cradling an M-16.

The next day was brighter. A new CAT scan showed no evidence of additional PEs. I'd have to stay on anticoagulant drugs for six months to stop new ones from forming. But I had a reprieve from death row and a pass back to 57. Amputee Alley was the home of survivors. With technology and determination, we had the potential to lead full lives. I couldn't wait to get back to the land of opportunity.

4.
HOOKS AND HEARTS

Christmas had never been more hectic for Pete Damon. He had gone home on a holiday leave from Ward 57 in mid-December and left his shopping to the last minute. Wandering into a store in Brockton, Massachusetts, he picked out a camera for his fiancée. When it came time to pay, Pete closed a pen in his prosthetic hook and signed the credit card slip. The salesman regarded the scrawl curiously. "You couldn't read it before," Pete cracked.

The signature marked a big breakthrough for a man without hands. Pete was relearning survival skills. When he landed at Walter Reed on October 27, he couldn't do a thing for himself. Nurses fed, bathed, and dressed him; they brushed his teeth and wiped his backside after bowel movements. It was humiliating and frustrating. Sometimes his food arrived and got cold because no one came to feed him. But he had no choice and saw no point in feeling sorry for himself. Pete was a realist. He let others be his hands until he learned how to use fake ones and told himself that maybe that day wasn't too far off: another soldier with the same injury had come to his room for a visit carrying a cup of iced tea in a prosthesis. Even more encouraging was a video he saw in mid-November of a double amputee from the Vietnam War rock climbing with hooks.

Pete met the rock climber, named Jerry, in a hospital visit a couple of weeks later. He told Pete he could do anything he put his mind to, then demonstrated by reaching into a pocket for his wallet and peeling back dollar bills from it one by one—all using hooks. Pete was impressed by his dexterity and asked for a few tips on daily hygiene.

Jerry suggested a toilet paper routine that made Pete laugh. But the next time he had to go to the bathroom, he tried it. Pete pulled baby wipes from a package with his teeth, bent down, and dropped them along the edge of the commode. When a couple of wipes fell to the ground, he got on his knees, picked them up with his stumps, and used his teeth again to spread them across the porcelain. He sat down on the wet tissues, cleaned himself, and kicked them into the toilet. "I'm going to be doing this the rest of my life," he thought, a bit deflated. Still, Pete scored one for independence. He was determined to take care of himself and invoked his mentor whenever he faced new challenges: "If Jerry can do this shit, I can do it."

Pete had realized he had to invent new ways of doing everything. When he had worked on construction projects, he practiced a "get it done" rule. The same attitude would apply now. He targeted the things he missed most and devised how to get them done. Smoking topped the list. It was prohibited in the hospital, so he figured out how to transport his habit to the courtyard outside the fifth floor. He picked up a pack of cigarettes with his stumps and dropped it into a hat placed on his bed. He dove into the hat headfirst, flipped it on, and off he went. Once outdoors, he used his teeth to pry open the pack and tease out a weed. All he had to do was bum a match from another smoker. "Can you give a man with no hands a light?" he'd joke. The sight of Pete attached to an IV pole and a Marlboro became part of Ward 57 lore.

After weeks of spoon-feeding, Pete figured out he could use his longer stump to slide cookies across a bedside tray and shovel them into his mouth. He was soon expanding his diet with a cuff designed for him that boasted small, Velcro-fastened pockets for utensils. A toothbrush fit into one of the slots: another thing he could do for himself. To a man without hands, teeth were a valuable "third arm." Pete's choppers opened canned soda tabs, pried off pop tops, twisted bottle caps, and pulled off package flaps.

Another invention permitted Pete to bathe himself. Technicians stitched together two towels into a large terry-cloth mitt. Pete hoisted the double towel over his left shoulder with his teeth and stumps, and held it under his left armpit with his short right stump. He then stuck his below-the-elbow forearm into the mitt and cranked it, washing his front and back. To clean his buttocks, he placed the wet towel on a bath stool, sat down on it, inserted his heel in the mitt, and thrust his leg forward.

Gadgets aside, Pete played hooky from rehab more than anyone. He occasionally practiced how to operate a bionic hand. But a high-tech future didn't address the immediate problems he faced. He preferred to stay in his room and figure out ways to take care of himself. Other guys had at least one hand to perform day-to-day activities. He had to rely on his ingenuity.

He paid a price for dropping out before learning the electronic arm. When prosthetists rush-ordered one in late November, Pete had trouble getting the hand to open and close. Even when it did work, it was clumsy and imprecise. He couldn't even pick up a soda can with it. In the days leading up to his one-month leave, Pete had become anxious. He didn't have another hand to rely on while he experimented with this high-tech contraption. Jerry swore by an old-fashioned system of harnesses and cables operated by shoulder, chest, and back muscles. The body-powered prosthesis was cumbersome, yet effective and simple to use. "Look, I've seen it work with those hooks," Pete told the prosthetists. "I want to be like Jerry. Gimme those fucking hooks."

The day before Pete left, his wish was granted. The fiberglass shell was lighter than the electronic arm and easier to maneuver. Attached by straps that fit over the shoulders and under the armpits like a backpack, the prosthesis required Pete to do a little dance to get it on; but once on, it was easy to operate. He had only to thrust his left shoulder to open a hook. To close it, he retracted the arm. It was a big moment: for the first time in fifty days, Pete had the life-sustaining capability nearly everyone else took for granted. He celebrated at an airport bar on the way home. The first sip of Heineken tasted as good as ever, even if he raised the bottle with a metal clamp.

His first night home, Pete's mother threw a pizza party for the family. Pete was still too green to use the hook for eating, so he brought his mouth to the end of the table and shoveled the pieces in. A few days later he paid a visit to a rehab specialist at the local Veteran Affairs office. She gave Pete small pieces of pipe insulation to wrap around the stems of forks. The spongy surface provided traction for the hook. He went home that night and ate with a regular fork for the first time.

Every day brought a new milestone. One of the biggest was learning how to dress himself. He'd hold down a sock with one foot, insert his big toe, and yank up the top with his hook. Jeans he bought a couple sizes big, laid them on a bed, and used his teeth to button and zipper and to feed a belt through the loops. After wiggling into them on the bed, he'd tightly hitch up the belt to keep them from falling down. Without the towel mitt and soap dispensers of Walter Reed, he had to screw off liquid soap bottle caps with his mouth, lather up hand towels, and wash himself by holding the towels between his teeth and stumps. Drying off was more complicated because he couldn't wrap a towel around himself. So he sat down and air-dried. He turned his feet and toes into tools, using them to open doors, type, turn knobs on the radio, and punch buttons on phones and TV remote controls. He even lit a cigarette by holding the match between his big and second toe and striking it on a stovetop, tile wall, or brick. Then he'd cross his legs and lower his head with a cigarette clenched in his teeth, ready to be lit. To open plastic bags, he tore a small hole with toenail clippers and widened it with his teeth. When he bought a new CD, he stomped on the case to open it and then stored the disc on a spindle.

Over the holiday break, Pete had walked around Brockton in search of new challenges. One day he pulled out money from an ATM machine and bought himself a cup of coffee, making sure to double up the paper cups to keep the hook from crushing them. Another time he walked into a bar and ordered a beer. Despite his successes, though, he had a lot to mourn. He had been the lead guitarist and singer for a rock band called D-Minus. Now all he could play was a harmonica gripped between his lips. He was an inveterate Mr. Fix-It who had worked with tools since he was a kid and could electrically wire a house in an afternoon. When something broke now, he went crazy watching others fumble when he could have repaired it in minutes. His impatience landed him in his share of power struggles, particularly with his wife-to-be, Jenn Maunus.

One afternoon in particular, Jenn was trying to put a flint in a lighter. Pete had done it a million times: just remove a screw and drop in the flint. She was taking all day. If he still had hands, he would have ripped his hair out. He started screaming at her, and she screamed back at him for screaming at her.

Jenn was no pushover. She had grown up in Brockton four years behind Pete. Even women had to be tough in the "City of Champions" where Rocky Marciano was raised. The twenty-seven-year-old daughter of a bank security guard, Jenn once broke up a bar brawl by whacking a man over the shoulders with a pool stick. She was blond, hazel-eyed, and no-nonsense. When Pete first spoke to her over the phone from Iraq, he said he hoped she could live with the fact that he'd lost both of his hands. Jenn set him straight. "How can you even ask me that? Don't you know me by now? I'm just happy you're alive." She and Pete had lived together intermittently for ten years. They never had enough money to pay for a wedding, so they had put it off. But from the moment he had awakened in the Iraq hospital and heard of the benefits that a disabled veteran and his family would receive, Pete knew the time had come. He proposed over the phone from Germany.

On December 20, Pete and Jenn were married in his mother's small living room by a justice of the peace, an ordained nondenominational minister who happened to be Jewish. The couple wasn't, but it didn't matter for a secular service. The Reverend Ivan S. Fleischman knew Jenn from the pharmacy photo lab where she worked and considered it an honor to marry a wounded war veteran for the price of one dollar. Jenn put on makeup and a simple white dress she picked up the previous day. She gelled Pete's hair, brushed his teeth, and dressed him in a dark shirt and a left hook. He wore nothing on his shorter right stump.

More than ever, Pete was aware that he had responsibilities. His kids looked to him for strength, not bitterness and depression. Pete wasn't a mope anyway. But he had new reason to prove that people could deal with whatever life threw at them.

When he thought of his family, Pete always channeled the nineteen-year-old specialist killed in the tire explosion. Paul Bueche hadn't lived long enough to have a wife and kids. What if he and Pete had changed places and it had been Pete who died? What if Pete had moved a foot closer to the wheel rim and taken the full brunt of the blast? He might no longer be able to hold hands with his children, but Pete could still read to them and take them on walks. He might not be able to do heavy lifting, but he could show them strength of character. He still had his eyes, his brain, and his heart. He had been given a huge gift: a second chance.

★

It arrived in a thin, black, rectangular box the day after Christmas. David Maraniss hadn't bothered to wrap it. The gold embroidery and inscription were all the decoration a Purple Heart needed.

The heart-shaped medal was embossed with a gold profile of General George Washington. It had been awarded "For Military Merit" to Thomas M. Hinger, a name I recognized from my pal David's epic on Vietnam, *They Marched into Sunlight.* Hinger was a medic wounded in a heroic struggle to save his comrades from a 1967 ambush. He had read of my ordeal and called David in mid-December. "I've got something for your buddy Weisskopf," Hinger had apparently said. "I really want him to have it. I don't want to talk about it. I don't want him to say no." When David received it in a brown padded envelope a few days later, he called Hinger to make sure he really wanted to part with what most soldiers consider the highest military honor. "It means more for me to give it to him than for me to have it," the former medic replied.

I was overwhelmed by conflicting emotions, honored by the generosity, but uneasy about accepting the symbol of another man's valor. The beautiful medal also underscored unresolved feelings I had about my own actions and others' interpretation of them as heroic. Hinger had intentionally risked his life to save his comrades. I had acted reflexively for reasons I still didn't understand.

David insisted I accept it. We had been best of friends for twenty-six years, meeting as young reporters at the *Washington Post*. He had been poised to fly to Landstuhl until *Time* decided to send an escort. Since his visit on my first day in the hospital, David had been urging me to record my experience in case I ever wanted to write about it. When I shrugged off the idea, he offered to be my Boswell and interview me on tape. After a disjointed first session, he relaunched the oral history on December 26.

Placing a chair at the foot of my bed, David started at the beginning: "Why did you go to Iraq?" An hour into the interview, I reached the point in the story where the grenade exploded in the Humvee and I was fearing imminent death. "The first thing I thought of was . . ." My voice cracked and eyes watered. I paused to regain my equilibrium.

David looked up.

I continued, biting off each word. "That I was going to do to Skyler what my father had done to me . . ."

David broke into tears before I could finish.

". . . that I was going to leave him."

We were both sobbing, caught up in one of those moments where life is distilled to a single thought: what it meant to be a father. It conjured loss for both of us—my late father, David's ailing dad, and my near miss. David and I cried for a good minute, then, with a nodding acknowledgment of the emotions we shared, picked up the narrative where it dropped off.

I hesitated in the same place I always did when I told the story: what I was thinking before I grabbed the grenade. I had a detailed memory of what happened before and after the attack. I just couldn't remember what motivated me to get in the middle of it. I'd been credited with heroism by everyone from the chairman of the Joint Chiefs of Staff to friends who half-jokingly compared me to Admiral Nelson. But I continued to be mystified by the question of intent. I kept deconstructing the event, second by second, frame by frame, looking for clues in the position of my body when I picked up the grenade, the place I landed in the Humvee—anything to shed light on why I had acted.

Shortly after arriving on the ward, I had a vivid dream of the Humvee ride: I was leaning against the wall of the truck when I heard a thunk and saw an object. It was small, dark, and puffing smoke, gauzy wisps that quickly dissipated into the night air. I clung to the image when I woke up. "I think it looked like it was smoldering a little bit," I told David. "It didn't look good."

I couldn't stop replaying that vision after David left. If the object had looked ominous, I must have assumed it was deadly and sought to protect myself from it—if not everyone else in the Humvee. Did I have it right? Or did I dream it up to help square my account with the heroic labels? I remembered something that made me question whether I had indeed recognized danger. The soldiers in my Humvee had collected incoming rocks like Mardi Gras trinkets. Did I simply grab what I thought was a harmless stone to keep as a souvenir? Or had I in fact detected a smoking device and realized it had to be ejected? I owed it to Hinger to get it right. Either I did the honorable thing by accident or I had acted with "military merit," as the inscription on the back of Hinger's Purple Heart read.

★

One of my biggest fears in the immediate wake of the accident had been losing my half-time custody of Skyler and Olivia. It was a job that required both hands to make their staple of peanut butter sandwiches, wash clothes, and chauffeur them to school and soccer games, and there was no telling whether I'd still be considered fully qualified.

I didn't have to wait long for an answer once I reached Washington. Judith Katz walked into my room and presented me with a "Left-Handers' Calendar" to mark the days the children would live with me after my discharge. Her confidence in my fathering capability lifted a dark cloud. And after an initial period of awkwardness, the kids themselves had reverted to form, a reassuring sign of life's continuity. My southpaw daughter gave me daily lessons in using my left hand. My irrepressible son required a few stern lectures about hospital etiquette. We spent a lot of time picking the nickname for my withered right arm and settled on "Stumpy." Judith, from whom I had separated in 2002, brought them almost daily and sometimes let the visits go on too long. But I was happy to resume a semblance of life with my kids, even from a hospital bed.

I kept a greater distance from my professional brethren. The first day on 57 I had received flowers from the *Today Show* with a personal get-well note from co-anchor Matt Lauer. By the second day, his producer was on the phone asking if I would tell my story on the popular morning show.

A cardinal rule of reporters is never to become the *story*. We covered the news; we didn't make it. The principle suited me. I wanted my work to speak for itself. But the events of December 10 cast me in a new light: a reporter who had saved soldiers. It was a man-bites-dog story, the kind the media can't resist. I was pursued for interviews with an intensity usually reserved for avalanche survivors and celebrities. *Time*'s publicists in New York were fielding requests from virtually every network and cable news show, scores of newspapers and media outlets as far away as Japan. So was the public affairs office at Walter Reed. When I agreed to see Congresswoman Eleanor Holmes Norton, who had helped me get into Walter Reed, her aide asked if I'd permit local TV cameras and reporters to cover it—a request I granted only to still photographers standing no closer than my room door.

I refused all of the interview requests not only because I felt crowded and depersonalized, but because I couldn't honestly characterize what motivated me to snuff the grenade. And until I could, I didn't want to answer questions about it or fuel efforts to lionize me.

Finding myself on the other side of the camera was intriguing. The media often trample the traumatized in the name of "news." But my story wasn't merely a case of journalistic lust; my colleagues were proud of what I had done. We don't always act in ways the public considers honorable; so when one of us does, it's a time to show off. Ben Bradlee, my former boss at the *Washington Post*, sent me a note in which he recalled his own World War II military service in the Pacific. "Your courage has moved us all—to tears, to pride, to wonder. I remember wondering as I went into battle off Guadalcanal whether I would be brave. All of us do, but few of us get a chance to prove it the way you did."

Bradlee's note choked me up. But such praise only deepened my increasing sense of conflict. The seconds it had taken to seize a grenade brought me more attention than the thousands of articles I had written. I wanted to be recognized for reporting, not soldiering. I felt torn.

The Cookie Lady walked into the middle of my identity crisis. Marje Hoban was a great-grandmother in her seventies who served up heaping plates of homemade chocolate chips and gratitude. Marje felt a special debt to soldiers, whom she had seen as protectors ever since she laid awake at night as a child listening to German bombers strafe her native England. She married a U.S. Air Force officer and moved to this country, finding her way to Ward 57 through her participation in a computer network of people who asked for prayers for friends. A few months after the war started, Marje saw a request for a critically injured soldier at Walter Reed. She set out from her home in suburban Maryland to pay him a visit. Meeting other patients who had no family at their side, she became a regular caller, always bringing her delicacies.

Marje was making her New Year's rounds when she popped into my room to introduce herself. "Thank you for the sacrifices you made on behalf of all us," she said. "I'm here to visit the troops and bring around cookies."

"I'm not a troop," I said, in what I realized was a cold voice.

Undaunted, she pressed ahead in her lilting English accent. "You were over in Iraq, weren't you?"

"Yes."

"I understand you saved several lives," she remarked.

"Well, that's what they say."

When she offered me cookies, I suggested she give them to the soldiers in other rooms. "They're more deserving."

A few days later she returned. "I know you don't want any cookies," she said. "I just came to tell you people out here are still thinking of you. We appreciate the sacrifice you made. You saved lives."

I brushed it off. "I did what I had to do." Unwittingly, I was echoing the response Marje typically received from real soldiers: "I was just doing my duty, ma'am."

I was no more forthcoming with hospital professionals. Every few days the psychiatry service sent someone to my room. I'd summarily dismiss the person, and, after a while, someone with a different specialty would show up, offering to treat post-traumatic stress disorder or feelings of victimization from violence or depression. I had the same message for each: "I'm unconflicted." I had no regrets about going to Iraq or picking up the grenade. So we had nothing to discuss.

Of course, I completely missed the point. Within a few days of my arrival on the ward, I was feeling conflicted—if not over what I had done, then why I had done it and what it meant. By the end of my first week, I had worn myself down with the constant weighing of contradictory versions. I spent long periods staring out my window at the barren frozen courtyard below. A great oak spread its leafless branches. I melded into the still life and waited for the sun to return.

Walter Reed had tripled its staff of psychiatrists to deal with baggage from the Iraq war. The service was headed by psychologist Hal Wain, a thirty-year veteran of the hospital who urged his staff to watch *The Best Years of Our Lives* as a training tool. The 1946 film on the wrenching homecoming of World War II servicemen, including one who had lost both hands, deepened Wain's understanding of the feelings of futility that every amputee was facing. The therapist's job was to stop such negative thinking. The quicker his patients realized they could resume normal lives, the quicker they would adapt and move on.

But it was hard for us to leave the past behind, to stop recounting the moment that had forever rearranged our lives. The flashbacks were obsessive, a constant rewinding of the tape to alter the outcome. We lived in a world of "if onlys"— if only I had missed the call for a patrol, or ridden in another Humvee, or released the grenade a few seconds earlier, none of this would have happened and I'd still have my right hand. Sergeant Pete Damon asked himself over and over how differently things might have been if only he had known about safety problems with the equipment he used to inflate the helicopter tire that exploded and severed his arms. For Sergeant First Class Luis Rodriguez, the question was what if he had driven the Humvee, as he usually did, rather than ride shotgun, where the bomb that ripped off his right leg had detonated.

Wain tried to draw out those visions in hospital rounds three times a week and a group therapy session—dubbed "Cripples' Cavalcade" by one amputee—every Thursday at lunch. The soldiers opened up, sometimes tearfully, revealing their fears about life after 57: Who would marry a guy with no legs? How am I going to get a job with one hand? What a dies in Iraq going to do without me? How am I going myself in a tough neighborhood? Who is going to help me when I live alone and fall out of my wheelchair? How am I going to carry my baby with no hands?

★

Pat Isaacs leaned forward in a recliner and watched her son sleep. It didn't seem so long ago that Bobby was a chubby baby hospitalized for pneumonia in western Pennsylvania, where the family was then living. Doctors had prescribed Tylenol, which made him hyperactive: the eleven-month-old toddler stood up and walked for the first time. Now, twenty-one years later, the bacteria coursing through the veins in those same legs threatened to kill him—if the narcotics didn't get him first.

Bobby was so pumped full of painkillers Pat feared that he'd overdose. His eyes often rolled up and stayed open as he drifted off. Whenever he acted out of the ordinary, as he did on the afternoon of December 28, Pat became anxious. At about 1 P.M., Bobby suddenly extended his arms rigidly and convulsed all over, as if he was having a seizure. "Bobby, wake up, wake up," Pat yelled, shaking him. When he didn't respond, she ran out in search of a nurse. By the time they got back to the room, Bobby had mysteriously awakened. Pat took the opportunity to rant about doctors who overprescribe narcotics.

Bobby didn't like what he heard. Drugs were easing his pain, and he was happy for any relief. "Butt out," he snarled.

That was the last thing Pat would do. At forty-four, she had little in her life that could compete with the care of her only child. Her ex-husband, a trucker, was long gone; so was her career as a nurse—a back injury had put her on total disability fifteen years earlier. Bobby had always been the center of her life. They looked alike—though less so since she had begun going gray—and both had a laconic and modest manner. Pat had been a protective mother who insisted on a say in her son's religious training, choice of friends, and the cars he rode in. Even when he was six thousand miles away in Iraq, she couldn't let go. Television news ran twenty-four hours a day in her bedroom, kept on mute at night so she could catch the crawl on the bottom of the screen in case she suddenly woke up. When casualties in Bobby's battalion were reported, she made a note of it on a USO calendar she stored in her nightstand. She would say a prayer for her son and, every time the phone rang, worry that the army was calling with bad news.

The morning of December 10, 2003, had started with an early-morning TV report on a roadside bomb assault in Mosul. Pat added a note to the calendar—"Convoy attack, one dead, three injured"—and left for the day. She was so busy running errands that she didn't think about it again until the phone rang just after six o'clock that evening. It was an army captain calling from Fort Campbell, where Bobby's 101st Airborne Division was based. He said Bobby had been injured and was in serious condition, with shrapnel wounds to his lower limbs. Pat broke into tears and called her brother in western Pennsylvania, who dialed up Fort Campbell for more information. He was asked to verify Bobby's home address. The request touched a raw nerve. Bobby always said if he got hurt, the army would phone home. If the family got a knock on the door, he'd be dead.

"You're not telling me you're going to their house, are you?" Bobby's uncle asked. The officer didn't respond. Nor did he pass on that army doctors in Iraq had given Bobby less than seventy-two hours to live.

Pat phoned Liberty Baptist Church in Durham. Her pastor, Jack Cox, was getting ready to preside over his regular Wednesday prayer meeting. After hearing the news, he called his hundred worshippers to the altar and led them in prayer for Bobby. "God, we don't know where he is," Cox said. "We don't even know the extent of his injuries. You do. May your will be done." Then the pastor and his wife, Renée, drove twenty-eight miles to Roxboro to console Pat.

The captain from Fort Campbell promised Pat that he'd update her as information became available. She didn't leave home or even use the phone for fear she'd miss his call. He phoned the next day and asked for a way to reach Bobby's father, a tip-off that the army was getting ready to notify next of kin of his death. The only hard information the officer offered was that Bobby would soon be moved to the army hospital in Landstuhl.

Pat obtained a phone number for it and called Germany just after Bobby arrived on the morning of December 12. An orthopedic surgeon told her that he had suffered serious injuries to his legs but wouldn't lose them. He was heavily sedated and relying on a respirator to breathe.

Five days later, the Coxes drove Pat to Washington for Bobby's arrival at Walter Reed. She had asked the preacher to accompany her into the intensive care unit. They found Bobby grinning and talkative, but badly torn up. He was bloated, tangled in tubes, and streaked in dried blood and iodine. His swollen, battered legs were held together by titanium pins and black metal rods. Pat felt faint but pulled herself together. She knew Bobby had a long, painful road ahead and needed all of her strength to get through it. She vowed not to leave until he could walk again and moved into the Malogne House, a residential hotel on Walter Reed grounds for outpatient soldiers and visiting families. By her second day, Pat had established a routine. She showed up at five o'clock for morning rounds and stayed until 10 P.M.

Over the past three weeks Pat had faced constant tests of her will, none more trying than the January 6 amputation of Bobby's right leg. The surgery went well, but doctors discovered that the antibiotics prescribed to combat the Iraqi bug *Acinetobacter* had failed. Only one drug, Septra, was left to try, but Bobby was allergic to it. He would have to be desensitized to the drug, administered tiny doses over several hours. The trouble was, the process might induce anaphylactic shock.

Doctors called Pat at Malogne House and asked for a signed consent to proceed. The request pushed her over the edge; as she hung up the phone, she was crying so hard she had to gulp for air. After all the blood spilled and bone lost, Bobby could die from an allergic reaction. Renée Cox brought Pat's mother to Washington to be with her during the desensitization process. They sat by a phone in Pat's room, bowed their heads, and prayed. The five hours it took to administer twenty-six doses of Septra were torture for Pat. It was no easier for Bobby. He had to make it through the postsurgery period without painkillers. Doctors feared anything that dulled his senses might also dull his ability to recognize—and to convey to the staff—an allergic reaction to the antibiotic.

★

Sergeant Luis Rodriguez's wife, Lilliam, left Ward 57 every night about midnight. Since early December, she had taken to stopping at the first-floor entrance to count the gurneys lined up outside. Invariably, another bus from Andrews Air Force Base would be unloading a new batch of amputees. Lilliam figured that for each gurney that was waiting, another woman would soon be retreating to the wall flanking 57's northeast side and unleashing her anguish.

Fathers and sons looked stricken as they moved through the ward. But the women flocked to the wailing wall in open despair, leaning or pressing their foreheads against the hard plaster as if it might support the crumbling foundations of their lives: mothers wept for their sons, wives for their partners, and sisters for their childhood pals.

Although female soldiers had been injured in combat, only men occupied the ward in the first year of the war. Once strong and independent, they were as helpless as babies now. They couldn't walk, eat, or, in some cases, urinate by themselves. But at least they had narcotics and a hero's welcome. Their visitors bore only the burden of carrying the fears and confusion of their loved one. Worst of all, they had to shoulder it in silence. Their role was to be resourceful, reassuring, and omnipresent.

By the time their men checked into 57, usually the women had already arrived. Many of them never left, piecing together arrangements for their jobs and children back home. They'd spend all day running after nurses, pushing wheelchairs, warming up meals in the little kitchen across from my room, cheering on physical therapy or prosthesis training. Some slept in chairs next to a patient's bed. Others lived in residential facilities, like Malogne House. Late at night, they'd straggle back wearily, exchange disheartening stories, and get ready to do it again the next day.

Pat Isaacs knew her way around hospital rooms and served as Bobby's private nurse. When he wanted to turn in bed, she gently rolled him over. When he had to defecate, she brought a bedpan. She kept his linens fresh, his IV unclogged, and his dressings clean. Every other day, it seemed, Bobby had surgery, more often than not a routine procedure called irrigation and debridement, in which surgeons dug out shrapnel and contaminated tissue, then rinsed the wounds with a high-pressure jet of saline. Pat watched the hours pass without a word, not knowing how much of her only child would come out of the operating room. She'd wait at Malogne House for surgeons to call, an eternity that she passed watching TV news shows, reading the Bible, Andrew Carroll's *War Letters*, and magazines, updating relatives on her cell phone, or brewing coffee in an electric pot she'd brought from home. Most days, she would kneel at the side of the bed and pray for the surgeons to perform well and for her son to return better than he'd been when he went in. One hour. Four hours. Six hours. Then a doctor would call with no definitive information.

She recorded every day's events in a loose leaf "Top Flight" notebook. Writing became her therapy. By reducing every tragic turn to the written word, she could depersonalize it. Her entries resembled a bed chart, a bare-bones factual account of bowel movements, menus, blood pressure numbers, visitors, temperatures, hours of surgery, and dosages of medicine. The jottings betrayed little emotion—from her or Bobby—beyond noting a "bad day" or the fact that she kept praying.

The caretaker's role was hard, heartbreaking, and sometimes thankless. Katrina Fair slept in a pullout bed next to her husband, James Fair, the blind, handless combat engineer. A recent high school dropout, she was eighteen years old and five months pregnant when the bad news reached her in Manhattan, Kansas, on November 12. She had arrived at Walter Reed five days later and was shocked by what she saw: James was lying unconscious in the ICU, his shaven head swollen as large as a basketball and implanted with metal staples, his eyes bugged out, skin burned, both forearms shortened and swaddled in dressings. His right calf muscle was open and raw from shrapnel wounds.

Katrina bit her tongue to keep from crying and decided she had to be strong. "Hey babe, I'm here," she announced, prancing into his room at 1 A.M. "Why don't you get up and talk to me?" She carried on a one-way conversation with her unresponsive husband all night and resolved to be his eyes and hands. She did everything for him when he regained consciousness—bathing, feeding, wiping up after bowel movements, shaving, positioning the urinal, cleaning ears, scratching, and reading.

Her job became tougher when James's brain trauma eased. He kept insisting that he still had his hands, that he was grasping a pencil or holding metal objects—a knife or carpenter's nails. When she tried to explain that he was experiencing phantom sensations, he lashed out: "You're calling me crazy." Raising his stumps, he got more agitated. "My hands are here, Trina." As his frustration escalated, so did his temper. He yelled at Katrina in front of others and banished her from his room.

Katrina's experience was not uncommon. Amputees often crossed from depression to rage and took aim at the nearest targets. Not everyone stayed the course. Some young women quickly realized they couldn't hack it. After a few days, their mood turned bitter—they hadn't bargained on an amputee for a husband or boyfriend. When they left, they took a piece of the soldier's heart.

Staff Sergeant Maurice Craft's wife showed up a few days after he arrived on the ward on December 3, his left leg cut off at the knee and his right knee connected to his hip by a titanium rod. Initially, Andrea Craft was supportive of the handsome, twenty-six-year-old paratrooper from New Jersey, who bore a close resemblance to Tiger Woods. But Andrea, in her early twenties, quickly made friends in Washington and was soon spending less and less time with her hospitalized husband, leaving their two young daughters with her mother, who lived nearby.

Craft figured that his wife saw him as a loser and began to view himself the same way. He got depressed, then mad. His anger drove Andrea further away, and she vanished for weeks at a time. Craft began to have panic attacks. He grew convinced that his life was over. He had reconciled himself to the fact that he would never be able to jump out of airplanes again or best his cross-country running records, yet now he faced another devastating loss. He and Andrea had had their ups and downs in five years of marriage. But surely she would see him through this moment of crisis, Craft felt.

When Christmas arrived, his grandmother and aunt traveled from New Jersey to visit. No sign of his wife. When he stood up for the first time on a prosthetic leg, he would have liked Andrea to have been there to cheer him on. She wasn't. Craft's amputation made him feel that he no longer fit in mainstream society. With Andrea's disappearance, he didn't even feel at home on the amputation ward. He was one of the only married amputees whose wife was AWOL.

★

Wives were usually informed of their husband's injuries by army officers specially trained to counsel the grieving. But no one prepares a woman how to deliver the news to her children. Everyone did it differently. Jenn Damon had taken a direct approach. When six-year-old Allura asked why her mother was crying, Jenn didn't mince words. "Daddy lost his hands," Jenn told her.

But Allura hadn't seemed to comprehend the loss until early November, when Jenn showed her a front-page *Brockton Enterprise* photo of Pete, his stubs wrapped in heavy bandages, meeting with Senator Ted Kennedy on Ward 57. Allura silently widened her eyes. Jenn tried to be consoling. "He might look a little different," she said, "but he's the same person." A couple of weeks later, their daughter had a chance to see for herself when Jenn brought Allura and one-year-old Danny to see their father at Walter Reed.

Allura walked to the foot of Pete's bed and froze.

"I'm still the same Daddy," he told her.

The little girl ran over and threw her arms around Pete's neck. Allura had begun to process the loss. But after returning to Brockton, she put an old picture of Pete in her backpack to show her teacher what he had looked like with hands. Noticing that her daughter looked troubled one afternoon in December, Jenn inquired why. Allura was worried that Pete wouldn't be able to play their favorite card game, Uno. "How is he going to hold his cards?" she asked. When Jenn explained that he'd have a hook, Allura demanded to know how he'd be able to pick a card at the same time. "He'll have two hooks and use both," Jenn reassured her.

Pete had done his best to comfort Allura during his home leave. He took her for a walk in the neighborhood and said that when he thought he was dying, he focused on her. "I'm really happy that I didn't die," he told her, then promised he wouldn't disappear again for a long time.

Lilliam Rodriguez had taken a more gradual tack with seven-year-old Michelle and five-year-old Melanie. Rod had lost his leg just three days before Thanksgiving, but she waited until after they finished their turkey to break the news. Their father had fallen and badly hurt a leg, she gently told her daughters. The next day, she added an important detail: doctors had to cut off his leg to keep him alive.

At first the girls were inconsolable. They wanted to know if someone could donate a leg to him. When Melanie asked if her father would return to Iraq, Lilliam saw a chance to change the tone. "No, never," the thirty-four-year-old mother shouted joyfully. Her daughters took the cue, parading up and down the small living room and cheering: "Daddy's never going back to Iraq again."

Michelle and Melanie traveled with Rod's father to Washington on Christmas Day. Melanie immediately pulled the sheets off his stump and kissed it, telling Rod not to worry. The little girl appeared to have found all the proof she needed that Daddy wasn't going anyplace soon.

5.
HORNBOOK FOR
THE HANDICAPPED

Room 3J04 pulsated with the sounds of heavy metal, wailing electric guitars and crashing drums. I entered in a manual wheelchair pushed by a hospital orderly, and was greeted by a black, soul-shaking colonel and a pair of one-legged soldiers playing foosball. No, it wasn't a morphine dream. I had landed in occupational therapy.

Located two floors below Ward 57, OT might as well have been another planet. The name made it sound like a job training center. Instead, it helped to get bodies working. This was boot camp for amputees, training for life without limbs. The clinic held out potential to patients who thought they had none, a place to stop grieving and learn how to compensate with technology and ingenuity. The motto was, "Whatever Works."

Usually that meant use of artificial limbs. But when a prosthesis couldn't help the legless take a shower or the one-armed tie a shoe, therapists offered new strategies, from bath stools to elastic shoelaces. Leg amputees learned how to jump out of bed without falling on their faces and get in and out of a model car from a wheelchair. Arm amputees practiced hanging shirts, cooking, and sweeping the floor of a mock apartment named Fort Independence. OT returned the real world to patients who had dropped out of it. Everyone trained together in an atmosphere set up for comradeship and comfort. No one paid attention to rank or age. They bonded over a common plight and debated endlessly which limb was worse to lose: an arm or leg. The patients got to play their favorite music and help themselves (if they could) to candy bars, gum, and beef jerky from a cabinet. A bulletin board posted hometown newspaper reports on their injuries.

Captain Katie was the queen of OT. When she came to 57 on my first day for an assessment, she asked for my recovery goals. "Return to my abnormal life," I told her. By the time I started OT in the late afternoon of December 26, she had drawn up a baseline charting the distance I had to go. I still needed supervision to safely reach a toilet and "moderate" aid in unbuttoning and zipping after I arrived. I couldn't bathe or put on pants without help.

ed me up from the wheelchair to check my
d down the hall with my stump folded like a
sting badly to my right side. She directed me
p, raise my head, and swing my short right

arm as freely as I did my left. My port side was getting a lot of attention. Now that I was a southpaw by necessity, I had to get my brain used to the new boy in town. Katie gave me shoestrings to lace, buttons to close, and sentences to write on notebook paper. I'd do it, and she'd have me do it again— only faster. On December 30, I was promoted to her hottest class: Bionic Hands 101.

Myoelectric is the non-sci-fi name for bionic. A myoelectric hand works off tiny electrical signals released when muscles (*myo* is the Greek word for muscle) are contracted. The signals are picked up by electrodes that line the inside of a prosthesis and cover the muscles of a stump. Electrodes send the signal to a computer chip that instructs an electronic hand to open, close, or rotate—depending on the muscle flexed and the speed and intensity of its contraction.

For long stumps like mine, forearm muscles located three inches below the elbow drove the process. Flexing the one on the outside of my forearm signaled a hand to open. Tensing the inner muscle would close it. The technology mimicked nature. Katie held out a cup and told me to grab it with my good left hand. I felt the inner muscle tighten as I grasped it. The outer muscle relaxed when I let it go.

The first lesson focused on how to isolate those muscles. Captain Katie had a tool, called "Myo-boy," as high tech as the device I hoped to incorporate. She strapped electrodes onto each forearm muscle and plugged the other end of a cord into a laptop computer. The object was to generate a spike on the monitor by flexing the right muscle. It was more difficult than it looked. I jerked, twitched, and turned my stump. Nothing happened. I pumped again, hunting for the right spot, but the monitor stayed blank. When I grew frustrated, Katie had me close my eyes to map the muscle in my mind. I contracted. She let out a cheer: "You did it."

I opened my eyes and saw a tiny streak on the monitor. I squeezed, again, sending the spike higher. I was getting stronger. Unfortunately, as I kept practicing, the computer indicated that I was firing both muscles at the same time. I closed my eyes again and accessed my outside one. Katie released another yelp of encouragement. I finally managed to distinguish one muscle from the other and triggered each separately so as not to send conflicting signals. Manipulating those tiny muscles was exhausting. I felt as if I had pressed two hundred pounds. My hospital gown was soaked in sweat.

Over the course of the next week, I spent at least an hour a day working on the Myo-boy, graduating to new levels of virtual reality. One was a monitor that showed cars careening toward a brick wall. I could lift the car and avoid disaster by flexing the right muscle. I took turns connecting the electrode to the inside and outside of my forearm, compiling a good enough driving record to increase the challenge. Katie ran two cars at the same time, each controlled by a different muscle. Finally, I simulated the mechanics of a virtual hand, including the wrist rotation I had paid so dearly for. It took an extra step, hitting both muscles at the same time. That would change the gears of the hand, preparing it to turn clockwise when I squeezed the outer muscle and counterclockwise with the inner muscle.

Katie spent the last ten minutes of each session massaging my stump. She pressed hard on the scar tissue to keep it flat and supple. The kneading also gave me comfort. Once the pain of surgery had subsided after Christmas, I began to suffer the bane of amputees: phantom limb pain. When I first heard the term, I thought it sounded like a form of self-delusion, a mind game of amputees who couldn't accept their loss. How could something that didn't exist hurt? The name recalled a favorite childhood action figure, the Phantom. But I certainly wasn't fantasizing the deep ache in what had been my right hand. Sometimes I felt as if my fist was clamping tighter and tighter until my fingers were ready to explode. The pain brought back memories of that horrible night in the Humvee. In those moments, my hand felt as if it were cupped around a hot object, burning and throbbing as it did after the explosion. At other times, the Phantom could create the sensation of twisted fingers or a bent thumb. Sometimes, it was an annoying tickle on the heel of my hand.

Virtually everyone on Ward 57 had some phantom limb pain. Its cause remained as mysterious as it had been when a Civil War doctor coined the term to identify the complaints of soldiers whose injured limbs had been sawed off. Their symptoms had been dismissed as psychosomatic, but today's doctors recognized the pain as a bona fide neurological condition. Nerve endings that had naturally extended to the fingers of my right hand no longer had a place to go; they were frantically crashing into one another, sending pain signals to my brain and tricking it into thinking I still had a hand. Some experts believe the brain has a blueprint of body parts that persists even if they've been cut off. According to one theory, when the brain sends signals and receives no feedback, it bombards the missing limb with more signals. That aggravates the swollen nerves that once served it, inducing pain.

Doctors were as hard-pressed to treat phantom pain as they were to explain it. They resorted to trial and error, using remedies originally intended for other ailments that seemed to relieve nerve pain. I had a sampling on my nightstand: pills to combat seizures and depression, lozenges for bronchitis, allergy nasal spray, arthritis cream, medicated patches for shingles, and an electro-stimulation device. It was hard to tell if any of them worked. The crushing, stabbing pain in my right hand flared and subsided—but never went away. Doctors said it might last a month, a year, or a lifetime. Every amputee was different. I had resolved that 2004 would be the "Year of the Phantom."

Phantom pain was a daily topic at OT, the whittling porch for amputees. I made my first friends there. I'd been in no mood for small talk the first two weeks on 57. Most of my neighbors were half my age and from different backgrounds, small-town boys who had passed up college or blue-collar trades for a military life. I was urban, overeducated, untattooed, and distrustful of uniforms and blind patriotism. But I soon discovered that I shared something with those soldiers larger than the differences in our biographies. We were men struggling for identity. The psychological scars of amputation ran deeper than those from conventional wounds of war. The blasts took away something deeply personal. None of us felt like the man who had gone to Iraq. We possessed the same minds; they just resided in different bodies.

The loss of my writing hand launched an assault on my self-image. If I couldn't be a reporter, then who was I? What would I do? The questions left me raw and wide open, no more so than my new friends who had honed their bodies for a completely different cause: war. The military represented the perfect synthesis of muscle and discovery, a place to play out feelings of invincibility. Now they confronted the world from a wheelchair or without an arm. Life looked different with no war to fight, orders to follow, and comrades to love. The question was how to fill the void, and with what.

No one knew what to make of me at first. I was rumored to be a colonel who had stumbled into harm's way. Fortunately, the suspicion was short-lived—soldiers had even less regard for officers than for reporters. Once word got out that I had coauthored the *Time* cover story on the American soldier and saved a couple of privates, I was let into the club. No one knew my name—I became known as "the reporter who ate the grenade." Most of my interactions with other amputees took place off the ward, in more friendly territory like OT or the hospital cafeteria. We swapped stories of our injuries, compared notes on painkillers, and competed on the Myoboy. The arrival of someone's prosthesis created a lot of excitement. Everyone would wait for him to strut into OT to show it off. I felt at home in the small universe of men, who, like me, were trying to figure out what was left of them and the lives they once led. We had the privilege of working through our pain, insecurity, and clumsiness without the stares and questions of outsiders.

Not everyone enjoyed the company. The tone in OT could shift from laughter to grave silence in the moment it took a soldier to scream in pain or explode into anger. Captain Katie segregated the angriest amputees. If they wanted to poison the atmosphere, they'd have to do it together. Her morning sessions bristled with tension. Metallica and Motorhead blared from speakers. Amputees leaned back in their wheelchairs and spun the wheels. One specialist who had trouble picking up a peg with his above-the-elbow prosthesis flung the $115,000 device against a wall. "I ain't doing it anymore," he shouted. Another threw the metal pedal of his wheelchair into a costly exercise machine.

My own moods fluctuated between anger and joy, frustration and triumph. But a feeling of melancholy prevailed as I came face-to-face with the larger tragedy beyond my own: stolen youth. Specialist Hilario Bermanis, twenty-one, had been built like a fullback when he left his home in Micronesia to join the army. Now, he hunched in a wheelchair, a thick neck and broad shoulders the only reminder of his once muscular body. He had lost his left hand and both legs above the knee to a rocket-propelled grenade in Baghdad. A photo of Bermanis taking the oath of U.S. citizenship hung in OT. He held up a right hand, his sole undamaged limb. I had seen the photo but hadn't taken a full measure of the devastation until the day I saw him wheeled into OT by his father. I couldn't erase the horrifying picture of a once strapping man reduced to a single hand.

Specialist James Fair had the cruelest of all fates; not only had he lost his sight, he had no hands for braille or a cane. Still recovering from a brain injury in late December, he was wheeled into OT for sensory perception tests. He rolled his head back and forth, unresponsive to the therapists. As I watched, I couldn't help but question if he would be better off without the capacity to reason.

By the end of 2003, the war had become little more than a distraction for most Americans, a faraway conflict fought by a volunteer army. The daily stories of soldiers killed in action began to blur and the statistics grew abstract. Few reports even mentioned the number of casualties, despite the fact that the ratio of wounded to killed was running 8 to 1, double that of Vietnam. But the onslaught was no secret to anyone entering Walter Reed, where the most seriously wounded were taken. Amputees occupied one of every five beds, alongside the blinded, burned, and brain-damaged. Every day, the *New York Times* published the names of U.S. soldiers killed in action. I began to read between the lines and calculate how many new roommates I'd soon have. For me, the Iraq war had become deeply personal.

Everyone knows that war has an ugly face. It's a different thing to wake up to it every morning. I had been in Iraq in April 2003 after U.S. troops had toppled Saddam Hussein and pulled back the curtain on his reign of terror. It had been exhilarating to see a nation break the bonds of tyranny, a victory that nearly all my new Walter Reed friends believed was worth their sacrifice. But my experience on 57 changed the calculus for me. A day of freedom for Iraqi youth didn't necessarily seem worth a lifetime of darkness for James Fair.

★

The orthopedic staff of Walter Reed couldn't read Bobby Isaacs. He so rarely complained that doctors feared he was covering up severe pain and directed anesthesiologists to monitor him closely. Bobby responded to every inquiry with an ear-to-ear grin and a soft drawl delivered from the back of his throat: "Aw, it ain't that bad." The young corporal had entered Walter Reed with all his limbs intact. The night we arrived,

Bobby had been rushed to the operating room for eleven hours of surgery. Over the course of the next fifteen days, he had gone back another seven times, for a total of thirty-five more hours under the knife, recovering in the ICU between operations. He finally received his ticket to Ward 57 on December 31. He still had everything but half of his right foot.

It was a medical feat just to hold his legs together, however. Each shinbone was broken and missing a three-inch segment. Pus oozed from open wounds, the skin surrounding them cracked and dried out. His left leg was fractured in a couple hundred places. Surgeons worried most about the infection that at one point had his temperature spiking to 104.

Bobby granted doctors the right to amputate as they judged necessary and hoped they'd get rid of whatever was causing his pain. He figured his legs had taken such a beating they wouldn't do him much good anyway. He wasn't worried about walking; one of his uncles had lost a leg in a hunting accident and got around just fine with a prosthesis. A couple of days after arriving at Walter Reed, Bobby told a therapist, "I'm going to walk out of here—either on my legs or a prosthesis." He didn't care how his body looked as long as he felt good.

On January 6, during Bobby's tenth operation, surgeons removed a titanium nail that had been holding together his right shinbone. The stench was overwhelming: infection had reached the bone. The doctors amputated eight inches of his right leg, from his ankle to halfway up his calf. Bobby may have been the first patient to cheer his own amputation: three days after the surgery he told his mother he was feeling so much better that "I may just tell them to take the left, too."

He was only half-joking. Doctors kept looking for a way to salvage the left leg, but in truth he had no use for it damaged. If he'd be better off with a prosthesis, then why not get on with it. The leg was severely infected and missing a long section of bone; the flesh around his wounds was unlikely to heal.

On January 12, surgeons laid out three options. They could splice a piece of his hip into the broken segment, which would require many operations. They could fuse both ends of the gap in his left leg and shorten his right to conform, dramatically reducing his five-foot-seven height. Both of those procedures were described as long shots because of the extensive damage to bone and tissue. Even if one worked, he'd always have pain and trouble using the salvaged limb. But that was a big *if*. Doctors told Bobby he was at the "very end of a high likelihood" of failing and would probably be back within a year for the third option: amputation.

Bobby decided on the spot. "Just take it," he told his surgeons. Three days later, they removed seven inches from his left leg.

★

The Walter Reed dietitian was in a panic. I had banned hospital food from my room a few days after arriving. It tasted bad and smelled worse, like old socks. My friends had filled in the gap, stuffing a giant refrigerator in the Ward 57 pantry with enough food for six meals a day. When the dietitian found out, she immediately assumed that I wasn't eating right and rushed into my room to confront me.

I informed her that the hospital cuisine brought down my

morale and everyone else's on the ward, then proceeded to tick off delicacies from the kitchen of my *Time* magazine colleague Judith Stoler, who was contributing 90 percent of my daily caloric intake. I must have made the dietitian hungry. "He is suffering no negative side effects," she wrote on my chart on December 29.

Nurses like it when patients begin to bitch. It's a sign they're getting better. By the last week of 2003, I must have been improving by the hour. The chaotic condition of my room—a nine-by-twenty-foot repository of flowers, books, magazines, cookies, dishes, luggage, games, letters, chairs, a carton of Marshall Field's famous Frango Mints, get-well cards, and toiletries—was contributing to my crankiness. Nurse Tami banished me to the corridor and restored order.

Although my pain hadn't eased, I was feeling stronger. I spent much of my waking hours pacing up and down the two-hundred-foot-long hallway for exercise, brandishing my IV stand like a mountaineer's pole. My flimsy hospital gown often flew open in the back, prompting nurses to hurriedly cover me in robes or sheets. Ward decorum had to be preserved.

Nighttime was gloomy. The visitors and volunteers had gone home, leaving the ward in silence, save for the strange noises of surgical equipment. Malfunctioning IVs produced a high-pitched ring. Wound vacuum machines swooshed. A depleted bag of liquid painkillers beeped rapidly. The nocturnal sounds reminded me of the cries of wild animals on long-past camping trips.

By New Year's, doctors had started talking about moving me out. It wasn't an eviction notice, but a hint that I had recovered enough to free up a bed for new amputees being sent from Iraq at a steady rate. Since I had been admitted, eighteen days earlier, five more soldiers had lost limbs in Iraq. When my buddies were released from 57, they got a room at Malogne House, a short distance from the hospital. Because I lived in Washington, my discharge meant a trip home. The thought terrified me. It wasn't fending for myself that worried me so much as dealing with my pain.

It was mushrooming daily. The greatest relief came from a peripheral nerve block, an anesthesia that numbed the nerves around my wound, not unlike the effects of novocaine on the gums. It was nonnarcotic, administered locally, and highly effective. Used in a handful of hospitals, the painkiller had been battlefield-tested in Iraq at the urging of a Walter Reed anesthesiologist. I received my first dose in Baghdad and lived off it in Walter Reed, as a supplement to the narcotics pumped into my veins by an IV to ease the relentless cramping and occasional electric jolts. If morphine didn't cut it, I had a Dilaudid chaser released by a button near my bed. I never became inured to pain, only more fearful of it. The hospital provided me defense on demand. I was afraid of losing it. What if I awakened in agony in the middle of night and had no emergency button to push, no nurse with narcotics?

Three weeks of hospital life had taken a toll. I was twenty pounds lighter, stooped, and as pale as a death row inmate. My eyes were bloodshot and puffy. Lacking a hand and three inches of forearm, my right limb hung almost a foot shorter than my left, the length of a child's arm attached to an adult's body. In a light-green hospital gown, I wasn't groomed for the runway or my date of January 2. My girlfriend, Rebekah Edminster, had flown in from California for a ten-day stint.

A professional singer who lived in the artists' colony of Ojai, Rebekah had kept her distance from Washington to avoid potential rivalry over my care. My sister had come for the first few days, and Judith Katz, to whom I had been married for a decade, had been a continuous presence. Patients often had to mediate between mothers and wives, girlfriends and sisters. I had been romantically involved with Rebekah for a year, but she had wisely decided to supply her love long-distance until things had settled down a bit. Her opening gambit had been a call to me at the army hospital in Landstuhl. "Does this mean I'm going to have to be on top for a while?" she quipped. It was just the tonic I needed to stop feeling sorry for myself. At Walter Reed, I had spoken to her almost every night.

I wasn't sure how she'd react when she actually laid eyes on me. But Rebekah arrived and kissed me as if nothing had changed. After a couple of hours, however, I sensed a little tension, as I had over the phone. I knew what was coming: a *Washington Post* story covering the Iraq incident had identified Judith as my wife. We were legally separated, but I had used the term interchangeably with divorce. Rebekah felt misled, telling a friend, "The grenade didn't kill him, but I'm going to."

I had avoided the subject on the phone but decided to broach it now, setting off a debate on the definition of marriage. I became angry and defensive. The room got close. I insisted I had never intentionally deceived her and couldn't operate from a "deficit" of trust. I needed support now, not doubt.

Rebekah could see the discussion was going nowhere fast and worried the confrontation would raise my blood pressure.

"Listen, are we not friends?" she asked, locking her eyes on mine.

I nodded yes.

"Then we'll get through this," she said.

I knew I had been wrong. Even those who go through hell have to deal with their dirty laundry when they return. My world had exploded into a thousand pieces. I didn't know which ones to pick up first and was hoping for a little slack from Rebekah. It felt good to stand up for myself, even though I was on shaky ground. When she left that evening, I was more determined and self-confident than at any time since my injury.

Before saying good night, Rebekah rubbed my back. "What's this?" she asked, pointing to a red, bumpy rash on my right shoulder blade. I shrugged it off as a likely reaction to medication and got ready for sleep. About one o'clock I awoke for a bathroom call. Trying to get up, I felt an intense pain in my right shoulder and upper back, like jagged glass ripping through the muscle. The night nurse wasn't sure what it was, but figured it didn't warrant a trip to the emergency room.

A doctor on morning rounds diagnosed it as shingles, a nerve infection. It was caused by the chickenpox virus, a childhood disease that had lain dormant in my nerves since I had it fifty years earlier, and reactivated by extreme stress to the system—a common plight of combat amputees. I was given an antiviral drug that quickly eased the pain.

Rebekah was relaxed when she returned. After leaving the previous night, she had called a psychotherapist friend for advice. He suggested that I was at a crossroads. One path was bitterness over what I might view as an unmitigated disaster. The other was emotional growth. Her job, the friend said, was to guide me to the positive road and put off our differences until later.

"Our relationship issues can wait," she said. "I want you to know that there's no part of me that isn't one hundred percent for you." It was gutsy and giving for a woman who had felt betrayed and unsure of her standing. She had lifted the pall and reminded me of why I had fallen in love with her. She looked sexier than ever in new black boots, her dark red hair offsetting large hazel eyes and pale coloring. A diplomat's daughter, Rebekah had Victorian manners and worldliness beyond her thirty-nine years. But she cared so little for convention she refused to marry the father of her son and routinely battled institutional powers, from banks to the traffic police, usually winning. Her humor was racy, her wit sharp, her heart vast, and her affection for me abundant. She was just what I needed to get me out of bed.

We strolled the corridors, talked about my good fortune to be alive, played Scrabble, and dined on chocolates, takeout Thai food, and Stoler's finest—teriyaki salmon, carrot and ginger soup, and Chicken Marbella—which Rebekah warmed up in the pantry. I introduced her to Captain Katie and the OT guys, to whom she donated one of her New Age albums to compete with the usual grinding sounds. Each night before she left, she massaged my ever-painful stump.

What had happened in the Humvee rarely came up. Rebekah cared more about the courage I needed to move forward. My confidence grew daily. I found myself yearning for regular time with my kids, my dog, my house, work, and a normal relationship with Rebekah. My recovery was far from complete—shrapnel wounds in my hindquarters had not healed and required daily treatment. I needed regular monitoring of my phantom pain, pulmonary embolism, and shingles. My rehab had just begun. There would be prosthesis fittings and training, not to mention physical therapy to build up my left arm and gain range of motion in what was left of my right. But I didn't have to live at Walter Reed for any of it. I could return every day for treatment and training. Most amputees became outpatients after a month on Ward 57. I was closing out three weeks and ready for it.

By Monday, January 5, I was plotting my departure. The thought still filled me with dread. Yet I gathered strength from the leafless great oak outside my window, noticing that its thick branches were shouldering drifts of snow, weathering the season.

Later that day, doctors removed my stitches and ordered up a new wardrobe for Stumpy. Thick bandages were replaced by an elastic "sock-aid" to reduce swelling. I would have to change it myself twice a day at home. The sock looked like two pairs of one-legged tights connected at the toe. I was supposed to double it over my forearm—no easy chore with one hand. Captain Katie, the Princess of Pragmatism, demonstrated how to do it using my knees, teeth, and good hand. I kept dropping the sock and biting the wrong side, cursing all along, until finally I mastered it.

My withdrawal from intravenous painkillers took place over a couple of days. Nurses pulled out the nerve block catheter and removed the narcotics pump. Little by little, the morphine drip was cut back. I broke loose from the IV pole for the first time since my injury, but I still had plenty of painkillers in the form of oral narcotics, principally the heroin substitute methadone, which I was gobbling.

A few logistical snags had to be ironed out. My bosses at *Time* eliminated the biggest: transportation to and from Walter Reed for my daily treatment and rehab. They agreed to put a car and driver at my disposal. Then there was the question of running a household. My sister urged me to get a housekeeper to clean and prepare meals. She had an ally in Tammy LaFrançois, who had witnessed firsthand my less than patient nature and had concerns about my ability to deal with the frustration. She called me into her office and warned that once-simple tasks would be more difficult. Instead of getting dressed in fifteen minutes, for example, I might need an hour. If I hired a helper I'd have the time and space to adjust to everyday life with a single hand.

The concerns didn't sway me. I already had Rebekah to help me settle in. My mother planned to visit from California immediately after Rebekah left. I wanted to regain independence as soon as possible. The more nursemaids I had, the longer it would take me to get there.

My discharge papers arrived the afternoon of January 8. Rebekah and I spent the day consulting doctors, packing up, and saying good-bye. I gave boxes of Frango Mints to my favorite nurses. We had only to wait for medications before leaving. I took one last lap around the ward, passing wall posters and pictures I'd grown to recognize as old friends. I hugged LaFrançois and Tami Barr, promising to stay in touch. When at last the pharmacy dispensed the sixteen different prescriptions and several pages of instructions in a brown paper bag and we got up to leave, Dr. Friedman walked in. He was accompanied by his eight-year-old son, Daniel, who asked me to autograph a copy of *Time*'s "Person of the Year" issue. It seemed a fitting occasion for my first left-handed signature.

I insisted on leaving Walter Reed on my own two feet, but quickly learned why the hospital recommends wheelchair departures. I hadn't negotiated stairs for a while. I was wobbly and spacey from the painkillers. Descending a concrete staircase to the lower-level parking lot, I lost balance and started to fall, my left hand reaching helplessly for the railing. Rebekah caught me before I did any real damage. It was just the first of many stumbles in the days ahead. She steadied me as I got into the car for the ride home.

Driving away was unsettling. For the past two months, the army had been home. When I climbed into a Humvee for the first time, I had felt no connection to the soldiers surrounding me; they inhabited a universe whose values and culture seemed foreign. And yet I ended up in my own platoon of wounded warriors, ordinary guys like me who had gotten hurt doing a job. We were fighting together to recover our strength and dignity, a moment-to-moment struggle. I'd be back every day, but it wouldn't be the same. I'd miss the little grievances, the triumphs and trials of a common experience. I was leaving the nest, entering a civilian world with its different truths and tempos.

The car drove down Washington streets I had taken many times before. But everything looked different, like a sepia photograph of a place I once had known. Maybe it was me. I had changed. Less than two months earlier, I had traveled to

Iraq as a diversion from an increasingly stale routine. The twelve-thousand-mile journey had been renewing in one sense. Now I was back home, where the everyday things I had once taken for granted had become an adventure.

★

No one looked twice at my shrunken, swaddled arm in the halls of Walter Reed. In the aisles of a Washington supermarket, however, I was a circus sideshow. I didn't know if people were staring out of recognition or pity. But I knew one thing after my first public outing January 9. I couldn't conceal my disability.

I had nothing to hide from *Time*'s managing editor, Jim Kelly, who came to my house for a visit the next day. Kelly had arranged to reach me by cell phone the moment my plane landed on U.S. soil, and he had called me often since then from his office in New York. But he had not come to see me until he sank into a stuffed couch in my family room, a bottle of pinot noir in hand. He said our "Person of the Year" story had rivaled top newsstand sales for an end-of-the-year edition, and he planned to nominate it for a National Magazine Award. He thanked me and pulled out a red Cartier box tied with a yellow ribbon. "I thought you'd like to have this," Jim said.

"What is it?" I asked, hoping that it wasn't a gold retirement watch. I found something far more precious inside. It was Olivia's little photo album. The tiger-striped fleece was flecked with shrapnel, the pictures inside torn. A soldier had recovered it from the first-aid station of Gunner Palace and delivered it to *Time*, Kelly explained. I had longed for the furry object in that cold wait for a medevac in Baghdad. To see it again filled me with pure joy. I called to Olivia in the next room. She couldn't believe her eyes. Her artwork had traveled the globe and passed through many hands before coming home.

The snapshots of Skyler and Olivia were the things I carried, to borrow a phrase from author Tim O'Brien, keepsakes of innocence transported through killing fields. In Iraq, they conveyed love. Now they represented survival. Like me, they came back ripped but not ruined. And they had belonged to me when I was whole. I was recovering the things I valued.

The person who helped shape those values arrived later that day. My mother, Marci Stillerman, had come to take over for Rebekah, who was due back in California. When I was born, Marci counted my fingers and toes. Now I had five fewer. At eighty-one, she knew a lot about loss—her father committed suicide and her first husband died prematurely—and about surviving it. I was looking forward to learning from her. But, always a strong-willed woman, she had a different idea: "I want you to pretend you're six years old again and let me do everything for you," she announced shortly after arriving.

Mothering was the last thing I needed. I had my own kids to raise, a living to make, and a house to run. I needed a crash course in independent living, a hornbook for the handicapped—not maid service. Eventually I'd have a prosthesis. But until my stump healed, I had to get by with one hand in a two-handed world. "I don't want to be babied," I told her.

Marci ignored me, and the battle was joined. I'd reach for something, and she would grab it first. We fought over the opening of cereal boxes and medicine bottles. When I'd put on a coat, she'd rush to zipper it. It was a struggle to leash the dog by myself. I got prickly and pricklier until she finally backed off.

On my own, I soon discovered the practical importance of a second hand—the hard way. Tying shoes. Flossing teeth. Buttoning shirts. Cutting meat. Unscrewing jars. Even washing hands. The more I took on, the messier it got. I managed to sink a corkscrew into a bottle of wine, but when I turned it, the bottle skittered off the counter and bounced along the floor, leaking merlot everywhere. I did only slightly better carrying a two-handled pot of water to the stove. I got halfway to the sink when it tipped. I was thankful the water was cold and easier to clean up than merlot.

Marci took me shopping for loafers, an electric can opener, and left-handed scissors. She recommended meals I could prepare with one hand and found a laundry bag to re- place a two-handed hamper. Frustrated and feeling sorry for myself, I couldn't wait to get back to occupational therapy.

My first day at OT as a civilian was unforgettable not only for the survival tips I would receive from Captain Katie. The place was quieter than usual, with a small group sitting around a swarthy man in a New England Patriots hat and a dark-blue tank top. I noticed he had no hands. His left arm ended below the elbow, his right at the triceps, just long enough to accommodate the tattoo of a she-devil. My heart stopped a beat. I had never seen anyone separated from both hands.

Sergeant Pete Damon, I soon discovered, had twice my loss and a lot more gumption. He had just returned from his first furlough and was reporting on life outside Ward 57. "I hear people whispering that they'd rather be dead than have no arms," Pete said, coughing his machine-gun laugh. "Well, I don't have no arms, and I'm glad I'm not dead, and so are my kids."

A few minutes with Pete stopped self-pity in its tracks.

★

Luis Rodriguez felt like a caged animal. He wanted off Ward 57. But after six weeks, his truncated right leg showed no signs of healing. For the first time in his life, hard work and perseverance weren't enough: he had to let his injury run its course. It was torture. He hated the hospital regimen. It wasn't logical. It wasn't efficient. It wasn't *his* regimen. He couldn't even get the rest that doctors said he needed to heal: the minute he fell asleep, he was awakened by a nurse wanting to know if he was sleeping. He had a drill sergeant's intolerance for sloppiness or incompetence. The stitches in his two cropped fingers had been left in so long that skin had grown over them. When Rod showed them to the doctor, she pulled out a pair of surgical scissors to snip. But it was too little, too late. "Get out of my freakin' room," he ordered. Grabbing a pair of tweezers, he frantically dug out the stitches himself. Another doctor overheard Rod's curses and poked his head into the room. "I don't want your help," Rod snarled. Wincing, he turned to Lilliam. "I don't want your help, either. Get out of here, too."

News from Iraq fueled his desperation. If he heard reports of casualties to the 101st, he called Fort Campbell for details of the location. Rod knew Mosul so well he could determine from the site of the attack whether anyone in his platoon had been hit. He dreaded that the most. The guys he had trained faced an ever more dangerous enemy, and they had to confront him without their sergeant. Rod had abandoned them. Sure, he had no choice. But they were alone nonetheless. His injury didn't absolve him of burden or guilt. He prayed for them every night.

Rod needed men to lead. He wouldn't let his injury stand in the way. If he lost his platoon, he'd find a new one. What better place than 57? Sergeants first-class had responsibility for the morale of their troops. One morning in early January he decided it was time to go to work. He turned a wheelchair into his Humvee, scooting down the corridor and poking his head into rooms to check on his men. Rod could be just one of the guys, bitching and rowdy. But he also assumed the role of protector. He knew it took another amputee to really understand what the soldiers were going through. He was part confessor, part cheerleader, and part benefactor—the consummate ward heeler. When Bobby Isaacs finally made it to 57, Rod brought him a cap with the "Screaming Eagles" emblem of their battalion. He saluted Pete Damon as he went outside for a smoke. Those in pain got commiseration. The depressed got a pep talk. Everyone else got a little bit of Rod-ribbing.

"Get down and do some one-armed push-ups," he teased a soldier who had lost an arm above the elbow. "One. Two. Three."

The soldier laughed and shot back, "Come on, Sergeant Rod, you don't have a leg to stand on."

When Rod needed bucking up, he had Derick Hurt.

Injured ten weeks before Rod's own accident, the twenty-five-year-old specialist was the first soldier in Rod's company to have lost a limb. Hurt had just been released as an outpatient from Ward 57 when Rod arrived. He limped into Rod's room on a prosthesis. Rod, who had orchestrated an airlift of Hurt and carried his stretcher into the Mosul field hospital, was thrilled to see his old charge walking. "I can't believe you're here," Hurt said. They hugged and grasped forearms for a full minute, repeating how happy they were to see each other alive. It was an odd yet poignant reunion—the rescued tending to his rescuer.

Hurt had been given a rare chance to pay back the support he received. He was a frequent visitor. The army may have brought them together, but adversity bound them. No doctor could be as informed as Hurt, no patient as trusting as Rod. When Rod complained of pain, Hurt could finish the sentence. "It gets better," he promised. "Remember what I looked like the last day you saw me? Now look at me."

"How does it feel to walk?" asked Rod.

Hurt responded with a wide smile. "Best feeling in the world."

★

The toilet was broken. I needed a card catalog to keep my medications straight. Laundry piled up. So did bills. My house smelled like a zoo; a pair of cats left virtually alone for two months could have that effect.

As of January 17, I was on my own. My mother had returned to California, leaving me alone for the first time since I was wounded. I wasn't in top form. My upper-body muscles had atrophied from disuse; raising my right arm set off waves of agony. I was in the grip of phantom pain so intense I needed a fistful of narcotics just to make it through the day. Still, I was committed to the goal of "returning to my abnormal life," and I rose every morning eager for the chance to get a little closer to it.

My kids resumed their half-time life with me. Victor Vorobyev, a Russian émigré hired by *Time* as my driver, chauffeured them to and from school. I overcame my nightmare of peanut butter sandwiches with the help of technology from Captain Katie's kitchen. A sheet of sticky, rubbery material held the jar in place while I twisted off the top with my good hand and scooped.

Skyler and Olivia had no adult notions of loss or judgments about helping me. Not long ago I had tied their shoes. Now they were tying mine. I had patched up their cuts and scrapes; now they were changing my dressings. Their sweetness permeated the house. Before Iraq, I had thought of parenting as another job—a lot of work with little payoff. Now, it was a love affair. Skyler and I picked up our running chess game. Olivia helped me cook dinners—"one-handed spaghetti" was our specialty.

A blizzard plowed into Washington one day in late January. We packed into Victor's car and went sledding. I stood at the bottom of the hill and watched. The sun sparkled on their snowsuits like tiny stars. They laughed and called out: "Watch this, Dad." "Did you see me, Daddy?" I waved and wept at these beautiful sounds, realizing how close I had come to never hearing them again.

Why did I risk it? I had scrutinized my motivation for picking up a grenade, but not the reason I had put myself in range of it. My rationale for going to Iraq as a career milestone no longer struck me as truthful. I already had scrapbooks full of big stories and enough money in the bank. I realized that something else had driven me, an old problem of self-worth: I was good because of what I did, not because of who I was. I had important roles as father, brother, lover, and son. But without achieving in some material way, I felt empty and unseen. Journalism had provided a regular opportunity to reinvent myself. I had gone to Iraq for another fix.

Like any junkie, I thought only of myself, taking on a dangerous mission as if others didn't deserve a say, as if the chance of success for me was more important than the certainty of fatherhood for my kids. I didn't weigh the risk to them until I lay bleeding in the bed of a Humvee, too late to spare them the fright.

It had taken a major loss for me to understand what I meant to others. Relationships rescued me. They got me out of Baghdad, into Walter Reed, and back home. I received that help not because of a grade I had earned, a story written, or lives saved; it was for being me. I resolved to return the love by being less self-absorbed. I promised my kids I would stay out of war zones. My brother-in-law, Michael Flesch, came for a three-day visit, the longest time we had spent alone together in years. We hung out at Walter Reed by day and frequented Washington haunts by night.

And then there was Rebekah. I had finally realized why the divorce flap was so upsetting. Relationships meant everything to her. I had glossed over an important distinction in ours, shortchanging her on candor. The open heart she had brought to Walter Reed deserved better. I apologized in a couple of long phone calls to California, promising full disclosure as the bedrock of our relationship from here on out. She accepted my apology and an invitation to Washington, where I'd have a chance to put my new commitment into practice.

6.
NEW MUSCLES

Body parts lay everywhere: plaster arms and thighs, electronic hands, and spindly metal legs sporting Reeboks. The room looked like a morgue for mannequins. But these were no props for store windows. They were appendages to imitate life's functions as well as its forms. They delivered dexterity to the handless and mobility to the legless.

The prosthesis shop on the third floor of Walter Reed was a throwback to the Vietnam War, a large, dingy room cluttered with boxes dating back forty years, file cabinets, old newspapers, and sheets of plastic stacked on a yellowed linoleum floor. It was just the kind of place where the frazzled graduates of Ward 57 felt at home. Amputees wandered in all day to pull up a chair at the crossroads of industry and medicine. They came for repairs. They came for fittings and batteries. They came to watch technicians stoop over worn wooden benches, file plaster casts, program devices, and fire propane torches. Prosthetists were re-creating a birthright in body parts, like the one that was ready for me on February 4.

Nearly two months after losing my right hand, I couldn't wait to try it. I was tired of reaching for objects and coming up a foot short. I missed being able to do more than one thing at a time, like carrying groceries and opening a door. I hadn't even tried to push a broom or cut a steak, activities requiring two hands. Losing a forearm had thrown off my balance. I looked like a penguin when I walked, my stubby right wing flopping foolishly.

I had no idea if a myoelectric hand would make me whole. I'd never seen one before I was injured. Fewer than 10 percent of the 150,000 new amputees in the United States every year lose an arm, and only half of them wear a prosthesis. The Iraq war had dramatically narrowed the disparity—a third of Ward 57 patients during my stay had at least one arm missing.

Walter Reed had received bad publicity in 1991 for scrimping on the best prosthesis technology for Gulf War amputees. The hospital's current leaders were committed not to let this happen again and had laid plans for a first-rate program even before the Iraq war had started. Not long after the September 11 terrorist attacks, they hired an expert in artificial body parts to revamp hospital policy. A well-known Virginia prosthetist, Joe Miller took one look at the prosthesis shop, known as the "Dungeon," and could see why the hospital had taken a PR hit a decade earlier.

A thirty-eight-year-old second lieutenant in the army reserves medical corps, Miller convinced Walter Reed to spring for state-of-the-art technology—myoelectric arms and computer-programmed C-legs. With its approval, the army gave birth to the first generation of war veterans to return home with bionic limbs. In the wake of the Afghanistan invasion, Miller himself worked on a few leg amputees. But when a batch of soldiers missing arms arrived a year later, he called in John Miguelez, a renowned upper-extremity specialist who heads his own prosthesis company based in California. In July 2003, Miller asked him to take on six patients. "I can't guarantee any more work," Miller said.

But then another upper-extremity amputee arrived, then a couple more, and Miguelez's company, Advanced Arm Dynamics, was hired full-time. He came up with a plan approved by the army to provide each patient with three types of prostheses—myoelectric, body-powered, and cosmetic—at an average cost of $150,000 for below-elbow amputees and $185,000 for above-elbow. Miguelez sent two teams a week to take care of Walter Reed's ever-growing caseload. He employed people who could relate: a male technician who had lost a leg above the knee in a traffic accident and a female patient liaison who was born missing half of her left forearm.

Miguelez, a bearded, forty-one-year-old Southern California native, had chosen his unusual field because it combined a childhood love of electronics with a desire to help people. After earning a graduate degree in prosthetics from Northwestern University, he decided to specialize in arm amputees, a smaller but more dynamic class of patients. Most lower-extremity amputees fall on the downside of life, elderly victims of diabetes or vascular disease. By contrast, 75 percent of Miguelez's patients had lost their arms in work-related accidents in textile and lumber mills, meatpacking plants, and farming. They had most of their lives to live with an injury that couldn't be concealed.

Ward 57 was stocked with Miguelez's kind of patients: twenty-something, athletic, and hardworking. Making rounds in a white lab coat, he pushed them to the casting room less than twenty-four hours after their stitches came out. Most civilian amputees waited months to be fit. But Miguelez figured the soldiers were too aggressive to be kept waiting for long. They might get used to one hand and face problems of overuse later in life. By then, it would be harder to learn how to use a prosthetic arm.

I didn't fit the soldiers' profile—one of my doctors referred to me as a "unique demographic." But it wasn't my age and occupation as much as pain that kept me from the preparatory phase. In mid-January, I finally allowed Miguelez to roll on a "shrinker," a silicone sleeve tighter than a sock-aid, designed to reduce swelling of my stump. I was ready for a visit to the casting room, a brightly lit space off the Dungeon barely big enough to hold a couple of folding chairs and a stainless-steel sink. Wrapping wet plaster gauze around my stump, Miguelez created the mold for a "test socket," a hard plastic vessel that slipped onto my forearm to determine the fit of a prosthesis.

The myoelectric arm I received in the first week of February came in three parts. A hard, clear plastic shell housed a flexible sheath with electrodes aligned to touch my forearm muscles. The last piece—an electronic hand covered in a flesh-colored latex glove—screwed into the frame like a lightbulb into a lamp socket. Fully assembled, the artificial limb was haute high tech. Its guts—blue electrode wires, silver electrodes, and black wrist rotator—were visible through the shell. Protruding from the top of the forearm was an inch-square tan box containing batteries that had to be removed daily and dropped in a special charger, like a cell phone.

The prosthesis's arrival was more exciting than a new pair of shoes—but no more comfortable to wear. Just getting it on was painful: my stump was still incredibly tender. The apparatus was designed to pull over the elbow, which anchored and kept it on. I was presented with a piece of blue, resistance-free parachute silk to ease the shell over the bone. Draping the silk over my stump, I then dropped an attached cord into the vessel and out a "pull hole" on its side. By plunging my stump and tugging the cord at the same time, I finally got the prosthesis over my elbow.

That was the easy part. The rigid frame made it impossible to bend my elbow more than a few inches and pressed against the sensitive tendons and tiny bones around the joint. Miguelez's technicians spent hours tweaking the prosthesis, curving plastic here, cutting it there. Nothing worked. Easing pressure from the elbow loosened the suspension. Either it pinched or it slid off. The best they could do was reach an unhappy medium. It hurt some and it slipped some.

If my former right hand had floated lightly, the fake one moved like a dumbbell—fat, clunky, and heavy. Its two and a half pounds were concentrated in the electronic hand—the place farthest from the half forearm. The prosthesis made my arm crook out like Popeye's; my range of motion was so limited that I couldn't raise the hand within a foot of my mouth. I kept bumping it into things. I gave up on long-sleeved shirts. They didn't fit over the bulging battery box or couldn't be buttoned over the thick prosthetic wrist. I named it Ralph, after the clumsiest kid in my grade school.

Ralph didn't work any better than he looked. The thumb and first two fingers opened and closed like a claw, the grossest of motor skills. The third finger and pinky, which are employed by natural hands to carry things, were frozen. Ralph's wrist didn't bend. Despite weeks of training on a computer, I had difficulty with the basic functions: my stronger outer forearm muscle kept flexing and involuntarily opening the hand—even when I was trying to close it. I had no more success with the mechanism to rotate the wrist. The simultaneous contraction of both muscles was unnatural and hard to remember in real time. When I did it right, I couldn't keep the hand from spinning 360 degrees, an annoying loss of control—and embarrassing in public.

I was also a menace. After wearing the prosthesis for a week, I decided to take it for a test drive—literally. Climbing into my 1992 Volvo station wagon to go pick up my kids, I ran into trouble right away. The ignition lay on the right side of the steering wheel. I couldn't turn the key with my fake hand or easily snake my left one around the steering column to reach it. I had to get into the passenger seat and start the car with my left hand, then slide behind the wheel of the now-running car. But I had no right hand to move the automatic gears. I enlisted my left hand again to cross over and shift into drive.

Off I went, steering with my good hand. As I headed for the first turn, I closed my electronic hand on the wheel to steady it. The prosthesis froze at a 90-degree angle parallel to my lap. I tried to open the hand, but couldn't convince my forearm muscles to cooperate. The pincers had a death grip. Idling in the intersection, I created a rush-hour backup, complete with blaring horns and angry motorists. I panicked, and my muscles tensed up. The microprocessor read the spasms as a signal to co-contract and launched the wrist rotator. The hand tried to spin but couldn't break the iron clamp on the wheel. My only option was to yank my stump free of the prosthesis.

The electronic hand was still locked on the wheel, with the fake arm attached. I couldn't get the right leverage to separate them. I had one move left. I shifted to park, got into the passenger seat, and pulled down on the prosthesis. The wheel turned enough to get my car around the corner. I hurriedly jumped back into the driver's seat, hit the gas pedal, and completed my first one-handed right turn.

The entire ordeal lasted less than three minutes but seemed like forever. Fortunately, I had no more turns to make before I reached my destination. Skyler figured out how to free the hand from the wheel by manipulating the electrodes inside the shell. I felt rattled, not to mention incompetent. My eleven-year-old had had to rescue me. But it wasn't for nothing. It was a good reminder that I couldn't do everything alone, a lesson every amputee learns sooner or later. I was lucky I had someone to assist me. We drove home with the prosthesis in the backseat where it could do no harm.

My disillusionment with Ralph grew daily. It seemed like technological overkill to replace a hand with the full-length artificial arm. No one had told me it would trap my elbow, a sensitive and pivotal spot. I couldn't keep my anger from Captain

Katie, with whom I was supposed to enter a new phase of rehab to adjust to the new prosthesis.

I learned from Katie that my original decision to have another three inches cut from my stump to accommodate a wrist rotator had larger consequences. If I had refused it, I wouldn't have been able to turn the electronic hand, but I might have worn a shorter, lighter prosthesis that stayed on by suction and freed the elbow. I had never been informed of that variation. If I had known of the trade-off between facility and comfort, I would have elected the latter. If I had known the full costs of the rotator—a heavier, elbow-trapping prosthesis—I would never have chosen it. I felt hoodwinked.

Katie urged me to forget the past and focus on training Ralph. She walked me through a few exercises, but I struggled with even the simplest ones; picking up blocks and putting plastic rings on a pegboard stymied me. I succeeded one of every ten times with the co-contraction of muscles necessary to rotate the wrist. I could bear the prosthesis for only thirty minutes at a stretch. By the fifth day I was so frustrated I was ready to quit. "What's the point?" I asked Katie. Pain was too high a price to pay for such limited facility. I'd be better off with one hand.

My old friend and coach was sympathetic. Every amputee had an angry phase, she told me. It usually set in after the narcotics wore off and the harsh realities began to resonate. I had deferred my rage, believing naively that technology would fill the breach.

Now I felt like the Tin Man without an oilcan. There would be no easy fix. I was out of options.

Katie didn't want to see me quit and reported my anger up

the line. I had rarely complained at Walter Reed and never flaunted my journalistic card. But I wasn't just any patient. Katie's report reverberated. On February 11, I was invited to meet with my rehab team of eight people, who crowded into a small examination room in the amputee clinic. Joe Miller was there representing prosthetists. Katie had a seat, as did a physical therapist, a rehab nurse, and several physiatrists who specialize in restoring function to the traumatically injured. Lieutenant Colonel Paul Pasquina, medical director of the army's amputee care program, led the group.

"We hear you have some concerns," Pasquina said. After I listed them, he cited a few options to the myoelectric arm, including a body-powered prosthesis like the one worn by Pete Damon. They were lighter, unencumbered at the elbow, and ended in a hook. Pasquina said I might adopt a hook as a trademark that people would come to respect for its straightforward honesty.

I bristled. I wanted a prosthesis to disguise my deformity, not spotlight it. "The circles I travel in wouldn't be amused," I told Pasquina, dismissively. I still was banking on an easy-fitting, lifelike substitute. I asked whether the briefer prosthesis mentioned by Katie might work. He explained why it had never been proposed: even before my last surgery, I lacked sufficient wristbones for the suction to hold.

Only one question remained for me: whether a myoelectric arm was better than nothing at all.

★

Staff Sergeant Andy McCaffrey thrust out his right hand to introduce himself. It was prosthetic. The thirty-one-year-old

Green Beret had lost his real one seven months earlier in a hand grenade accident in Afghanistan. After recovering at Walter Reed, he joined a Special Forces unit at Fort Bragg, North Carolina. McCaffrey had come back to the hospital for a visit in late February. I met him in the occupational therapy room, which I entered dejectedly, ready to pitch my $92,000 myoelectric arm.

The Special Forces soldier couldn't get enough of his. He wanted to be the first amputee to return to combat and pushed John Miguelez to help make it happen. The prosthetist took it as a challenge. He customized a flexible plastic hand that allowed McCaffrey to do push-ups when he still had stitches in his stump. When McCaffrey got stronger, Miguelez designed a "war hand" fortified with steel strips and carbon-fiber fingers that withstood the tough treatment it would undergo in active duty.

McCaffrey applied a basic military doctrine to the devices. Soldiers made their weapons a part of them. He did the same thing with a prosthesis. He drilled with it until he automatically performed functions required of behind-the-lines forces. He could take apart a rifle, open a parachute after jumping out of an airplane, and thread an IV needle into someone's vein.

The Long Island native had a rough exterior. He cursed with every breath, spit tobacco into a Styrofoam cup, and swept his black mustache across the shoulder of his uniform to wipe it. But he managed social graces with his prosthesis. His electronic hand was covered in a lifelike silicone glove with etched fingernails and knuckles. He operated it as if it were real. He talked with both of his hands, gesticulating as naturally with the fake one as he did with the real. He even affected a nonchalant pose of hooking the thumb of his prosthesis in his pants pocket. If I hadn't looked closely, I would never have known McCaffrey was an amputee. He became my new hero. I was amazed by his deftness and inspired by his resolve. I pressed him for his trade secrets.

The first thing McCaffrey suggested was physical training to restore range of motion and strengthen my injured arm. His dominant right hand had been blown off in the same place as mine. Forty-eight hours after the wound was closed at Walter Reed, he began lifting weights. He agreed to introduce me to his physical therapist, whom he described as "one tough son of a bitch."

We walked down the hall to the physical therapy room and found a short, barrel-chested man in a brown T-shirt and camouflage pants. Justin Laferrier hugged his old patient. The twenty-nine-year-old lieutenant was a former marine with little patience for wounded soldiers who felt sorry for themselves. Laferrier made sure they didn't have time to wallow in self-pity when they came to his PT. He refused to accept limits for the limbless. "Impossible just means that someone hasn't done it yet," he'd say. Laferrier had never before applied his principles to a fifty-seven-year-old, one-handed reporter who didn't like to take orders. But he was happy to try and signed me up.

I had reservations. The idea of lifting weights and tossing medicine balls was daunting. Although I had been in top shape before Iraq, ten weeks of inactivity had turned me to Jell-O. My right upper body was so atrophied I could barely raise my stump. But I wanted to look good the next time I saw Rebekah. I showed up bright and early the next morning.

Laferrier was waiting for me with a blue, cushiony disc. "Let's start with push-ups," he said.

Even the words hurt. "Push-ups? I can't put pressure on my stump," I protested.

"Prove to me you can't do it," the lieutenant said. I knew in those first few minutes he would be known to me as "Muscle-ini," for his pint size and his categorical dictates. He marched over to a wall and pressed the four-inch-thick disc against it. I had to step back and push my stump into the cushion and left palm onto the plaster.

"Now gimme some push-ups," barked Muscle-ini. I said I couldn't do it.

"Oh boy, was that the wrong thing to say," he dead-panned.

I grimaced and slowly leaned forward, then pushed back. I did it again. The end of my stump burned. My forearm muscles ached. But I had passed my first test. Pain was the point. Laferrier was trying to desensitize me, getting my nervous system used to it.

He sought to do more than rebuild my broken wing. My newly dominant left arm had to be prepped for double duty. The trainer had an assortment of tortures, starting with the Total Gym, an adjustable bench that rolled back and forth as the exerciser hoisted his own body weight with a pulley system. The equipment required two hands to operate the pulleys. I grabbed one side with my left hand and held out my stump for Laferrier to wrap it in a nylon cuff sealed by Velcro. He hooked the cuff to the machine and set the resistance to 10 percent of my body weight.

"Do some curls," he ordered. I did a set of twelve and moved on to other exercises designed to strengthen the muscles supporting my shoulders and upper back. When we moved on to barbells, I donned a clawlike device known by the German word for grabber, *Greifer*, for my right side. Laferrier wound elastic material like an Ace bandage around the plastic hand to keep it from flying open as I curled a three-pound weight—I used to lift twenty-five pounds. I was sweating and straining as I reached my last curl, an hour after I started working out. He ordered up another set.

"I don't know if I can do another," I whimpered.

"Then do two more," countered Muscle-ini. "You might not be able to do one, but I bet you can do two."

Laferrier knew that before he could push amputees past their limit, they'd have to trust him. He used teasing to bond. He hopped from me to other patients, ribbing here, coaxing there, keeping up a running banter. Sergeant First Class Luis Rodriguez was one of his favorite sparring partners. Laferrier knew that "Hot Rod," as he called him, was as competitive as he was. He enjoyed throwing on a few more push-ups to get the joshing started. But the diminutive sergeant always took the bet, proving he couldn't be burned out by a former "jarhead."

"You can't smoke a rock," Rod said in one session, barracks braggadocio that he was as untouchable as a rock to fire.

"I bet I can break one," Laferrier countered. Then he ordered a few more push-ups, determined to have the last word. But Rod wasn't easy to one-up. Sergeants first class didn't answer to low-ranking officers. "Take your ass back to the Marine Corps," joked Rod, catching his breath. "Obviously, they kicked you out for some reason if you ended up as a physical therapist in a hospital."

Laferrier exhausted me, but I returned every day for at least an hour. I came as much for the comradeship as the workout. PT was the locker room of Walter Reed, a place to remember what it was like to be lighthearted among other guys.

A lot of serious physical therapy took place as well. Lower-extremity amputees walked for the first time on parallel bars, holding on as they tried to balance themselves on an artificial leg. Double amputees started out on two-foot-high "stubbies," wooden pegs in tennis shoes, before progressing to full-length prostheses. Other patients, like Bobby Isaacs, had major medical issues to resolve before they could wear fake legs. Bobby turned up in PT the same time I did in February.

Bobby's routine was agonizing. Unable to bend his knees due to the buildup of scar tissue, he sat at the edge of padded therapeutic platforms with his two stumps jutting straight out like forklifts. Therapist Isatta Jackson sat on a stool before him and pushed down on the limbs with her full weight. The pain ripped through Bobby's legs. He let out gut-wrenching screams and cried, which often led Isatta to sob in sympathy. She tried ultrasound and heat treatments to dissolve the tough bands of tissue. But nothing worked. He couldn't bend his knees enough to walk in prostheses.

Doctors decided to operate. On February 17, they anesthetized him and bent his knees until the scar tissue broke. When he woke up, Bobby had to drape his swollen and sore knees over a bolster to keep the scar tissue from re-forming. The pain was excruciating.

The next morning, Bobby's knees were wrapped in ice to alleviate the agony. But he went back to PT, lay down on the platform, and allowed Jackson to push his stumps toward his chest. I watched his strawberry-blond hair darken with sweat as he grimaced in pain. Every few minutes, a therapist removed bandages on his stumps to sop up leakage from wounds that refused to heal.

★

Pete Damon didn't get many out-of-town visitors at Ward 57. So he was a little wary of the man from Massachusetts who had asked to meet with him. John Gonsalves had first phoned the day before Pete got married in December and told his fiancée he wanted to build them a home. "Jesus Christ, gimme a break," Pete said when Jenn relayed the message, assuming it was some kind of con.

The old saying—"If it wasn't for bad luck, I'd have no luck at all"—was made for Pete. Nothing had ever come easily. It figured he'd lose his hands right after landing the perfect job as a civilian helicopter mechanic. He would have full military disability payments for life, but with two kids and a wife, a government check would barely pay the bills. Pete had always dreamed of having his own home, a hope ever more pressing now that he had to put everyone under one roof. While he was hospitalized, Jenn and the kids were squeezing into his mother's two-bedroom house in Brockton, along with Pete's brother. When Pete came home in December, the little

place burst its seams. A new home would solve a lot of problems, especially if it were adapted to his handicap. So, when
Gonsalves kept calling, Pete figured he had nothing to lose
from a visit.

Gonsalves had everything to gain. At thirty-six he was
a laid-off contractor with an idea to build houses for wounded
soldiers and honor the memory of his grandfather who had
died in the invasion of Normandy. But he had no money
and no way to promote his organization. On October 31, he
had seen an NBC *Nightly News* story on amputees that featured a sergeant from Brockton, not far from Gonsalves's
hometown of Raynham. The image of Pete lying in a gurney
with no arms was powerful. Gonsalves knew right away he
had a poster boy. Finding Pete was another thing. Gonsalves
spotted the name of Pete's mother in the local paper. But her
phone number wasn't listed. He finally reached Jenn at her
mother's house on December 19. The builder spoke to Pete a
few days later and could hear his skepticism. By early February, Gonsalves had put up a Web site and found a law firm to
draft bylaws for his group, called Homes for Our Troops
(HFOT). He had something concrete to show Pete. If he
couldn't convince a man he wanted as his first beneficiary,
he'd never get anywhere. So he pushed persistently for the
meeting.

The afternoon of February 6, Gonsalves arrived at Ward
57 and presented Pete with a progress report. Pete remained
suspicious but was willing to have his picture featured on
HFOT's Web site. He laid out an idea: plugging the group with
his media contacts. Reporters were calling Pete all the time,
looking for stories on Iraq war amputees. If he could get them

to report on the special-needs home-building effort, the publicity might raise some money. Pete recognized how compelling people found the image of his double stumps. Every time he went on TV, letters and e-mails streamed in from across the country. "People will see me and say, 'Oh, fuck, this guy lost both his arms. We better send this organization some money,'" he told Gonsalves.

The tactic wasn't totally self-serving. Gonsalves planned to build as many homes for maimed soldiers as money would allow. The fact that his would be the pilot project attracted Pete to the venture even more. Yet he felt a twinge of guilt about accepting anything for his injury. After all, he had been hurt in a freak accident maintaining helicopters, not wounded in action. Weren't the guys who took enemy bullets more deserving? Whenever he thought that way, he reminded himself that he was doing his job just as they had been doing theirs. They all got hurt serving their country. No one was more worthy than another. If Pete helped put HFOT on the map, everybody could benefit.

His strategy paid off. Columnist Mike Barnicle of the *Boston Herald* requested an interview with Pete during a late February furlough to Brockton. Pete agreed and invited Gonsalves to sit in on the session at his mother's home. When the column didn't mention HFOT, Pete persuaded his partner to call in to Barnicle's live radio show. The Brockton paper did a story on it, followed by local and national media coverage. Money rolled in. A March 6 fund-raiser at Christopher's bar in Raynham, attended by Jenn, sold almost $5,000 in tickets. The proceeds didn't approach a down payment for vacant land in costly Massachusetts. But it was a start.

The future looked brighter from the cozier confines of Malogne House, where the army put up Pete after he moved out of Ward 57, the same day as Gonsalves's visit. It was the first time in three months he had the privacy and time to relearn basic skills. He set aside every afternoon in March to practice writing with his hook, an exercise that brought home his loss more profoundly than anything. Pete had a gift for drawing that he had first expressed as a young boy in sketches of a picnic scene copied from a picture book his mother gave him. As a teenager he amused friends with pencil profiles of beer cans that captured the shadows and textures of tin. In Kuwait, where he had a lot of time to kill, Pete turned out tattoo art and pinup girls with color pencils.

Even if he would never draw again, Pete figured, he could at least teach himself to write. It was an uphill struggle. Pete's hook was rigid metal, not exactly ideal for guiding a pen across a page. He had been right-handed; he wore the hook on his left stump, the only one with an all-important elbow for control. Pete sat down at the little desk in his room as determined as a first grader. Turning the hook at a slight angle, he clamped the Number 2 pencil and swept it lightly across lined paper: Capital *A*. Lowercase *a*. He completed a full sheet of *A*'s, covering two lines per letter. Every day he completed a different letter, until he had mastered the alphabet. Then he tried something new.

Pete rounded out a circle, then drew a triangle. "Wait a second," he said to himself, gaining ease with the hook. He outlined a square and colored it in. A little pink eraser fit into the hook and cleaned up the errors. Not bad. "Man, I can still do this." It felt as if an old friend had come back from the dead. Pete hit the speed dial with his hook to share the news with Jenn.

"I'm not surprised," she said. "It's all in your mind, not in your hand."

7.
A HERO'S WELCOME

The nightstand clock read 5:50 A.M. I had overslept. It was Valentine's Day. Rebekah had taken the red-eye from California; her plane was due to land in twenty minutes at Dulles Airport, which was a thirty-minute drive. Five weeks after I had last seen her, I was determined to prove I was no longer the frail, disoriented, and needy inmate of Ward 57. I had planned to get spiffed up in my new fake hand, but there was no time to primp; the prosthesis took at least fifteen minutes to put on. I wiggled into a pair of jeans, T-shirt, and a ski jacket and sped off to the airport. I got there in time to meet Rebekah at the luggage carousel. I threw my one and a half arms around her.

A series of long, sweet phone calls had revived our relationship after its bumpy January ride. But I was apprehensive about seeing her in person. I didn't have the strength to carry her bags. Having been out of the journalistic loop, I had no juicy stories to share. My arm was shriveled and my backside still bore deep purple gouges.

Rebekah had known me well enough before the injury to judge how much it had changed me. But I worked hard to obscure the differences. I was never inclined to divulge my insecurities. *Men's Journal* had just included me on its list of the "toughest guys in America," ranked number two after Green Bay Packers quarterback Brett Favre, for, among other things, "fearlessness" and a "high threshold for pain." It was a silly testosterone gauge, but a recurring characterization since childhood. I had returned to school a couple of days after my dad's funeral and acted as if nothing had happened. No one knew how scared I was to lose a father—not only financial providers, fathers physically protected their sons on the South Side of Chicago. No one knew how scared I was now. I was as determined as I was in 1957 not to draw attention to my loss.

That required some fancy footwork in Rebekah's company. I kept circling around to her right, lining up my good side for hand-holding. I wore bulky sweaters to conceal the bulge of my prosthetic arm and its stiff, unnatural angle. I stashed a tabletop of pills in a drawer to avoid drawing attention to continued dependence on painkillers. I slipped into the bathroom to keep her from seeing me button my shirt with a special hook and slip it over my head. I positioned the steering wheel of the car for left-handed access to the ignition, so she wouldn't see me struggle to start it. I took charge of social events, and ordered restaurant food I could cut with a fork.

But within a couple of days, Rebekah had convinced me the only body parts she really cared about were my heart and mind. What she wanted was commitment from them. I proposed on February 16. In a period of confusion and change, it was the one thing I felt absolutely certain of. So did she. We planned on living together for a year and getting married in 2006. I'd be seeing a lot of her in the coming months before she moved to Washington with her eleven-year-old son. In March, I planned to throw a fortieth birthday party for her in Ojai.

I redoubled my efforts to get into shape, pushing myself hard in Muscle-ini's gym, running three miles a day on the treadmill, and tripling the weight of my barbell and pulley exercises. I trimmed down to a thirty-two-inch waist for the first time in memory and bought a pair of black, pin-striped pants from Hugo Boss and a tight black sweater to show off on my West Coast tour.

But as my flight neared, I became increasingly anxious. I'd never worried about my looks before. They weren't good or bad enough to affect how others judged me. Now I evoked pity, fear, and curiosity—people couldn't hide their reactions. I might have been better off wearing a military uniform: there would be fewer questions. The prospect of all those new eyes prying in Ojai, a center of New Age lifestyles, artists, and showbiz refugees seventy-five miles south of Hollywood, made me nervous. It would be my social debut as an amputee. When Rebekah had visited Washington in February, we spent almost all our time in private. We were about to go public. She was a beautiful woman in her prime. I was a knight in shining arm gear—not exactly glamorous. Was she ready to stroll down Main Street on my prosthesis? I worried that she might be embarrassed.

After a few sleepless nights, I decided to check it out. I called her the morning of March 6, asking if she worried about being seen with me. "All I feel is pride," Rebekah replied. I wasn't totally convinced.

I had one last bit of preparation before my coming out, following up on a fashion tip from my amputee hero, Staff Sergeant Andy McCaffrey. I remembered the lifelike glove of his prosthesis, with its well-defined knuckles and fingernails. Mine was a baggy, pink latex that picked up stains from food and newsprint. I went to Walter Reed prosthetist John Miguelez and asked for an upgrade.

★

My train pulled into Fairfield, Connecticut, on a snowy morning, March 8, long after the last commuter had left for Manhattan. I walked off the platform and was greeted by a man with the compact build of a wrestler, wearing half-glasses and a closely cropped salt-and-pepper beard. Mike Curtin was a prosthetic artist who created silicone replicas of body parts so close to the original they could almost fool the wearer. He had agreed to do a rush job for me if I came to his studio.

We drove to a colonial farmhouse in the adjacent town of Southport, where I caught my first glimpse of Curtin's talent. Bronze-colored wax busts of the twelve apostles looked down from individual oak bases in his living room. Curtin had modeled them when he was a struggling young sculptor in New York. He began moonlighting in 1986 as a silicone pourer for a firm that made fake hands; he was amazed by the natural look of the products. Working his way up, he learned how to shape and paint hands himself, and eventually turned a temporary job into a career. What had attracted him to art was its mimicry of life. In prostheses, he could imitate reality in a different medium—silicone. It was an art form that drew an appreciative and high-paying audience.

Curtin worked out of a cedar-sided carriage house behind his home. Part artist's studio and part hand museum, the first-floor room boasted hundreds of nickel-plated master casts of all hand sizes mounted on wooden pegs, palms up. It looked as if they were applauding our entrance. We moved to a winding staircase and climbed up, reaching the loft where he spun his magic.

I had come to model the colors of my hand. Curtin had already produced the canvas: a thin, translucent glove. It was a replica of my former right hand, an eerily similar copy complete with raised veins, knuckles, palm creases, life lines, fingernail shape, wrinkles, and the bends of my fingers. The clone had emerged from a complicated process that had begun a week earlier at Walter Reed, where Curtin made an impression of my left hand. Back in his Connecticut studio, he filled the hollow, silicone rubber mold with hot wax and placed it in an ice bath. When the wax started to harden on the outside, he emptied the liquid residue, leaving a thin coating along the sides—a double of my uninjured left hand. Next, Curtin culled his well-stocked library of hand molds to find a right palm with similar characteristics to the wax double of my left. Casting the "donor" palm into wax, his assistants used an electric needle to weld wax fingers that had been taken from the original mold of my left hand and sculpted to simulate my five missing digits.

My injured hand had come back to life in wax form. But Curtin was creating a silicone glove, not a statue. His final step was to create an electroplated metal mold of the wax model and fill it with clear liquid silicone. It was rotated for evenness, heat-cured to rubber strength, and carefully peeled off—a thin, silicone rubber twin of my old hand.

The unadorned glove was waiting for me on a worktable in the loft, a slanted-roof garret lit by two skylights and occupied by a unique school of artists. A year earlier, Chuck O'Brien had been making cadavers in Hollywood for TV hits such as *The X-Files* and *CSI: Miami.* He set out to pursue a more serious use of his talents and went to work as a painter for Curtin's Alternative Prosthetic Services in late 2003. With his black spiky hair and goatee, the twenty-six-year-old former art major still had a showbiz look. But he studied my uninjured hand like a portraitist, placing it under a pair of drafting lamps—fluorescent and incandescent—to view within a full spectrum of light.

Before the coloring process began, O'Brien glued hair that had been shaved from my left hand to corresponding places inside the glove, where it couldn't be rubbed off. The interior was also where the colors were brushed, mimicking natural skin, which had a clear outer layer and pigmentation in the deeper levels. O'Brien examined the gradations of color, from the back of my hand to the fingers, and from fingers to the

Corporal Bobby Isaacs killing time in a makeshift barracks during summer 2003 guard duty in the northern Iraq town of Karakosh. Bobby loved the independence and comradeship of army life. *(Private collection of the Isaacs family)*

Sergeant Pete Damon surviving the 120° heat of Kuwait in August 2003 with a water bottle in one hand and the other pointing to a thermometer. A few weeks later, he would lose both hands in a freak accident in an Iraq aircraft hangar. *(Private collection of the Damon family)*

Sergeant First Class Luis Rodriguez lining up with Headquarters Company leaders in Kuwait during a March 2003 military exercise just days before the detail-obsessed sergeant led the best-equipped platoon up the Iraqi desert. *(Private collection of Luis Rodriguez)*

Specialist Paul J. Bueche (right) embracing his NCO, Sergeant Jason Roten, a few weeks before Bueche's fatal accident. *(Private collection of the Bueche family)*

The last jottings of my right hand, blood-streaked notes written in an open "high back" Humvee as it pulled out of a busy Baghdad marketplace. Minutes later, I used the same hand to pick up and attempt to eject a grenade. *(Private collection of Michael Weisskopf)*

Walter Reed Army Medical Center in the northern reaches of Washington, D.C., the most recent incarnation of the hospital that has treated soldiers in every major war since World War I. *(Photograph by Denease Anderson)*

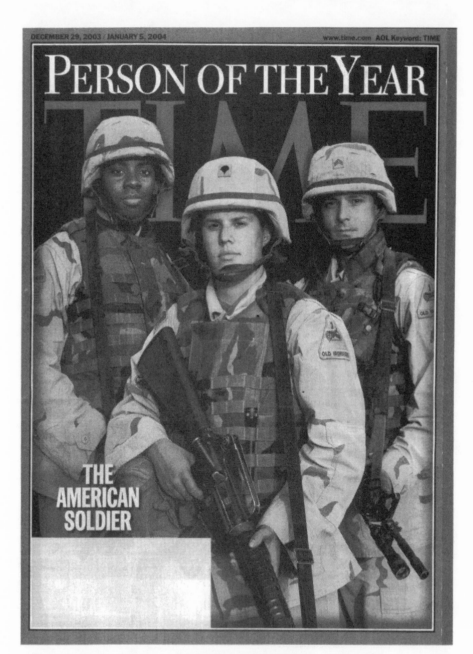

PERSON OF THE YEAR

THE AMERICAN SOLDIER

Specialist Billie Grimes occupies the center of *Time* magazine's "Person of the Year" cover in December 2003, a photo taken a few hours before she rescued me after the grenade attack.
(*Photograph by Jim Nachtwey for* Time *magazine*)

Bobby Isaacs building upper-body strength in Captain Katie's center for occupational therapy at Walter Reed, a clubhouse for amputees, in February 2004. *(Private collection of the Isaacs family)*

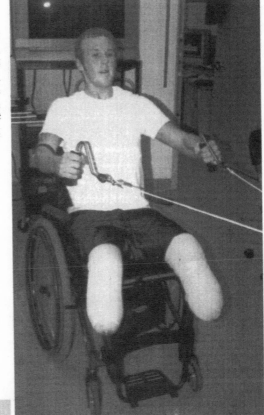

Bobby and his mother, Pat, greeting President George W. Bush on Ward 57 just after his re-election victory in November 2004. *(Private collection of the Isaacs family)*

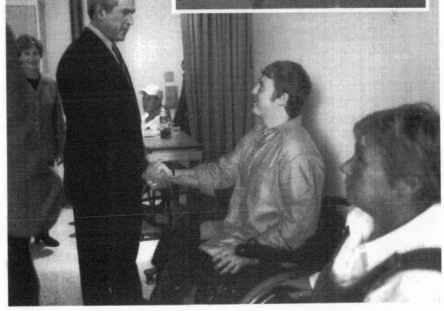

Pete Damon waves to Fenway Park fans after tossing out the ceremonial first pitch at a Boston Red Sox game in June 2005. He was proud to hear fathers in the stands telling their kids, "There's a real hero." *(Jim Davis/*The Boston Globe*)*

Luis Rodriguez standing on his C-leg at Fort Campbell's granite memorial, dedicated to the fallen soldiers of his beloved "5-0-Deuce" Infantry Regiment, September 2005. *(Private collection of Luis Rodriguez)*

Maria and Paul Bueche posing with their son, P.J., at his graduation from army basic training at Fort Sill, Oklahoma, in August 2002. *(Private collection of Bueche family)*

"WARRIOR"

DAMON 10-05

With the aid of a hook, Pete Damon rediscovered his childhood love of drawing. "Warrior," illustrating his "handless art," was presented to the founder of Homes for Our Troops when the Damons moved into their special-needs house in October 2005. *(Private collection of Pete Damon)* palm. He mixed little plastic cups of colors to capture the range of pigments, dipped in a small brush, and painted in tiny strokes. The brush penetrated the wrist of the glove and down holes in the fingertips where nails would eventually be inlaid.

The three primary colors—red, blue, and yellow—were all O'Brien needed to match the shades of my hand, with white mixed in for opacity. He added transparent colors for the deep highlights in the knuckles, fingertips, and pads of the palm, infusing each layer with increasingly subtle transparencies. My knuckles needed more red, my veins a purplish blue, my palm opaque. If he wasn't satisfied with the results, O'Brien scraped out the residue with a skinny spatula. The process went on for five hours, interrupted by an occasional request for a second opinion from Curtin.

"A little more of the purple-pink as you paint it in," kibitzed Curtin at one point.

Forty-five minutes later, the master looked down again and critiqued the shading. "It looks a lot more beige on the side." He pointed to the knuckles and said, "You could go a little redder there."

After four coats of paint, the glove came alive with color. It had to dry before the final assembly and insertion of fingernails, a custom-made acrylic that would be matched to my skin tones.

I returned home that night, leaving the last touches to Curtin. The next day, he stretched the glove over an electronic hand that I had left with him and shipped it to Washington, where I was anxiously waiting. The package arrived March 12, the day before I left for California. I had goose bumps when I opened it.

The prosthesis looked so real it could have been my old right hand retrieved from the rubble in Baghdad and sent back by snail mail. It was frozen in a claw position, but looked completely natural when hanging by my side. I immediately screwed it into the shell and went out for a test run. For the first time since my injury, I walked down the street without drawing stares. I boarded the plane to California the next day psychologically prepared for my unveiling. No one had to feel sorry for me or single me out for special treatment.

I settled in comfortably in the land of silicone enhancement. With a long-sleeved cotton sweater draping my wrists, I could pass for two-handed in most social settings. I even managed a convincing clap at a folk music concert the first night. Of course, appearance wasn't everything. My right arm still operated robotically. The prosthesis remained heavy, clunky, irritating to wear, and obviously ersatz to anyone who was standing within two feet of me. I couldn't greet Rebekah's friends with a natural handshake or, for that matter, with my left hand if I was carrying a cocktail in it; the fake hand wasn't facile enough to hold a tumbler, so I had to put my good one to use. I nicknamed the glove "Pretty Boy"—all looks, no brains. It was a mama's boy when it came to strength. The silicone index finger tore after a few days and threatened to fall off.

Otherwise, the seven-day trip was a great success. The birthday party I threw for Rebekah and twenty-five friends at a local art center featured a performance by traveling folksingers and a cake inscribed *Diva*. Rebekah and I took long walks in the mountains encircling Ojai, dined with her friends, and mapped out the details of her move to Washington. Four months after my injury, the event had begun to recede in importance. No one paid much attention to my new right hand.

Even banged up, Curtin's copy passed for real. On my flight home, I landed at Dulles and descended an escalator to retrieve my baggage. A woman behind me fell, knocking out my legs. I tumbled and started a chain reaction. A Good Samaritan planted himself at the landing and uprighted people as they arrived feet first.

When it was my turn, the rescuer grasped Pretty Boy and pulled. The prosthesis slipped off my elbow into his outstretched hands. I quickly grabbed it back and got out of the way. Looking a bit flustered, the man was fortunately too busy to be interrupted. I was too embarrassed to explain. So I proceeded to the luggage area as if nothing had happened.

I was Curtin's first client from Walter Reed and a living example of his artistry. Miguelez soon put him on contract to sculpt and paint all the hands—and a few feet—of Iraq war amputees, at a cost to the army of about $15,000 each. Curtin patched up Pretty Boy after I returned and was soon finding new ways of making his gloves more durable as the demands of his new subjects grew.

★

Not long after I arrived at Ward 57, Rebekah wrote a song titled "Baghdad Is Never Far Away." On March 24, I was

reminded of just how close it was. *Time's* chief Iraqi translator, Omar Hashim Kamal, was gunned down gangland-style
as he drove his rusted jalopy to work.

Only forty-eight years old, Omar was a bear of a man with
the soul of a poet, a free spirit who loved adventure, story-
telling, and whiskey. Brian Bennett had brought him into our
little circle during my first trip to Iraq. Brian returned to
Baghdad the day Omar was shot. He found him in a coma at a
familiar place, the 28th Combat Support Hospital, in a room
next to the one I had lain in fifteen weeks earlier.

The news hit hard. Omar represented the best hope of a
new Iraq, a man educated in the West who appreciated the
ancient culture of his native land, a trained computer engineer who understood political subtlety. Anti-U.S. rebels apparently had targeted him as a "collaborator." Doctors held
out little hope for the translator, who was breathing through
a respirator. He had a bullet in his brain.

I was so heartbroken by the news that I woke up Rebekah
in Ojai, where I had left her a few days earlier. She knew of
Omar from stories and from a large close-up photo of him
taken by Brian. Rebekah sat down at an upright piano still in
her nightgown and composed "Ode to Omar." It was as sooth-
ing as a lullaby.

Loved are you

Blessed are you

By all that is good

And all that is True

I know strength is yours

As is all that is True

Omar,

We are taking a stand for you.

Rebekah raced to a local recording studio and put it on a CD to be sent to Baghdad. The studio managed to e-mail the sound file to Brian, who downloaded it from the hospital computer to his laptop. But he couldn't get his portable computer to reproduce the love song for Omar before his mighty heart gave out, four days after the shooting.

Brian put "Ode to Omar" on his iPod and hooked it up to speakers at an impromptu memorial service in the Palestine Hotel following his burial. Omar's cousin and colleagues listened in silence.

Transmitted through the ether, Rebekah's hymn reached the land where I, too, had fallen. Omar's death was a reminder of how lucky I was to have left Iraq for a better place.

★

Sergeant First Class Luis Rodriguez practically shot his way out of Walter Reed. Even as an outpatient, he couldn't stand the pace and inefficiencies of hospital life. When a psychologist tried to draft him for the Cripples Cavalcade therapy group, Rod informed the man in no uncertain terms that he just wanted to go home. The shrink tried to play hardball, threatening not to sign his release papers. "Let me tell you something, I'm going whether you sign that shit or not," said Rod. "I'm fed up with this place." He was gone in a matter of days.

He had imagined landing at Fort Campbell and walking off the plane in desert camouflage with a rifle in one hand and his rucksack in the other, amid a sea of balloons and banners. His kids would be waving American flags, his wife running toward him with outstretched arms. The whole town would turn out for a parade with patriotic music and proclamations recognizing the combat valor of the medic and his men.

Instead, on the morning of March 19, Rod hobbled up to his Clarksville, Tennessee, house, accompanied only by Lilliam. He had worn his artificial leg for the benefit of his two young daughters so they could see him return the way he left—in one piece. But one was in school, and the other didn't hear him enter. Only Blackie the family dog came to the door to welcome Rod. He stuck his nose against the prosthesis and kept sniffing: even a dachshund could spot a fake. The tepid reception left Rod feeling empty and depressed. When his battalion came home from Iraq in February, the brass band had played and people cheered. Where was everyone now?

Neighbors from his modest subdivision of mostly military families stopped in to welcome him. After an uncomfortable few minutes, however, they didn't know what to say to the returning warrior whose facial wounds were still visible and who was a good twenty pounds lighter than when he left. Fortunately, they didn't stay long. Rod had constant pain in his right stump—electric shocks, cramps, vicelike clamping—and a backpack full of narcotics he wanted to dip into.

Home didn't feel right after nine months of war and four of the hospital. Civilians went about their daily lives as if they had no stake in Iraq, no concern for the young soldiers who were getting killed and killing every day. The defenders of American freedom were living in peril and discomfort. Beneficiaries of their sacrifice lived for the latest clothing sales, radio shock jocks, and electronic gadgets.

Even family life was awkward at first. He felt guilty about saddling his already overburdened wife with his household duties. His daughters didn't know what to make of their daddy who had been away from home for so long. Everyone's roles had reversed. Instead of Rod taking care of his girls, they fetched him a glass of water or his crutch. When they asked what had happened to his leg, he said only that a bomb had gone off and "bad guys" had taken it away. The youngest wanted revenge. "I hope they die," said Melanie.

The single-level house became Rod's fortress, as he hunkered down to plot his next move. Decorated for bravery, he worried about rude stares and questions now. If he went to the post gym where he used to work out, it would be annoying. People would go out of their way to help him or make a big deal when he lifted a ten-pound dumbbell. His biggest fear was blowing up at well-wishers. He didn't want to be patronized, and he didn't want to hear the inspiring stories people liked to pass on about amputees who had run marathons or flown airplanes. He needed to figure everything out by himself.

Nothing had been done to adapt the house. He had left Walter Reed before learning how to operate an artificial leg, and the wheelchair was too wide to fit through doorways. He relied on crutches, which often caused more damage than good. A few days after he came home, Rod shuffled outside his front door for a breath of fresh air. He placed his good left leg on the second of three steps, leaned on his crutches, and let go of the storm door just as his oldest daughter, Michelle, was walking outside to join him. He moved instinctively to catch the glass door, letting go of his right crutch.

It was a perfect pirouette, except that Rod had no way to stop himself. He fell backward on the concrete landing, twisting his ankle. The medic who could once jump out of planes lacked the strength and the will to get up. He had never felt so helpless, so out of control, so despairing. He broke down, howling in pain and frustration. Terrified, Michelle ran for her mother. Lilliam offered a hand. "Just leave me alone," Rod insisted. "Go away. I'm going to do it by myself. I have to learn." Lilliam brought the girl inside the house. Rod wept for thirty minutes before pulling himself up and limping inside.

On his first public outing, a trip to Wal-Mart, Rod decided to use an electric cart to conserve his energy. But when he opened the throttle, the thing barely moved. "Even Grandma can probably take advantage of me," he muttered to himself. "Here I am, a thirty-four-year old guy, and I feel like I'm eighty." He lasted for less than ten minutes. "No, baby, I can't do this," he told Lilliam. "Stop, stop. Get my crutches. I don't care if I break my arms, I'm not going to ride in this stupid cart all around this place." He hopped around the store for a half hour of shopping until his armpits were rubbed raw.

Rod had always set seemingly unobtainable goals for himself and persevered. The son of a cashier who worked his way through the University of Puerto Rico, a low-ranked enlistee who earned the right to lead his own platoon, he wanted to take control of his life again. He started by buying a Total Gym to rebuild his upper body, setting it up in the garage. Every morning he raised himself from the seat of his wheelchair to the bench of the weight machine and worked out for twenty minutes. He traded in his stick-shift truck for an automatic that he could drive with one leg. He took it to Nashville, where the army had signed up a specialist to refit his prosthesis.

The C-leg was still so new, exotic, and costly—about $50,000 apiece—that only the most able-bodied civilian amputees wore them. As of May 2003, Walter Reed had made a decision to automatically issue them to every Iraq war casualty who had lost a leg above the knee. Nothing else would be as stable or predictable, a necessity for soldiers who might not be able to bear weight on the other leg if it was injured. A microprocessor programmed in a software language named "C" operated the knee, the breakthrough component. The force of push-off from an artificial foot, transmitted through sensitive gauges, cued the knee to stiffen or release for walking. Electronics monitored changes in the foot and knee fifty times per second, recalibrating for different speeds and terrains.

Rod had seen C-legs at Walter Reed and thought they looked easy to operate. His own arrived just a few days before he left. It fit so poorly and uncomfortably that he could barely stand to wear it; when he did, he could only drag it like a dead weight. Back home, he picked up basic techniques from a Fort

Campbell therapist, though Rod quickly got fed up with his theoretical approach. "How can *you* teach *me* how to walk?" Rod asked. He had never liked to depend on others. Everything else he had learned in life he had taught himself. Why should this be different?

He would master the C-leg his way, turning his small living room into a training camp. His first challenge was learning how to push off without a knee. Although the prosthesis was programmed to bend, it didn't thrust like a real knee. Rod had to jerk his right hip to move forward, a function he had difficulty learning. He had never had to isolate a body part to do something as natural as walking. After a few days, he came up with a formula: if he swung his arms just the right amount, the hip would follow. Next he taught himself how to flex the knee, experimenting with putting pressure on the toe of his artificial foot. Balance was essential: if he leaned too far forward with his torso, the knee wouldn't budge; if he angled himself back too far, he would trigger the knee before he hit his stride. Rod's left leg had a role in the choreographing. He had to plant it forward to steady himself. Then he could pull back his stump and drop the fake toe.

Whenever he tried something different, he practiced on crutches. If he had success, he moved to a supporting wall and took small steps. Sometimes he learned the hard way, like the time he tried to walk unassisted from the brown love seat in his living room to the kitchen—a distance of five yards. The prosthetic knee buckled. He fell forward, smashing his head on the linoleum kitchen floor. He sat up in exasperation. "It's going to take me a lot of work just to walk," Rod muttered.

He wasn't exaggerating. According to oxygen-consumption studies, it requires 60 percent more energy to walk with an over-the-knee prosthesis than on two legs.

Rod found a more forgiving arena in his backyard, where the grass could cushion his falls. The uneven earth made for tricky balancing, but he gained confidence and moved on to the long, downward slope in front of his house. Soon he was making a daily trip to the mailbox at the foot of the hill. If he could master the decline, why not stairs? He faced the five steps leading down from his wooden deck, gripped the railing, and slowly put down his fake foot, careful not to hit the toe. If he did, the knee would buckle and he would tumble. Leaning on the heel, he kept the prosthesis stiff and landed his good left leg on the next step. His body weight naturally caused the prosthesis to bend, completing the descent. One foot after another, he reached the bottom. He was conquering the C-leg.

But the progress produced as much pain as pride. The hard plastic socket that covered his stump didn't fit well and caused bruising. His leg was constantly cramped. When his pain became unbearable, he closed himself in a room so his wife and kids wouldn't see him suffer. Once Lilliam opened the door of the bathroom and found her husband balled up on the bathroom floor, crying.

It was nothing compared to the psychological stress. Rod kept running into the limits of anatomy and technology. Even simple tasks, like changing his shoes, tested his patience. He had to take off the artificial leg, lay it in his lap, and pull the shoe off a rigid carbon fiber foot. The tongue of his army boots had to be cut out to fit over it. The prosthesis itself required time to put on: a silicone liner had to be pulled over the stump and a pin aligned with a locking device in the shell. When his nub of a leg swelled up, he had to jam it painfully into the hard plastic. If the stump shrank, he had to add cotton socks until it fit snugly.

Rod's self-administered boot camp made him tense and volatile, causing quick shifts in his normally upbeat mood. Lilliam complained he was "too aggressive," jumpy, and bossy. "You talk to me like I'm one of your soldiers," she told him after a couple of weeks. In return, Rod begged for space. "I understand I'm not the same," he told his wife. "I just need time and I'll get back to normal."

He tried to stay positive, focusing on his rehab. But the outside world had a way of pressing in. On April 11, the *Clarksville Leaf Chronicle* ran a special section on the Iraq war dead. Rod brought the paper into the bathroom to read, sitting on the toilet as he flipped through photos and short profiles of fallen soldiers from nearby Fort Campbell. His eyes fixed on a twenty-four-year-old specialist killed November 15 in a collision of two Black Hawk helicopters in Mosul. The name jumped off the page: Ryan Travis Baker. Rod burst into tears as his mind traveled back to Iraq, nine days before he was wounded.

It was 10:30 at night. He had been sent to recover remains from one of the crash sites, an otherworldly scene that reeked of charred flesh. Stepping over body parts, he reached a heap of burned debris wrapped in blankets and set aside for disposal. The beam of his flashlight revealed what looked to be a headless human torso. Unwrapping the blankets, he turned it over. Velcroed to the remnants of an orange jumpsuit was a name tag. Rod tore off the tag and read it: Specialist Ryan Baker.

Four months later, Rod stared at the newspaper photo of an earnest young man in what looked like a tuxedo from his high school prom. The scorched specimen now had a face. Rod breathed deeply and looked at the picture again. It transported him back to the battlefield. He had never wanted to be anything but a combat medic; it was all he had done in fourteen years of army life, a sacred duty reserved for one soldier per infantry platoon. Rod cried now for the lives he hadn't saved—not just Baker but all the dead comrades in his unit. And he cried for his lost love of the job.

A few days later, Rod ran into his former commander and pal, Captain Dan Morgan, at a service station in Clarksville. Morgan told him that he might be redeployed to Iraq, along with other old buddies. Rod's blood rose. For a moment, all he could think of was shipping out with Morgan. No thought of his wife and kids who already had suffered so much. No thought of his own limitations on one leg. "I'll take my leg as is," he told the captain. "Strap my ass to the fucking top of a turret in a Humvee. I'll be your fifty-cal gunner." Rod caught himself, shaking his head and smiling wistfully. The testosterone was still there. He just needed a new place to channel it.

But first Rod wanted a last fling with his old crew, the Third Battalion of the 502nd Infantry Regiment, known as the "Widow Makers." He finally felt like socializing. He and Lilliam hosted a barbecue at their home April 18, a reunion of Iraq war comrades and friends. Ninety people showed up. Rod had not yet mastered his prosthesis, so he parked it out front like a door prize and hopped around on crutches. His guests got drunk quickly and, in typical military affair fashion, wives gathered on one side of the room with their men swapping war stories on the other.

It was a bittersweet moment for Rod. He was happy to see everyone and to let them know he was still kicking, albeit with one leg. But friends noticed the strain after a couple of hours. Rod used to be the life of the party, guzzling rum and coke, moving around and cracking jokes. Now he was stuck in a chair, exhausted from the crutches.

Everyone left around 9 P.M., except for a couple of Rod's platoon members, who kicked back on the deck under the stars. It started as light joshing, young subordinates trading anecdotes about the "hard-ass" boss Rod had once been. Then Specialist Nicholas Cutcher, a twenty-three-year-old medic from Port Huron, Michigan, dialed up the emotion. Cutcher had been trained by Rod, followed him in the Bronze Star rescue mission, and survived the roadside bomb explosion in the Humvee.

Cutcher noted that Rod had mentored his soldiers so well that everyone came home with all their body parts—except for their mentor. The specialist coughed out his words: "You're the one who always protected us, and you're the guy who got all fucked up, Sergeant Rod." Cutcher saw Rod as a father figure ripped from his family. He told him how much he respected and owed him.

The words comforted Rod. He had made a difference by pushing young soldiers to excel. His eyes filled up. But he restrained himself. Sergeant Rod would never lose his composure around soldiers he might lead into combat. Leaders didn't do that.

★

Liberty Baptist Church in Durham, North Carolina, was dressed up like a Fourth of July picnic. Patriotic bunting lined the pulpit. A choir belted out "The Star-Spangled Banner" as a giant American flag emerged from behind crimson curtains. Pastor Jack Cox knew how to wave Old Glory as fervently as any fundamentalist Christian. But his Sunday service on April 25 had a more personal billing: "A Grateful Church's Tribute to Its Own American Hero."

Bobby Isaacs had come home on a weekend furlough from Walter Reed to be celebrated by people who had watched him grow up, sent him off to fight in Iraq, and prayed for his recovery.

The three months since his amputations hadn't been easy. After a couple more surgical cleanings and a skin graft, Bobby was still battling pain and chronic infection. Doctors had finally discharged him from Ward 57 on February 12. He moved into Malogne House, where he wasn't much more mobile. His girlfriend Krystal—the sister of an army buddy whom he had met on the webcam while stationed in Iraq—had come for a visit about the time he was released. But their activities were limited to watching DVDs in the small outpatient hotel room that he shared with Pat. Bobby was still tethered to the hospital, going every day to see doctors, physical and occupational therapists, and prosthetists. By early April, Pat decided to drive Bobby home for the first time since his injury. He received a warm welcome at Liberty Baptist on Easter Sunday.

Bobby returned two weeks later to full honors. The celebration kicked off on Friday night, when he and Pat appeared as special guests of a church women's meeting hosted by Renée Cox. Bobby received a computer, a special set of Double Eagle Liberty Coins, and a surprise that threw open emotional floodgates. The church had flown in his best buddy, Jordan Caldwell, who had been discharged from the army after his tour in Iraq and now lived in Utah.

The tall, twenty-two-year-old Jordan walked onstage and locked eyes with Bobby. Both men instantly broke into sobs. The last time he had seen Jordan, Bobby had two legs and few cares in the world. Now the sheer joy of hugging a friend he had almost lost forever was overwhelming. Bobby had not let down like this since his injury; it was as if twenty weeks of suffering and sacrifice had coalesced in a single moment of emotion. He cried for the reunion and for much more—for his missing mobility and independence, for the fact he would never again enjoy the brotherhood of army life, and for the miracle of his survival.

Pastor Cox had no difficulty matching that emotional pitch in his Sunday service. It opened with a film montage of Bobby's life: as a seven-year-old initiate at Liberty Baptist, a soldier in Iraq, and a Walter Reed amputee who told ABC News *Nightline* in March, "I believe that God's still got some use for me." As the clip ended, Bobby rolled himself onto the pulpit in a wheelchair. The overflow audience of eight hundred burst into applause. Despite the major medical issues he still faced, Bobby looked handsome and fit after two months of physical training. He wore his dark green dress uniform, the empty pant legs draped over the edge of the chair.

Cox reminded his followers of the first news they had of Bobby's injury, when "we were trusting the Lord to take over where we couldn't do anything about it. . . . We prayed and prayed."

"I'm going to tell you all something quickly," he said. "Bob is going to be walking again. Aren't you, buddy?"

Sitting at Cox's left elbow, Bobby was nervously watching the pastor. He nodded yes.

"Yes, he will be walking again," Cox picked up, noting that Bobby had a couple more months left of therapy at Walter Reed.

Cox had another surprise for the young soldier. He launched into an account of Bobby's rescue. "Man, for somebody to save your life, that is something else. I know you told your family that one day you'd like to thank him."

Bobby nodded again.

"You can do it today. Let's welcome Dorian Perez."

Bobby's face lit up. The man who had breathed life into him six thousand miles away took the stage from the choir entrance. "Doc" Perez bent over the wheelchair and hugged Bobby for a full ten seconds. He raised Bobby's left hand like the winner of a prizefight and placed both hands on Bobby's shoulders.

Doc spoke into the microphone in a heavy accent. Describing how he had found Bobby "almost gone," he cut away to his own religious experience. He had lost an injured soldier three months before Bobby's ordeal in December, Doc said.

He recognized afterward that he was "just a tool" for the Almighty. But he had a question. "God, why me? I don't want this to happen again, please. Don't do it again."

Doc recalled that just before he began to apply CPR on Bobby, he told Bobby under his breath, "You're not going to die in my call."

"Ladies and gents, you've got a miracle right here," Doc said.

Bobby kept his head bowed. If he looked up, he'd have to meet all those eyes. It wasn't that he was sensitive about his legs. He simply didn't like the attention. He nodded at Doc when he used the term "miracle" and shook his hand. A few seconds later, he wiped away a tear.

Perez had come for more than religious testimony. He had been authorized by his military command to present Bobby with a Purple Heart, which had eluded him twice. Arriving at Walter Reed, he had found the prestigious medal in a manila envelope strapped across his chest. A general apparently had awarded it in Landstuhl, but didn't leave the paperwork necessary to make it official. President Bush had planned to pin it on Bobby when he visited Walter Reed; the young corporal was stuck in surgery that morning.

He would have preferred that his platoon be there for the award. But so many of his supporters were present at Liberty Baptist. He sat proudly at attention in his wheelchair, eyes straight ahead, as Doc took up the microphone and made the official presentation.

Doc opened the black leather case to display the gold medal, then handed it to Bobby. The congregation was on its feet, applauding. A few minutes later Bobby was wheeled offstage. The celebration ended as abruptly as it had begun. Jordan and Doc returned to their lives. By Tuesday evening, Bobby was back at Malogne House, just another amputee on a long road to recovery.

8.
"LOOK BACK, BUT DON'T STARE"

For nearly six months, Pete Damon had been grappling with what had gone wrong that fateful day of October 21, 2003. Helicopter tires don't routinely blow up. Maybe the rim had been faulty. Or maybe the wheel had been improperly assembled before he tried to inflate the tire. Whenever he asked army officers, they shrugged or gave lip service to his theories. Nobody had an explanation for the devastating explosion that had ripped off his arms.

Pete knew he could drive himself crazy trying to get to the bottom of it. And he had enough on his plate trying to figure out how to function as a double amputee and get strong enough to return home. In a special event the first weekend of April, the Massachusetts National Guard invited Pete to a welcome home tribute for the "Awesome Eight," his group of mechanics who had volunteered to service helicopters in the Persian Gulf. Pete, still a sergeant and an outpatient at Walter Reed, looked forward to it. Everyone else who had lost limbs in Iraq was being honored. He wasn't wounded in combat, but he played no smaller role in the war, priming its transport workhorses. The April 3 ceremony finally recognized his contribution. His wife helped dress him in a desert camouflage uniform and drove him to his old unit at Otis Air Force Base on Cape Cod.

It was a bittersweet day for Pete. He received a folded American flag, for which he crisply saluted with his left hook, and was singled out by the state adjutant general as the embodiment of "awesome." But he also saw something that stirred up old ghosts.

The March issue of *Flightfax*, an army journal on aviation risk management, was being passed around at the event. Someone handed it to Pete, opened to an article on the dangers of overinflating aircraft tires. Without identifying the unit or soldiers, the piece described a recent case in Iraq. But it was obvious from the details that it was an account of Pete's accident. Upon first glance, Pete grew excited—maybe he would finally discover what happened that day. He was surprised by a couple of facts: the nitrogen tank regulated to fill a Black Hawk tire had apparently been broken and a safety device used to prevent overinflation in the breach had been missing.

Pete focused on a reported exchange between him and his supervisor. According to the article, Pete had discovered and pointed out the equipment problems to the noncommissioned officer in charge, who asked if he had ever operated a nitrogen system in that condition. After Pete replied, "Lots of times," the NCO ordered him to inflate the tire.

"What the fuck is this?" Pete said angrily. "I didn't do this."

He was horrified. He had no memory of what led up to the accident. But he knew one thing for sure. He never would have claimed "lots of" experience inflating a tire that way. The little he knew of nitrogen tanks came from other mechanics, not instructors. He had never used the tanks to fill a tire by himself. Why would he tell his supervisor otherwise? That wasn't his style—he wasn't reckless. He never pretended to know how to do things. If he had faked it as an electrician, he would have been electrocuted long ago. He had heard about the dangers of bottled nitrogen. Why would he risk everybody's life, including his own?

Pete suddenly lost interest in the ceremony. His anger was building. The article suggested he was responsible for the accident. His old sergeant, noticing Pete's mood change, told him, "We know that's not what happened. You don't work like that." His words were reassuring. The sergeant ought to know. He had worked alongside Pete. Pete was the last guy to take chances.

The ceremony ended, but Pete's obsession with the *Flightfax* piece did not. He returned to Malogne House, where he had been spending a lot of time by himself while his family stayed in Brockton. Pete's mind began playing tricks on him. Maybe there was some truth to the story. He was the new mechanic on the job. Had he been trying to impress his supervisor? Maybe he had gotten cocky and persuaded himself that he knew enough to handle the unfamiliar equipment. If that's what happened, he was responsible for blowing off his own arms and killing his partner, Paul Bueche. The problem was, he had no way of knowing for sure what actually transpired that day.

Pete had no more to go on than a magazine article written by an officer who hadn't even contacted him for his side of the story. He didn't see any point in protesting the article. That would only draw more attention to its unfavorable and anonymous judgment. Pete knew the army had launched its own investigation and figured it would eventually get to the truth of what happened. An investigator had come to Walter Reed January 15 to interview him. None of the questions had been incriminating. They seemed pretty generic: How many times had Pete used nitrogen inflation equipment? What did he think caused the accident? Pete had heard nothing about the investigation since.

★

The label "hero" was the only four-letter word never uttered in Amputee Alley. None of the wounded soldiers needed a medal to demonstrate bravery. Nor did they like Hollywood dramatizations of it. The soldiers talked about buddies they had left behind, cities they had marched through, weapons they had fired, even Iraqis they had known, referring to them by the derogatory name "Haji" after the Muslim pilgrimage to Mecca. Only reluctantly did they discuss their valor.

The topic intrigued me because I was struggling to vindicate my loss. I had saved lives, to be sure, but the personal cost was so great that I was looking for psychological compensation. Viewing myself as lionhearted would go a long way. I had always wanted to be a hero, the guy who defended the weak or drove in the game-winning run. But what I did six months earlier still seemed abstract, someone else's story. I continued to be haunted by the question of intent. Did I act out of pure reflex or purposely grab the grenade to protect everyone?

My fellow amputees didn't need a rationale. They believed in the nobility of sacrifice, a traumatic loss for a just cause. Bobby Isaacs felt only pride when he displayed his stumps at church. It was his patriotic tribute, even more symbolic than a Purple Heart. He gave up his legs for love of country in a time of need. He was happy to have everyone know what happened to him when he served America. He wouldn't be covering his prostheses in flesh-covered silicone to make them look more lifelike. It might divert attention from his membership in the proud club of wounded veterans. But he didn't like being called a hero. It embarrassed him.

In Bobby's estimation, there was nothing noble about standing point in a Humvee, the last thing he was doing before the bomb went off underneath him. He couldn't see the larger picture, as if joining the army after September 11 and riding shotgun through the bomb-pocked streets of Mosul was just a job. He believed he had paid a small price for the honor of serving. "I still love my country, and I'd do it again," he told me.

For obvious reasons, Sergeant Rod never wanted to earn a Purple Heart. But the sacrifice it represented made his chest swell more than the Bronze Star he earned for bravery. He didn't sacrifice himself for patriotism or fealty to the commander in chief. He did it for family. If he hadn't been hit on November 24, 2003, it would have been one of his brothers.

When I asked what made him proud of his Purple Heart, Rod pointed to the risks his comrades had taken in fighting off the enemy and maneuvering him to safety. "My life was on the line," he said.

Even if there were no medals for those injured in accidents, Pete Damon was just as worthy as anyone on Ward 57. Volunteering to work in Iraq, he had sacrificed his arms to keep vital aircraft flying. He had lost more than many soldiers who had been decorated as heroes. He felt lucky to have been spared and wondered if the ordeal wasn't part of a divine plan to give his life meaning. When people called him a hero, he appreciated the sentiment: there was valor in the enormity of his loss.

I found no solace in sacrifice. I didn't have Bobby's patriotic cause, or Rod's dedication, or Pete's fatalism. Nor did I share their belief in the war as a justification. The mantra of 57 was "Freedom isn't free." I myself was increasingly skeptical of the U.S. role in Iraq. But it had nothing to do with my current crisis of conscience. I hadn't gone to Baghdad to fight insurgents. I was reporting on the fight, regardless of whether I approved of it. I had a good cause, just not good enough to give up a hand for it. Few stories are. It may have been worth losing a body part to uncover a terrorist plot or a case of child abuse or an egregious human rights violation. But there was no compelling public interest served by a profile on the American soldier in Iraq. There were other ways of telling the story beyond following a platoon into danger. Like so many journalists in this war, I had fallen into a snare known as embedding.

By the time I arrived for my second tour in November 2003, the Pentagon's policy of placing reporters in military units to provide close-ups of the U.S. invasion was well established. Every reporter lives for unfettered access to his subject. As I later suffered the consequences of that access, I was amazed by my shortsightedness. For proximity, I had traded a bigger principle of journalism: autonomy. When I moved in with a platoon, I forfeited my critical edge. It was impossible to be an impartial judge of soldiers who were feeding, sheltering, and protecting me.

I also sacrificed independence of action. The unpopularity of U.S. soldiers should have been part of the story. But I was in no position to document it from the seat of an army vehicle. I might as well have been slinging an M-16. No wonder I was wounded like a soldier: I was indistinguishable from one. The journalistic payoff was meager. I didn't learn much more than I would otherwise have gleaned from a few visits to the platoon; except for one thing—what it meant to be wounded in action. For twenty days, I had eaten, bunked, and patrolled with soldiers to sketch the portrait of a platoon. Once I grabbed the grenade, I crossed the line from observer to participant.

★

The ornate Empire State Ballroom of the Grand Hyatt New York had darkened. I struggled to strike a match with my left hand, securing the flint of a matchbook with the curled fingers of my Pretty Boy prosthesis. The Overseas Press Club, a prestigious group of foreign correspondents, had invited me on April 21 to light a candle at its annual banquet in a tribute to the fallen journalists of 2003. The group had awarded me and Brian Bennett honorable mention for our Iraq coverage.

The banquet official who introduced me recalled the night I had lost my hand, adding that "were it not for his bravery, three other people in the Humvee all certainly would have died." Fumbling with the match, I finally managed to light the candle for seventy less fortunate colleagues worldwide. Several hundred journalists, a hard-bitten crowd that rarely cheers anyone publicly, left their seats and clapped for almost a minute. The applause enveloped me like a warm wave. I was being honored by peers for intrepid reporting, the one thing I always had hoped would speak for me.

The generous reception gave me a new perspective. I had been holding myself up to a high standard of heroism. Perhaps it was the company I had been keeping, soldiers who aspired to a different ideal. The gold standard of journalism is truth telling, not bodily sacrifice. I felt more comfortable in that company.

I couldn't say the same for the actual job of reporting. I had returned to *Time* in late March and found my office in a dismal time warp, the evidence of a mad dash to make my overseas flight in November: ATM receipts, a list of items to bring scribbled in my old hand, maps of Iraq, news clippings, passport-size photos, the jacket of an Air France ticket.

My bosses spared no cost to ease my adjustment after three months of recovery. But it wasn't easy to perform most basic journalistic tasks. Never much of a typist, I found one-hand pecking straining and inexact. Left-handed keyboards were no panacea; they jumbled letters and numbers in a disorientingly different order than standard keyboards. I tried voice-activated software, a maddening technology of new commands requiring weeks of training to get words "right," instead of "write."

The telephone, a reporter's principal tool, became a liability. Instead of holding it in one hand and jotting notes with the other, I had to resort to a headset that picked up every noise and spooked sources. Note taking was no easier. Either the conversations moved too quickly or I wrote so unintelligibly that I couldn't dicipher my own chicken scratch. I grew so frustrated trying to read one notebook that I hurled it against an office wall. I resorted to taping everything. But the interviews then had to be transcribed, a time-consuming process. Not everyone consented to the intimidating process of talking into a box, and when they did, their words didn't always transmit. The playback of one lunch conversation with a high-level defense official was inaudible above the din of the restaurant.

I stormed into the office of Washington bureau chief, Michael Duffy. "I can't do this anymore," I said.

Duffy told me to take it easier on myself. I had been back only a few weeks. "It's going to take time," he said. He calmed me down enough to attempt a second effort. I phoned the official under the guise of clarifying a few points. He patiently repeated his earlier spiel. I had what I needed for a story.

I gradually adjusted to work with my left hand and to praise that I continued to receive for the last act of my right. At the annual White House Correspondents Dinner on May 1, President George W. Bush got up to launch a humorous retort to critics. He started out on a serious note, however, commemorating "great war journalists" of the past, such as CBS's Edward R. Murrow, photographer Joe Rosenthal, and Scripps Howard's Ernie Pyle. He cited a pair of American reporters who had died in noncombat events in Iraq: NBC's David Bloom and *Atlantic Monthly*'s Michael Kelly. Then, he said, "Others, like Michael Weisskopf, have shown incredible presence of mind and courage that won our admiration." The room erupted in applause.

Triumph is short-lived in journalism, a fact that editors love to rub in by the line "What have you done for me today?" Reporters don't get medals. Most earn less money than the people they cover. The biggest reward is the respect of other "hacks." I had declined to receive Bush on Ward 57—a military setting where I didn't really belong. But at a professional dinner, where I held my own among my own, he paid me a great honor.

★

In the Mobile Bay town of Daphne, Alabama, 850 miles south of Walter Reed, Maria Bueche was trying to make sense of her only son's death. The day of the accident, October 21, 2003, the army had informed her only that Paul had been killed in an aviation maintenance accident. The next day, Maria learned from authorities that a helicopter tire had exploded and that the incident was under investigation. She was promised a full report in about three months.

The *Flightfax* article that had inflamed Pete was published in March. The journal was authoritative, produced by the Army Safety Center. Based at Fort Rucker, Alabama, it had sent a team to Iraq to collect evidence and report its findings to the army's chief investigator. The major who authored the piece had worked on the team. But *Flightfax* circulated almost exclusively within the army aviation community. Maria didn't see it, nor had anyone sent her a copy.

By April, six months had passed without a word. So Maria, a fifty-one-year-old Cuban-American who designed gardens for a living, did some digging of her own. Soon after Paul's National Guard unit returned from Iraq, she invited five of his buddies to a barbecue at her home. Over a few beers, they confided how poorly equipped the hangar had been where Black Hawks were serviced and Paul had been killed. Ten days after the May 1 dinner, she received an e-mail from one of the guardsmen she had hosted. He provided alarming new details: the company's command had known of "faulty" tire-inflating equipment and "did nothing" to fix it. "To me it was just an accident that could have been prevented by having the right equipment on hand to do the job," he wrote.

Maria had heard enough. In mid-May, she called the Alabama National Guard for an update on the investigation. Officials told her the army was coordinating it. Contacting the army, she was told the guard was in charge. Maria knew she was getting a runaround. She also knew how to stop it: she called the *Mobile Register* later that month and passed along the reports of equipment and leadership failures at the Iraq air base. The newspaper ran an article June 19, echoed by TV reports on all three local channels. Instead of fending off calls from an unhappy mother, the guard and army now had reporters asking questions. The publicity-shy military got the message.

On the morning of July 5, Army National Guard Colonel Ernest T. Erickson arrived on her doorstep. Erickson, who had commanded aviation maintenance crews during Paul's tour, brought along the investigation report and a nine-page compilation of "facts and findings" in bold black print specially assembled for the Bueche family. Erickson also gave Maria a copy of the *Flightfax* article, which was published about the same time the investigation had concluded—four months earlier.

The report cited so many lapses of command that Maria quickly realized why it had taken so long to get her hands on it. Two names were blacked out, but it was clear from the narrative who they were: Pete and the noncommissioned officer in charge of the Alabama National Guard unit, Sergeant Jason Roten. The twenty-eight-year-old Roten was an aviation mechanic who had mastery of the nitrogen-inflation system and usually operated it in Hangar 13-B of the Balad Army Airfield.

Nitrogen was supplied from tanks wheeled around on metal carts. Each so-called nitrogen cart carried two tanks: a low-pressure vessel regulated to shut off once a Black Hawk tire reached its capacity and a high-pressure one designed to power heavy aircraft parts. For reasons the report failed to explain, the low-pressure tank was not used on October 21. (*Flightfax* said it was missing "proper fittings.") Instead, the tire was hooked up to the high-pressure side that had a capacity to spew nearly twenty times more nitrogen than was needed to inflate the car-sized tire.

The Black Hawk technical manual, the bible of repair crews, required the use of a fail-safe device for high-pressure tanks. The tire servicing kit, known as the "yellow box" because of its color, was supposed to be connected to the helicopter tire on one side and the tank on the other. The kit could be calibrated to automatically vent excess gas once the tire's capacity was reached. But Hangar 13-B had no yellow box. One was available next door, according to the report, but Roten made no effort to borrow it.

Instead, investigators found, he had directed Pete to use the tank without a yellow box. Pete never questioned the "improper directive" and was overheard saying that he knew how to use the equipment. He hooked up the hose directly to the tire while another crew member—investigators were unable to determine who—turned on the tank that was located several feet from the aircraft.

The report concluded that Roten and Pete "cut corners in the interest of speed." Pete was specifically cited for neglecting "by the book" procedures, including use of a regulated tank and inflating the tire only to its capacity.

Maria spent close to four hours studying the materials in the presence of the colonel, two military attachés, and an army chaplain who had gathered around her formal dining room table. The revelation of equipment shortages infuriated her the most, and she unloaded on the senior officer who had commanded her son's unit from Kuwait: "These young men were dispensable to you. You knew they didn't have operable equipment, but it was cheaper to kill a soldier and have him replaced than to get it. You were so cavalier about their safety. These people were nothing but a number to you."

Erickson took umbrage, pointing out that Paul could have refused the order. The teenager, said the report, was so inexperienced he probably had been "reluctant to challenge" his two senior officers. Maria also laid into them in absentia—Roten for ordering his men to work without safe equipment and Pete for professing knowledge of nitrogen carts and subsequently botching the job.

Pete had heard from an Alabama soldier at Walter Reed that Maria possessed the report. Pete hadn't received a copy himself, nor had he sought one from the army. He was in a bind, yearning to know what caused the accident and fearful of what he'd learn. He was uncertain about whom he could trust to give him the facts. Army investigators may have gotten to the bottom of it. Or they may have found a scapegoat to cover up shoddy safety practices at the army airfield. Pete was the perfect fall guy, the Yankee outsider who had only recently joined the Alabama unit. No one from Roten's crew had called Walter Reed to check on his well-being since he had arrived. Pete wondered if they blamed him for the accident and for surviving while their buddy perished.

The memory of Paul haunted Pete. The specialist had reached out to him before anyone else in the unit had. He was an endearing kid who loved to laugh and help others. The fact that Pete had survived and Paul hadn't racked Pete with guilt. When something good came along, like the Homes for Our Troops project, the undeserving feelings welled up: Why should he get a break when Paul never had a fighting chance? Pete thought of him all the time and never missed an opportunity in his increasingly frequent public appearances to note his partner's sacrifice.

He couldn't shut off the anxiety, even when he was sleeping. Pete had nightmares of narrowly escaping evil spirits that sought to take him away. Or he'd be watching helplessly as his wife and kids were being snatched by demonic kidnappers.

The events of October 21 kept replaying in his mind. No matter what *Flightfax* suggested, he couldn't believe he had been reckless or had followed orders he thought might result in disaster. Still, he couldn't help but feel somehow responsible. He was the man in charge of inflating the tire, the one closest to it at the time of explosion. He questioned whether he had done enough to avoid Paul's death. The survivor's guilt was eating him up.

That summer at Walter Reed Pete and I had struck up a friendship. We saw each other every week or so, in doctors' waiting rooms or the prosthesis shop. Occasionally, we'd grab a bite or I'd go with him for a smoke outside Malogne House. Invariably, the subject of his accident came up. It didn't take a genius to figure out why I was interested in Pete's struggle. It was familiar. We faced a common obstacle in our recoveries. Neither of us had reached an understanding of what role we had played in the sudden violent events that had drastically altered our lives. The inconclusiveness kept us from fully embracing our losses and moving on. Pete needed to know he had acted prudently, exposing no one to undue risk. I needed to know I had acted courageously, with the conscious intention of saving myself and others from danger. Each of us wrestled with a sense of guilt. I felt guilty for being rewarded for what I wasn't convinced was an act of true heroism. Pete faced a more difficult dilemma. He felt guilty for failing to save a life and questioned why he hadn't.

We stumbled over the same problem: memory gaps. Neither Pete nor I could recall what moved us in a defining moment. Why did I grab a grenade? Why didn't he prevent the tire explosion?

"I'd love to know what happened," Pete told me repeatedly.

★

Throughout the spring, Luis Rodriguez was haunted by a recurring nightmare. He was back in Iraq in a familiar role, scurrying to save three wounded American troops. He pressed a field dressing on the chest of the first patient and cleared his airways, fighting to stabilize him. But it wasn't enough. The soldier died. The medic moved to the second patient and patched him up in standard fashion. He died, too. The pattern continued a third time. Rod did everything by the book, practicing time-tested methods. Nothing worked. He stood up and realized he had lost them all.

The image would abruptly waken Rod, heart crashing against his chest. His nightmare anxieties mirrored his daily fears. No matter how hard he tried, he couldn't influence events as he once had. His power had gone the way of his right leg. The reality was gradually sinking in. He had to accept the limitations of his injury and get on with his life. He kept thinking about a line from a book he had read on Ward 57, the memoir of a Black Hawk pilot who had been shot down over Somalia. Author Michael J. Durant wrote that while recovering from his wounds, he received a letter from a cancer survivor who advised: "Look back, but don't stare."

By May, Rod had resolved to stop staring. He knew he had seen his last combat. But the army was still family. He had to find a new way to dedicate himself. He turned down a promotion to first sergeant of a company, the NCO in charge of 120 soldiers, knowing that he could no longer lead by example. How could he send them on a five-mile run and not head the pack? After a few days of soul-searching, Rod came up with an idea and walked into the office of his brigade commander to try it out. The colonel asked Rod if he had decided what he'd like to do.

"I want to teach," replied the sergeant.

The 101st Airborne offered an advanced course for medics who already had sixteen weeks of training. Rod saw this job as a way to satisfy his twin passions: leading troops and saving lives. If he couldn't be in the battlefield, the medics he taught would be there. He already had ideas about passing on the lessons he learned in Iraq, bringing combat into the classroom. He was hired on the spot. From that day on, he stopped staring at the past and thought only of his new mission. Pencil and paper in hand, he camped out at his dining room table to map out ideas for his curriculum.

Fort Campbell's Rascon School of Combat Medicine, named after a decorated Vietnam War medic, had a new noncommissioned officer in June. Rod pulled his SUV up to a tan cinder-block office in sprawling Fort Campbell. He opened his four-day course with tough talk, illustrated by a PowerPoint presentation and videos from Iraq. One of the first digital photos he displayed was a close-up of his bombed-out Humvee. The side where he had been sitting looked like a crushed beer can. "This is not a joke; this is not a story about your dad when he went to Vietnam," Rod told one group. "If you don't do the right thing here, somebody is going to die. When somebody dies or gets blown up because you didn't do your job, because you didn't make sure you had the right equipment, because you were too lazy to pay attention when it was time to pay attention, that's on you, and it will stick with you the rest of your days. You don't want to live with it."

His combat experience consistently informed the course. On the importance of tourniquets, he spoke of his own injury and how he had avoided shock despite heavy bleeding only because "Doc" Perez had quickly tightened one on his leg. On the unpredictability of warfare, he noted how he had been "blown up" on a noncombat mission when he least expected to engage the enemy. On the need to master weapons, he related the story of his Bronze Star rescue when he fired a semiautomatic to cover himself as he ran for a truck of medical supplies.

Rod supervised first-aid techniques in a simulated emergency room. Uniformed rubber mannequins hooked up to computers were stretched out on gurneys and programmed to mimic human responses, from dilated pupils to breathing to secreting fluids. Without enough liquids, the dummy's blood pressure rose. If a tourniquet wasn't properly tied, the dummy continued to bleed.

As the practice intensified, so did Rod's participation. At one of the sessions that I attended, he started out instructing medics on how to haul heavy bodies up a steep hill behind the school. "Put that weapon around your neck so you can use your hands," he yelled at an exhausted soldier.

Rod stopped briefly to introduce me. "Even though he's not in uniform, he's been there. Hooah?" Rod said, using the universal army term of approval.

"Hooah," came the echo.

Rod asked me to describe what had happened to my arm.

"Did you hear that?" Rod asked. "Keyword—if the medic didn't get the tourniquet on there, he would have bled to death. That's a fact of life."

We moved indoors to the "war room," where his students administered first aid in an atmosphere designed to replicate the aftermath of a roadside bomb blast. They worked in darkness and billowing smoke. Flashing lights and the noise of automatic fire and grinding vehicles—compliments of the sound track for *Saving Private Ryan*—contributed to the sensory overload. Dummies with computer-generated wounds and moans littered the concrete floor.

A twenty-year-old private from Washington State performed for the master medic. With a green phosphorescent chem-light in her mouth, she tightened a tourniquet over an amputated leg, applied a large bandage to a chest wound, and punched a needle into the lungs for air passage. Ten minutes later, taps played over a boom box. The patient had died. Rod pointed out to his pupil that she had failed to treat an exit wound. He ordered her to write a letter to the dummy's parents informing them that their young dummy died because she had failed to do her job.

"I guarantee you, the next time you'll do it right," Rod told her.

Rod discovered a love for teaching. Off-duty, however, he was learning. When Melanie decided she wanted to ride a two-wheeler that summer, she asked her daddy to teach her, as he had her older sister Michelle. As Rod grabbed the back of the bike and began pushing, his C-leg buckled and he landed on his knee. Frustration welled up. But he controlled his anger. This was something he couldn't do alone, he realized. He called on Michelle to run with the bike as he barked out commands. "I'm going to be right here," Rod assured his younger daughter. "When I tell you to let go, let go." The duo triumphed. Melanie mastered the bicycle and Rod the ability to ask for help.

He even made concessions in the macho world of military training. Rod had been a rappel master, certified to teach soldiers how to climb down ropes from flying aircraft. In early fall, he headed to the forty-foot rappelling tower at Fort Campbell to test himself on one leg. He reached the ladder and looked up at the steep incline. Holding on to the railing, he anchored his good left leg on the first rung and hoisted himself, the C-leg dragging behind. The climb was exhausting, but Rod was thinking about the bigger challenge at the top. Step by step, he finally reached the platform where the instructor, First Sergeant Ray Fulks, was waiting. Fulks had been Rod's company leader in Iraq. He had raced to the scene of Rod's roadside bomb attack and helped drive off insurgents firing at the convoy. It was Fulks who had told Rod his leg was gone.

Rod had jumped out of planes dozens of times by himself. But before leaping this time, he asked Fulks to make sure his harnesslike seat was properly buckled and the rope firmly secured. Moving to the ledge, Rod discovered that he couldn't push off. His C-leg was a dead weight, and if he tried to launch himself from the left leg alone, he'd lose control of the prosthesis. He enlisted Fulks to shove the fake leg off the platform at the same time he pushed off with his good one.

Rod made it down to the ground safely. But he couldn't have done it without a friendly push.

★

The dead never pick up their trophies. I couldn't drive the idea from my mind the morning of June 11, the day I was traveling to receive an award that memorialized the late journalist Daniel Pearl. While I waited in the Ronald Reagan Washington National Airport lounge, TV screens carried live coverage of Ronald Reagan's funeral with all its pomp and circumstance. It occurred to me that Nancy Reagan gladly would have traded all of the eulogies for another moment of the former president's warm breath on her cheek. Posthumous honors seemed like paltry compensation for dying.

Pearl had been executed by Islamic extremists, with whom he had prearranged an interview in Pakistan in January 2002. Like me, the thirty-eight-year-old *Wall Street Journal* reporter had been trying to get closer to his subjects. Both of us played the odds of returning safely. Tragically, he lost the bet and left a young wife, pregnant with their first child. I survived to pick up the Daniel Pearl Award for Courage and Integrity in Journalism at a posh Ritz-Carlton banquet in Los Angeles, accompanied by my family and fiancée. The plaque did not represent a prize to me, as much as a reminder of life's fragility.

I fought to reconcile our conflicting fates when I met Daniel's widow the next night. Marianne Pearl and Daniel's parents had established the annual award to commemorate the courage that he exhibited when he set out for his interview. A French journalist, Marianne stood behind a small podium and explained why I had been chosen for the clear Lucite plaque etched in Daniel's likeness.

"It is my conviction that physical courage at crucial moments comes from the sum of intellectual courage and integrity that you muster at that moment," she said. I had proven my mental grit, she explained, by trying to toss back a grenade that was intended to "silence" me, using the very hand with which I broke silences. I had sacrificed my means of expression in defense of the larger need to report what was happening. "I felt how strong that man must be in terms of intellectual courage."

I was moved by the idea. I didn't buy it as an explanation for why I had grabbed the grenade; whatever impelled me clearly had more to do with defense of self than of the public's right to know. But Marianne gave meaning to my sacrifice as profound as the lifesaving result of it. She linked the loss of my hand to a principled cause: freedom of speech. It took me a minute to follow her logic, but I eventually got it. In fact, I did stand for more than myself at that moment. I represented the principle of inquiry into matters of importance—in this case, the U.S. role in Iraq. I protected my ability to perform in that role by limiting the grenade's damage—regardless of the reason I picked it up.

The wife of a journalistic martyr opened my eyes to the significance of my actions in terms I could grasp, a nonmilitary context. "I would like Michael to consider this award as a metaphorical handshake between [him] and Danny, not because you both confronted terrorism, but because you offer an example for others to follow."

I cringed a little when I heard those last words. I had no interest in being a journalistic Billy Graham. I got paid well to do what I enjoyed—poking into other people's business, changing the scenery and shaking people by the lapels with a good story. I had never aspired to be a role model—the term "junkyard dog" had always seemed well suited to me. But Marianne's words provided new insight. Even if I inhabited a world of self-interest, I acted on a larger stage with consequences reaching far beyond me. I didn't have to be altruistic to have done something good.

9.
STANDING UP

The Fort McNair Officers Club was a relic, a nineteenth-century, plantation-style building in southwest Washington. On August 17, soldiers in dress uniforms and wives in party gowns gathered for a reception on the top floor, forking roast beef and shrimp from a buffet amid crystal chandeliers and mirrored mantels. I felt as out of place as a bulldog at a cat show. But I was the main attraction. The army had chosen to grant me its annual Fourth Estate Award for my Iraq coverage.

I almost declined the award. Reporters don't usually accept honors from the subjects of their stories. But my stint at Walter Reed put me in an unusual position. I already had taken so much from the army, it felt safe, and I had a new appreciation of its dedication to saving lives. Soldiers might not be freethinkers or humanitarians. But their sense of duty ran deep. So did their respect for mine.

The event had allowed me to do something special for Skyler and Olivia, who had lived through every minute of my injury. I brought them along to share this honor. Accepting the plaque from a brigadier general, I thanked the army "most of all for returning me to my beautiful children."

From the reception we drove in buses to the National Mall, where we were seated in the front row to hear the U.S. Army Band's annual *1812* Overture concert. The performance was rousing, the summer night perfect. The conductor interrupted the music between movements to announce my award. I heard applause and looked behind me. Walter Reed had sent a busload of soldiers. I couldn't imagine a more fitting group to join the celebration.

I was lost in the moment, only to be brought back by the firing of cannons at the end of the performance. The battle sounds were a harsh reminder of why I had been invited. I looked down at Pretty Boy and thought how lucky I had been to have lost only a hand.

★

Pete Damon used his backpack as his pockets. He filled it with his basic necessities, from cash to smokes, stashed in little compartments he could easily dip into with a hook. The knapsack was as vital to him as a cane to the blind. He brought it everywhere, especially when he ventured from Walter Reed; he felt more secure with a backup prosthesis inside. So when Pete had walked into a Toys "R" Us store in

Brockton on the evening of August 6 to buy his daughter a birthday gift, he had been shouldering a full load.

Pete and Jenn got as far as the customer service desk when a young woman stopped them. She announced that he would have to check his knapsack while he shopped.

Pete couldn't believe his ears. No one had ever made such a request before. With one arm cut off at the biceps and the other sporting a clawlike Greifer, Pete hardly represented a shoplifting threat. Indeed, the previous night he had browsed at the same store wearing the bag and had not been stopped. He explained this to the customer service worker. She replied blankly that maybe no one had noticed it the previous night.

"Nonsense," Pete said. He had asked several salesclerks for assistance and even received directions to the bathroom from the store manager. "Nobody said anything to me." His tone sharpened.

Her reply was almost robotic: No shopping with a backpack on.

Pete took another approach. "I don't have any arms," he said in a low voice. "I need the backpack. This is where I keep my money."

She repeated the store policy once more.

At that point, Pete lost his cool. Threatening to issue a complaint, he stormed out of the store, leaving a wake of expletives, only to turn around and see the woman snickering with coworkers. Enraged, he charged back in and demanded to see her supervisor.

The night manager was braced for confrontation. Before Pete could open his mouth, he issued the same edict as the woman. When Pete asked him why he hadn't stopped him twenty-four hours earlier, the manager replied that he hadn't noticed the backpack.

"Fucking retarded, I was standing right in front of you with my backpack on," said Pete. "I'm going to sue you and your fucking store. It's discriminatory."

What Pete heard next were fighting words: "You go right ahead, tough guy. Don't get too tough now, tough guy."

"Why? What are you going to do?" Pete snorted.

"You don't know what I'm going to do," warned the night manager.

In the old days, Pete would have knocked him down and started pummeling before he had finished the "tough guy" taunt. No one pushed Pete around then.

Nor would anyone now. Pete was armed with something mightier than fists. He had suffered a great loss in the service of his country and was proud of the sacrifice. Nobody was going to belittle him. He shouldn't have to wear a uniform to get his due; anyone disabled deserved the benefit of the doubt. If he didn't get it, he'd strike back as forcefully as he once had in street fights. Pete had discovered a new knockout punch: moral outrage.

He had a lot to stoke it that summer. A week before the Toys "R" Us incident, Pete had left Walter Reed for a furlough home, accompanied by Jenn. They reached Baltimore/Washington International Airport too late to make their Southwest Airlines flight. The gate supervisor offered to put them on standby for the next plane. Pete had never flown standby before and asked for details. The woman told him to have a seat and listen for instructions, then looked past him to the next person in line. Pete had just watched her take a long time with a couple of young, well-dressed people. Perhaps he wasn't enough of a yuppie, he thought. But he wasn't about to be brushed off. "Who the hell are these guys ahead of me that you can spend ten minutes with them, and you tell me to get out of here?" he asked the supervisor.

"I've got a lot of people here in line," she said. "Go sit down, sir."

Instead, Pete went to the Southwest customer service desk. He reported that the clerk had rudely treated an injured Iraq war veteran. The customer rep left to talk to the supervisor. She returned, apologized, and handed him two open tickets worth $300 each.

The Toys "R" Us brouhaha was not handled as smoothly. Pete's first thought was to enlist his old friends to teach the night manager some manners. Returning home that night, he decided on another course. Jenn dialed the company's twenty-four-hour hotline and issued a formal complaint. The next day, a corporate official called and promised to investigate. Pete told the man he wanted two things: an apology and the dismissal of the night manager.

No action was taken, and Pete returned to Walter Reed a few days later. But he told everyone how the nationwide toy chain had mistreated him. Soon he had reinforcements from a different group of friends. A veterans' activist from Virginia who had gotten to know Pete on 57 called the Brockton store and threatened to organize a Massachusetts veterans boycott and protest in the parking lot unless Pete's demands were satisfied. The night manager's boss called Pete to complain of harassment. Pete couldn't believe his gall.

The Toys "R" Us corporation took a different tack. A

regional executive called to apologize and told Pete the night manager had been "taken care of." The conversation went well and ended with a promise to send him company gift certificates. Pete thanked her and asked that she extend the same apology to Jenn, who was out at the time.

When she found out, Jenn berated Pete for falling for the sweet talk. He had done nothing to keep the same thing from happening to the next disabled person. "You can't let them get away with it," she told him.

Jenn got a chance to speak for herself. When the company executive called again for Jenn, she told her not to bother sending gift certificates. "We won't be accepting them. It doesn't begin to cover the damages and the embarrassment you put my husband through. And by the way, the next time you hear from us, our lawyer will be calling."

No one ever had to encourage Pete to make himself heard. He just never had a megaphone before he landed on Ward 57. The place crawled with national media, and Pete was a favorite subject. He had a devastating injury and a way with words. For him, it was love-hate at first sight. Reporters told him how articulate he was. He wrote it off as fake flattery, their way to persuade a soldier with no arms to go on camera; Pete knew the impact of his injury, especially on TV. He had made his debut in an NBC News broadcast October 31, ten days after his accident. He lay on a gurney, both arms heavily bandaged, and described phantom limb pain. Sympathy letters flooded the ward from almost every state. His stumps ensured high TV ratings.

Pete quickly realized the street ran both ways. His image sold. The media were like a cash register for Homes for Our

Troops. Less than two months after he signed on with the group, publicity he had sowed reaped $30,000 in gifts and pledges by local unions and contractors to build three-quarters of a house for him. All HFOT needed was more cash to buy the land. Pete could open the till pretty much any time he wanted during the presidential campaign of 2004. Debate over the Iraq war was dominating the contest that summer. TV couldn't get enough footage of wounded U.S. soldiers.

Pete had had another reason to want airtime: he had a score to settle with filmmaker Michael Moore. In late June, shortly after Moore's *Fahrenheit 9/11* opened, Pete had begun hearing about his cameo role in the movie. Civilian support workers at Walter Reed teasingly addressed him as "movie star" and congratulated him for "taking a stand" in the controversial film. Pete thought they must have confused him with someone else. He had never spoken to anyone from Moore's crew and didn't like what he had heard about the movie's criticism of President Bush and his war in Iraq.

Jenn went to check it out at a Brockton theater. It was Pete, all right, but he wasn't talking to Moore. He was being interviewed by NBC News's Brian Williams for the October 31 story on the residents of Ward 57. Moore had spliced in the interview to underscore his larger point: American soldiers were bearing the brunt of the war. Pete appeared in a section that opened with a Democratic congressman saying, "They're leaving all kinds of veterans behind," and panned to Staff Sergeant Maurice Craft: "They've got a death toll, but they're not showing the amount of people that are being injured and amputated because of their injuries." The screen then flashed to Pete on a gurney, bare-chested, pale, and tangled in tubes. He tried to gesticulate with his bandaged stumps. "I still feel like I have hands," he said. "The pain is like my hands are getting crushed in a vice." The next scene drove home Moore's political agenda. A wounded soldier who suffered from nerve damage told an interviewer that the injury had caused him to stop his long-standing affiliation with Republicans because "they conduct business in a very dishonest way. I'm going to be incredibly active in the Democratic Party" and "definitely do my best to ensure that the Democrats win control."

In early July, Pete finally saw *Fahrenheit 9/11* in Washington. He went postal. He hated that Moore had run the interview without seeking his consent. (NBC claimed to have licensed it to Moore with the understanding he would have to obtain all necessary releases to use it.) Most of all, he hated that Moore used him to make a case against a president and a war Pete robustly supported. He would never criticize the cause for which he had lost his arms.

The filmmaker reminded him of playground bullies who didn't fight fair. But with millions of people flocking to see *Fahrenheit 9/11*, Pete had to combat him in kind. After giving an angry interview to the *Army Times*, he got a call from the more widely read *New York Daily News*. The reporter quoted Pete saying that he felt "violated" by Moore, who should be "ashamed of himself" for treating soldiers "like a bunch of idiots." A movie director named Michael Wilson saw the article and phoned Pete. He was making his own film called *Michael Moore Hates America*. Would Pete like a part? Before long, Wilson was filming Pete in Brockton with a hand-held camera. Sitting on a stool at the kitchen counter of his mother's home, Pete spoke directly to Moore: "I don't want any part of your propaganda. I don't agree with what you're doing. I'm really pissed off that you decided to use my image to sell your movie."

Pete became his own agent. He railed against Moore every chance he got. Having a cigarette behind the Malogne House in late August, he ran into another arm amputee who had wound up in *Fahrenheit 9/11* without his consent. Pete urged the soldier to go public with his protest. "If I put your words and picture in the movie presenting the Nazi point of view, it's the same thing he's doing," Pete roared. "All those idiots come out of *Fahrenheit 9/11* and say, 'That's the truth, man, Michael Moore tells it how it is.' I just want to tell those people no, it ain't. He's a fucking liar. This guy slanders people. He pulls every dirty trick in the book."

Moore's appearance at the Democratic National Convention in late July had pushed Pete's political button. He began angling for an invitation to the Republican counterpart to show his support for the president and the war. Democratic nominee John Kerry, one of Pete's senators from Massachusetts, claimed to speak for veterans because of his decorated service in Vietnam. But Pete had never seen Kerry at Walter Reed. George Bush had visited three times.

Pete even found a financial angle to his anti-Moore crusade. He began to publicly call on the filmmaker to give some of his millions in movie profits to groups like Homes for Our Troops to improve the lot of wounded soldiers and their families.

By late summer, Pete had become the Jack Welch of Ward 57, an entrepreneur with a sense of mission and belief in his own moral authority. But with so many balls in the air, he often felt overwhelmed. HFOT needed to raise funds. The media hounded him for interviews. He ran into red tape trying to secure his release from Walter Reed and his retirement with full benefits from the National Guard.

The stress kept him awake at night and by day had him puffing Marlboros, which he plucked from his backpack pouch and lit as adroitly as a skilled carpenter wields his tools. Pete's stub of a right arm never took to an above-the-elbow prosthesis, which was hard to operate and constantly bumped into his body-powered left hook. Although he maneuvered well with one fake arm, Pete encountered daily frustrations, from tying his shoes to turning a key. Eating a sandwich was a contact sport. He'd place it on a table, lower his head, and steer it into his mouth with his prosthesis. If the food veered off the table, he'd pin it with his right stump, often leaving a trail of mayonnaise on his sleeve.

Phantom limb pain hit in agonizing bursts. On bad days, he imagined one of Mafia boss John Gotti's goons tightening his hand in a vice to force him to talk. Sometimes he felt his fingernails digging into the side of his palm or his fingers scrunching up. He wiggled his imaginary fingers to ease the pain, pretending he was fingering a guitar solo. But drugs were the only real escape. He took enough methadone every day to keep a street user of heroin floating, plus a large dose of a nerve pain medication called Neurontin that was originally intended for seizures.

But nothing pained him more than the lingering questions of responsibility for the accident and feelings of guilt for surviving Paul Bueche. Pete used his role in the anti-Moore film as a pretext for addressing the emotional conflict. He obtained the e-mail address of Paul's father from the Alabama soldier, and on August 19 took the bold step of writing him.

Dictating the message to Jenn, Pete asked permission to mention "your son's sacrifice" in the new movie. He said he didn't know what the Bueches thought of *Fahrenheit 9/11*, but he felt that "it disgraces soldiers and doesn't honor the soldiers who have died in this war as they should be honored. I don't believe your son, or other parents' sons and daughters, have died in vain. I believe their sacrifices matter. . . . Your son is a true hero." Pete told me a few days later that he wrote the Bueches for approval because if he had named Paul in a film they disapproved of, "I'd be doing the same thing that Moore had done to me."

If Pete were ever to free himself of blame, he would have to pass muster with the toughest judges: parents of the young man who had died by his side. He knew the Bueches had been digging into the cause of their son's accident in an attempt to assign responsibility for it. His e-mail was an attempt to break the ice. Most of it focused on Paul—how he had befriended Pete, how the two men wound up as partners, and how Pete kept asking for him when he woke up at the field hospital in Iraq. Of the accident, Pete wrote, "I don't remember anything before or after" it.

He apologized for taking so long to reach them, explaining he didn't know what to say and had been struggling with his penmanship. "My thoughts have been with you ever since this happened. I often pray that you and your family are dealing with this terrible loss and are able to get by this awful time in your lives."

Maria Bueche replied immediately. She had been waiting

for this moment. Privately, she suspected Pete was to blame for the explosion, a cocky northerner trying to prove to Alabama rednecks how great he was, and ultimately screwing up. That's how she had read the army report and the statements from Paul's friends in the guard. But as long as Pete remained hospitalized, she didn't feel right attacking or demanding answers from him. She had decided to wait until he recovered sufficiently to field her questions, or until he reached out.

Her reply walked a fine line designed to open a dialogue without scaring off Pete. The Bueches were glad to hear from him, she wrote, and had no problem with his plans to mention Paul in the upcoming anti-Moore film. But, Maria said, she had read the army report and was "frankly troubled" by some of its findings. She was eager for Pete to read it and hear his "take" on it.

Pete interpreted the initial contact as favorable, a bridge to redemption. But he didn't write back. He decided not to try to cross the bridge until he fully recovered and had his discharge papers from Walter Reed and the army in hand.

★

On August 23, Bobby Isaacs finally hit his limit. For six weeks he had been back in 57, receiving intravenous antibiotics to stave off a bone infection in his left knee. Doctors doubted they'd be able to save the all-important hinge, further complicating Bobby's ability to walk easily. But his prognosis improved to "wait and see" as he responded to a new drug delivered through a special catheter. He faced a decisive blood test the next day to determine his progress.

Early on the morning of the twenty-third, the catheter

clogged. Bobby hit the call light for help. No one came. He pushed the button again, worried about a setback if the drug stopped flowing. The nurse responsible for the catheter had left the floor. No one else answered the call because Bobby wasn't on the critically injured list. The inattention exasperated him. He had worked so hard to get off that list, and now, at a decisive point in his recovery, he couldn't get what he needed. He broke down in tears, so livid he got into his wheelchair and pushed himself to the Malogne House room where his mother was staying. He figured the infection would return, that all was lost. The next day he'd tell his doctors to go ahead and amputate. Bobby had given up.

It was amazing how long it had taken him to reach that point. The just-turned twenty-three-year-old had suffered one reversal after another. In May, recovered from surgery, he stood up for the first time on a prosthesis that fit over his right stump like a boot. It raised him higher off the ground than he had been in months, albeit on one leg. Bobby walked with crutches, which he refused to put down. He hopped from one end of the corridor to another, every day a little farther than the last. But within a week he was back on wheels. The stump had sprouted bone spurs, a condition called heterotopic ossification, which is common in blast injuries. A bony protrusion from the side of his right calf rubbed against the hard plastic shell of the prosthesis, making it painful to wear.

Returning to Ward 57 five months after his discharge was just the latest setback. After thirty-six operations—since his church had honored him in April, he had gone under the knife seven more times—Bobby still couldn't stand up to urinate or step into a pair of pants, much less walk. He saw the world from the height of a wheelchair or the unsteady tilt of a single prosthesis. Legless and marred by scars and skin grafts, he questioned whether a woman might ever find him attractive again. His girlfriend wanted more from the relationship than he was ready to give, so they broke up, and she started seeing one of his best army buddies.

Only a Zen master could have kept his cool. Bobby lost his occasionally. When technicians didn't make the right adjustments to his prosthesis, he'd curse and toss it to the side. He got angry if physical therapists didn't give him enough attention. He squabbled so bitterly with his mother that a good friend dubbed them "The Bickersons," after the 1940s radio comedy featuring a pair of battling spouses. Bobby refused to see an Iraqi general who had come to thank wounded troops. "Keep him the fuck out of my room," he told a Walter Reed official, not wanting to be reminded that he lost his legs because the Iraqi military couldn't hold its own against insurgents.

But aside from a few flare-ups, Bobby was still remarkably easygoing and upbeat. Other amputees I knew who had had to return to Ward 57 for follow-up treatment wallowed in anger and self-pity. I was in Bobby's room in August when a retired lieutenant general who worked for a veterans advocacy group came in to say hello and to offer Bobby a chance to grumble. He didn't bite.

Visitor: "How long you been here? Probably too long."

Bobby: "Eight months. I've been here since December, sir."

Visitor: "Have you? What does it look like for release?"

Bobby: "No telling. This is home now."

I was dumbfounded. We had been wounded the same day

in Iraq, treated in adjoining ICU rooms at the army hospital in Germany and transported in the same plane and bus to Walter Reed. I had left the hospital in less than a month and returned to work in three. But I was far less resilient and bullish than a man half my age who had no job nor any idea when he'd be going home.

Bobby, however, had a valuable asset: faith. He had an abiding belief in God's will to take care of him. He believed deeply in the power of prayer, a force his church had invoked to pull him from death's grasp. God had decreed that it wasn't Bobby's time to go. He was on Bobby's side. Although Bobby fell far behind the pace of recovery prophesied by his pastor in April, he never doubted that he'd walk again.

He had learned, however, to lower his expectations. He refused to set milestones. They'd just build him up for a fall. Even when he rose on his right prosthesis in May, he didn't allow himself to get too excited or he'd become "that much more bummed out" if it didn't work. According to Pat, pessimism ran in the family: "Expect the worst, so that it's better when it doesn't happen." Bobby discounted his hopes as a strategy for survival in a world where he had little control over destiny. He made up his mind that he'd be at Walter Reed as long as he was supposed to be.

For a brief moment it appeared that it wouldn't be much longer. A couple hours after his August 23 meltdown, the nurse inserted a new catheter. A blood test administered the following day revealed that the infection in his left knee had all but disappeared, a breakthrough that cleared him for a prosthesis fitting on his left leg. He was down in the Dungeon almost immediately.

On the morning of September 2, Pat tipped off a couple of Bobby's favorite therapists to wander over to the prosthesis shop about ten o'clock. "I think Bobby is going to be standing up," she told Ibrahim Kabbah, a Liberian-born occupational therapist who had worked for months with Bobby to strengthen his upper body.

The below-the-knee prostheses made for Bobby were not as high-tech as a C-leg. Basically, they were stilts with feet. The stumps fit into a plastic shell, which was connected to a running shoe by an aluminum rod. Bobby was already wearing his right one when he pushed his wheelchair into a small room off the Dungeon. He greased up his left stump with lotion, pulled a silicone liner over it, and lowered it into the shell. A suction cup kept it from slipping out.

Though Bobby had dreamed of this moment for almost nine months, he downplayed his excitement so as not to jinx himself. But the others who had gathered held their breath as if they were watching an Olympic skater poised for a quadruple toe loop. Armed with a small digital camera, Pat Isaacs weaved through the crowd to get a good angle. Her skin was covered in goose bumps.

Isatta Jackson, the physical therapist who had done as much as anyone to prepare Bobby for this moment, was clutching her hands on the sidelines. A number of things might go wrong. The prosthesis might not fit. Or Bobby might get up, only to lose balance and fall over.

Bobby edged himself to the end of the chair and tightened his quads, rocked forward in a single motion, and sprang up. Everyone clapped and whistled as he steadied himself and haltingly took a step. Bobby blushed and grinned broadly. He had won the amputee's gold medal. At last, he was moving forward.

Kabbah was overcome with emotion. He ran back to the occupational therapy room and yelled, "You won't believe what happened. Bobby stood up. He's walking. He's walking." The entire room cheered, as if their own child had walked for the first time.

Jackson cried. She remembered seeing pictures of Bobby taken at the field hospital in Iraq. His battered young body, bloody and swathed in dressings, had broken her heart. Now his journey had come full circle. After ten months of frustration, failure, and pain, Bobby looked whole again. She thanked God they were able to give back to him at least some of what he once had.

Bobby tested himself on the parallel bars and found he indeed had good balance. The stumps hurt with every step. But the next day he pushed himself to walk the length of the corridor with the help of crutches, and the next day he expanded his range. He loved being vertical again. Unfortunately, the physical costs were mounting. His left knee was so arthritic and weak that he couldn't put weight on it for long. The bone growths in his right stump had become so pronounced they rubbed raw in the plastic shell of his prosthesis.

Full recovery was still uncertain. But for Bobby, the days of taking two steps back for every one forward were over. He was determined to keep advancing with or without his artificial legs.

10.
ANNIVERSARY

Ward 57 was a hard place to shake. By September, I'd been back to work for six months doing my best to focus on the 2004 presidential campaign or the American military's battle for Fallujah in Iraq. But nothing engaged me like the stories I had left behind at Walter Reed, or the lives of my fellow amputees.

I had more than a professional curiosity. How the soldiers worked out their struggles would provide clues to reconciling my own. I focused on Pete's situation in particular. I kept pushing him to dig deeper into the cause of his accident and grew frustrated with his slow pace of inquiry. If he wouldn't come up with the goods, I'd do what any reporter would—I'd find another way. On September 6, I telephoned Maria

Bueche, introducing myself as a reporter who had lost a hand in Iraq and befriended Pete at Walter Reed. I asked her for a copy of the army report on the tire explosion, which she agreed to send. Waiting for the document, I acknowledged to myself why I was pressing so hard. Reporters, after all, are licensed voyeurs. But I was chasing the wrong story this time. I couldn't depend on Pete to fill in the missing blanks for me. I had to act myself.

I decided to start with the three men who had been in the Humvee with me that chilly Baghdad night of December 10, 2003. Finding them wasn't easy. I had spoken once to photographer Jim Nachtwey, a quick springtime phone call. The only contact I had had with the two soldiers was a March e-mail from Private First Class Jim Beverly, thanking me for my "bravery and sacrifice," and concluding that "your actions that night saved the lives of everyone in that Humvee."

I found each of them back at work and in reasonably good shape. Nachtwey had undergone two operations to remove shrapnel from his left knee. Either because the fragments were harmless or because surgery would have done more harm than good, doctors had left pieces in his other knee, groin, stomach, left arm, and face. He had rested for a couple months in New York and decided that work would be the best therapy, though he was only up to light duty, as his knees weren't strong enough for combat coverage. Both soldiers had been decorated with Purple Hearts and returned to their unit's headquarters in Germany. Beverly had lost range of motion in his right knee and emerged with a crooked finger, two lost teeth, scarred hands and knees, and a missing chunk of his tongue. After four surgeries to repair his shattered left femur, Private Orion Jenks walked with a pronounced limp. He was still taking large doses of narcotics for the pain.

I had to screw up the courage to make each call, not knowing what I'd learn about the most important few seconds of my life. Initially, the conversations flowed smoothly, old friends catching up on time apart. When I began asking questions about the attack, however, the tone turned somber.

I was in for one major surprise. Everyone knew a foreign object had landed in the Humvee. I thought at the time that only I was aware of it and thus had sole responsibility for dealing with the thing—whatever it was. It turned out that Nachtwey and Beverly had also heard the grenade land in the truck. Both wrote it off as another rock thrown by Iraqi kids and didn't investigate further. Jenks, who was closest to it, had noticed an oval-shaped "black mass" on the seat between us. But he had turned away, "thinking it was nothing" after he heard Beverly say that we were being pelted with rocks.

The disclosure that I alone acted made me proud of my instincts: if I hadn't possessed the presence of mind to evict the grenade, we all would have been blown to smithereens. On the other hand, why hadn't the trained soldiers sprung to our defense? Why was I the one stuck with saving the ship and losing the hand?

Of course, the fact that I had acted quickly didn't necessarily mean I knew what I was picking up. Did I think it was a rock or an explosive device? Did I plan to collect it as a souvenir or toss it overboard? Nachtwey supplied the first piece of hard evidence, saying he had heard me yell, "They're throwing rocks." That suggested I had nothing courageous in mind when I seized the grenade. His account appeared to

confirm my worst nightmare: I picked up the object for frivo-
lous reasons and dropped it as soon as I realized it was too
hot to be a rock.

Upon hanging up, I searched my memory and couldn't recall saying anything about rocks. Beverly had, according to
Jenks. Maybe Nachtwey had attributed the words to the
wrong person. Even if I had referred to incoming rocks, no one
could pinpoint whether I had done so before or after seeing
the object. Nailing down the timing was crucial in determin-
ing whether I had deliberately intended to save the day when
I made my move.

Something Jenks said indicated I had known it was dangerous. The grenade landed two feet from me—far enough
that I had to leave my seat or bend over to grab it. Would I
have gone to that much trouble to pick up a rock? In three
weeks of patrols, I had never reached for one before. The object must have aroused my suspicion.

A pair of Nachtwey's photos taken in the immediate aftermath of the explosion provided supporting evidence.
Digitally transferred to me by a *Time* colleague a couple of
months earlier, I had put off a viewing until now. I immediately felt nauseated and light-headed. But I soon spotted
a possible clue in the location where I had landed in the
bed of the vehicle. I was lying in the corner farthest from
the point of detonation. To have ended up there, I must
have known that I was handling a dangerous object and
needed to jump as far away from the imminent blast as I
could. If I had thought I was picking up a harmless rock, I
wouldn't have lurched away from it. I would have bent

over and inspected the object. In that case, I would have suffered different wounds. My face, neck, and chest would have taken the brunt.

Nachtwey and the two soldiers had seen postaccident photos of the Humvee that suggested another scenario. The blast had ripped a gaping hole in the thick bench and shredded metal parts below it. None of my fellow passengers had actually seen the explosion, but each had concluded that I couldn't have picked up the grenade. For it to have so thoroughly destroyed the wooden bench, the bomb would have had to detonate on top of it. Nachtwey speculated that one of two things had happened: I had placed my hand on the grenade as it went off, absorbing most of the blast, or that I had picked up the bomb and quickly dropped it to the bench after it scorched me.

The pain of melting flesh was so deeply ingrained I knew I had picked up the object. I also recalled swinging my arm to release it. After that, I passed out. If the hole could have resulted only from a blast on the bench, I must have released the grenade because of the heat—hardly a courageous act.

Hero or fraud? I went back and forth in self-analysis, a tiring and depressing effort. My inquiries brought me no closer to resolution. The evidence seemed contradictory. But at least I had begun to excavate my role in the attack, committing myself to the course I had prescribed for Pete Damon.

★

Maria Bueche was good to her word. The army report on Pete's accident—thirty-one pages, backed up by nearly two hundred pages of sworn statements, diagrams, charts, and forensic data—arrived in a few days. I found it detailed and candid, but it left many questions unanswered. Why wasn't the nitrogen tank regulated for Black Hawk tires used that day? Why did Pete's crew resort to the riskier tank and try to operate it without the fail-safe yellow box? Who turned the knobs to inflate the tire? Why did the crew's supervisor, who had wide experience and usually operated the system, leave it to amateurs?

I put in a call to Maria to see what she knew and learned she had many of the same questions. She did find out from a National Guard official that the regulated low-pressure tank had been broken—as *Flightfax* had reported—and was told that the crew acted out of expediency and carelessness.

To Maria, Pete looked like the chief villain. It was Pete, she said, who claimed he knew how to operate the volatile high-pressure tank. It was Pete and the NCO in charge, Jason Roten, she said, who ordered her son Paul to "proceed without proper equipment." And it was Pete, she believed, who manned the controls and opened the gas valve all the way, instead of turning it off.

Before passing final judgment on Pete, however, Maria wanted to have all the facts straight. If Pete had, as the report asserted, claimed proficiency with nitrogen carts at the time of the accident, why did he later tell army investigators he had never been taught how to operate them and never used them by himself?

I took her question as an opening. I didn't know the details of the case well enough to defend Pete. Nor would it have been appropriate. But I recognized a real commitment on Maria's part to get to the bottom of the circumstances surrounding her son's death and thought she should know as much as possible about the man she was holding responsible for it. I described Pete as a former electrician from a tough town who understood the danger of exaggerating his capability, whether it was on the job or on the street. Proclaiming knowledge of nitrogen carts would have amounted to a gross and dangerous exaggeration for Pete, and I told Maria that he vehemently denied ever making that mistake.

For the first time I sensed hesitation on the other end of the phone. Maria said she respected people who worked with their hands, especially electricians, who confronted danger in every move. Maria didn't mention the e-mail exchange she had had with Pete a few weeks earlier, but said she'd like a chance to meet him and ask a few questions.

I didn't hear from Maria for a month. Then, just after the first anniversary of the death of her son, she called me excitedly to pass on a tip. A reporter who wrote for a veterans' Web site had contacted Maria for an article she was researching on military maintenance accidents in Iraq. She told Maria that forty days before Paul died, a soldier was killed in a similar accident on the same air base in Balad. I decided to look into the September 11, 2003, death of Sergeant Henry Ybarra III. The thirty-two-year-old Texan was killed when a tire he was changing on a military truck blew up. His motor pool was missing a mandatory fail-safe: a cage that encased a wheel to prevent fragments of the metal rim from flying in all directions and hitting the crew if the tire blew up.

The incidents weren't identical, but Maria found it puz-
zling that Ybarra's death hadn't prompted army aviation authorities to ensure that their maintenance crews were
observing safety rules and that their hangars were well
equipped with tire inflation fail-safe devices. At the very least,
they should have redoubled precautions at the base in Iraq
where Ybarra was killed—and where Paul and Pete were both
posted.

I wanted to let Pete in on the discovery. On November 4,
I reached him at the Malogne House. He'd just come back
from a trip home and seemed irritable; he was nursing a cold
and was worried about a lump growing on his left stump. It
wasn't the best time to bring up memories of the accident.
We had talked before about broken and missing equipment at
the hangar. He hadn't registered much concern, taking the
view that soldiers always faced supply shortages in war. But
when I told him about Ybarra's death a few weeks before his
accident, he lost it. Authorities should have been "in a goddamn hurry" to make sure that every vehicle maintenance
crew in Iraq was equipped with working equipment and
safety devices, he said.

Pete knew I had been looking into his accident as well
and asked what I thought caused it. I told him that big questions remained, but everything I had read and heard bore out
the *Flightfax* article's implication that he had operated the nitrogen tank improperly, despite claiming proficiency.

"I know I would never say anything like that," he replied
defensively. When I told him that Roten had contradicted
that in a sworn statement, Pete accused his former supervisor
of "lying" and "covering up."

The issue consumed Pete. I thought it was less relevant than the lack of operable equipment, which would have prevented disaster no matter what he had or hadn't said. "It is relevant to me, very relevant to me," Pete shot back. "It means I'm fucking reckless. If I did do it, it was the first time in my life that I ever done anything like that. And look what happened. If I hadn't said that, right, Bueche could be alive today and I could still have my hands. But I don't think I did say it."

Pete sounded as if he were on the verge of tears, making me feel guilty for stirring up an issue he had hoped to avoid until his release from Walter Reed.

"This is why I didn't want to think about it," said Pete. "I just wanna think about getting the fuck out of here. But now I gotta think about this. I'm going to be thinking about it all the time now." He muttered to himself, "Jesus fucking Christ. I just want to get the fuck out of here. When I was out of here and well enough and ready to know what happened, then I'd find out what happened."

His voice cracked. "This is fucking eating me up on the inside, this whole *Flightfax* article that's saying that. The kid could be dead because of me. Look, as a mechanic, I had the power to stop everything. I had the power to say, 'No, I'm not fucking doing that and I think you guys are being fucking reckless by doing that and you're going to kill somebody.' I could have said that. I wouldn't have followed an order that I thought would get someone killed. Know what I'm saying? You could put me in front of the fucking president. He could tell me to do it, I still wouldn't do it if I thought it was going to get someone killed."

When I suggested we put off talk of his accident, Pete calmed down. But the conversation pulled an emotional trigger. Five days later, he decided to mark Veterans Day with a visit to Walter Reed's intensive care unit, where an army sergeant who had lost both legs and an arm in Iraq was fighting for his life. Pete struggled to find the right words: "These guys are going to fix you up, don't worry about it. You're going to be walking around in no time." But as he looked down at the patient whose wounds were still open and seeping through the dressings, he felt sick. The young soldier was so doped up he didn't seem to realize that half his body had been blown away. His eyes rolled back in his head, and he kept repeating the words, "Hey, man."

Pete's entire body started to shake. He had never questioned the Iraq war, nor the basis for the U.S. invasion or its aims. Now he wondered, "Is it fucking worth it?" He bolted from the room.

The stress seemed to compound Pete's phantom pain, which had become so unbearable that doctors had to double his daily dose of methadone to 30 milligrams a day. They did it begrudgingly; Walter Reed specialists worry that wounded soldiers will develop a drug habit. At least one of Pete's rehab therapists was alarmed by his sharply escalated use of the synthetic heroin substitute. That spring, I had had severe difficulty weaning myself off 5 milligrams a day, a low maintenance level. When I tried to go cold turkey, I ended up in the hospital's emergency room one night with shortness of breath and dizziness, and was told 5 milligrams amounted to the daily fix of a heroin addict. Pete and I also took Neurontin for nerve pain, which created a physical dependency. He had run out of pills during a recent visit home and suffered with-drawal symptoms, sweating buckets and recoiling from loud sounds. When he lost his temper with Danny one afternoon, he realized he had to do something to feel better, and called the local VA facility to refill his prescription of the drug.

On the night of November 23, two weeks after Veterans Day, Pete was sitting on his Malogne House bed. His heart started to race. Voices on the TV got louder and started to echo. He tingled from head to toe. Thinking he was having a heart at-tack, Pete tried to calm himself down with a glass of water. It didn't help. His calves burned. His tongue tasted metallic. Was it a stroke? he wondered. He left his room and walked around Walter Reed's sprawling campus, starting to enter the emer-gency room, then balking. He feared he'd be diagnosed with some new problem that would lengthen his stay. After a couple of hours, the symptoms subsided and he went to bed.

Two days later, when he and Jenn came to my home for Thanksgiving dinner, he seemed better. The food demolition specialist had become Mr. Manners in the past few months. He was a skilled practitioner of the hook, pinching almonds, forking turkey, and knocking back a few beers. His mood was relaxed, even expansive. He said the army medical board was getting ready to judge him unfit for service and retire him with full benefits. The unit to which he was assigned at Wal-ter Reed was going over his discharge papers. He hoped to be home permanently by Christmas.

★

December 10 marked the passing of a year since my injury. I al-ways hated the idea of anniversaries as milestones. I preferred to see life as a seamless web of indistinguishable days. But becoming an amputee brought changes measurable in time. The further I moved from that nightmare in Baghdad, the closer I returned to what I once had.

I'd never regain what I had lost in penmanship, tennis, home repair, lovemaking, freedom from pain, and dexterity. Even putting on a tie remained a challenge, one fraught with danger. Rushing to a TV appearance a few weeks earlier, I tried to knot one in the backseat of a taxi. I gripped the short end with my prosthetic hand, which began to spin uncontrollably, almost strangling me before I managed to extricate myself.

Despite occasional disasters, however, I was adjusting to a fake arm—thanks to certain modifications by John Miguelez's team. "Ralph" had bit the dust, replaced by a more tapered, slightly lighter shell made of carbon fiber and acrylic resin. Tired of my complaints about elbow-lock, prosthetists cut out a portion of the liner and shell that enclosed the joint, creating a "three-quarter socket" that soon became de rigueur on Ward 57. They also replaced the clunky batteries that had lain on top of the shell with a thinner model that fit inside it. The modifications improved my range of motion and wardrobe—I could now button a dress shirt. But I was hardly wearing a second skin. The rigid shell chafed my forearm and got so hot in the summer that sweat dripped out of the pull hole.

Before Iraq, the technology of arm prostheses hadn't changed much since World War II. The tiny population of amputees created little market incentive. Miguelez used the burst in demand from Walter Reed to lean on manufacturers for progress. Before long, he was outfitting Iraq war amputees with an electronic hand that opened and closed two and a half times faster and could be programmed to function at different speeds and grip strength.

But Pretty Boy, the lifelike hand in which I had placed so much hope, had lost my affections. The silicone kept tearing—it was constantly in the shop—and afforded the precision of a boxing glove. It was too spongy to grasp anything small and too slippery to hold most objects for long.

Function was only part of the problem. The idea of trying to pass had begun to trouble me. It made me feel as if I had something to hide or be ashamed of. When I started to go bald, I shaved my head. No comb-overs, transplants, or toupees for me. So why try to conceal a handicap? When I was given a choice of colors for the forearm shell, I picked black instead of a flesh tint. My new taste in prostheses reflected a larger psychological shift. I was now proud of how I had lost my hand. While I was still a long way from understanding my role in the Humvee, the stump had a story to tell, regardless of my motivations for grabbing a grenade. Why not draw attention to it?

No one could miss my disability now. I put on a hook for Thanksgiving dinner to match Pete Damon's, and never took it off. It twisted into the end of my myoelectric prosthesis and turned 360 degrees like an electronic hand. Only it worked better. Two silver talons opened like forceps, locked on to items, and could pick a dime off the floor. Occasionally, I screwed on the Greifer to move heavy objects, and I contemplated the long list of attachments—garden tools, spatulas, hammers, and pool-shooting bridges—that were available by special order. I usually sported the hook, however, even if it aroused more fear than friendship among people I passed on the street. Some kids cowered. Friends accepted it and greeted me with a high-two. Rebekah thought my choice impudent but sexy and advised me on clothing to complement it— black was obviously best.

A half year after I dismissed the suggestion from a Walter Reed doctor, the hook had become my trademark. It was brash, straightforward, and pragmatic, virtues I cherished. I had left a lot of me behind in the Baghdad grenade attack. By its first anniversary, I was starting to reclaim it.

★

Bobby Isaacs celebrated the first anniversary of his injury by packing. The next day, he would be permanently leaving Walter Reed, the only home he had known as an amputee. On the morning of December 11, Bobby climbed into the passenger seat of his mother's green Ford Explorer, his stumps in cutoff jeans elevated on pillows. Pat Isaacs, practically a graduate of Ward 57 herself, threw in a few last things and got behind the wheel. At 11:45, they pulled out in a cold driving rain, torn between expectation and regret.

It was one week short of a year since Bobby and I rolled into the hospital on our gurneys. Despite his rosy prediction about walking out of the hospital on two legs, he was still in a wheelchair, recovering from his thirty-eighth operation—this one to remove bone spurs from his right stump. The old prosthesis no longer fit. He'd need a new one. Only then would he be able to stand up and test whether his creaky left knee would hold up. Prosthetists had worked with him for months. But they couldn't provide anything more than he could get at the VA hospital near his home in North Carolina.

Bobby needed a change of scenery. A year of setbacks had knocked the smile from the man once known for his sunshine. After clashing with a physical therapist, he felt a chill from other hospital staff. On December 10, Bobby showed up to see a doctor at the weekly amputee clinic. Waiting for two hours, he wheeled over to the receptionist to complain. She told him there was no record of his appointment. Bobby's face reddened. He turned his wheelchair around and furiously pushed himself out of the waiting room. Walter Reed no longer seemed a friendly place. "I'll get my legs from the Yellow Pages if I have to," he shouted out as he departed.

On the day before he left, Bobby made the rounds to say good-bye to people he had seen almost every day of 2004. But with the large number of those who had departed or alienated him, he had a brief list of visits. Pat misplaced her truck keys the morning of their departure. The delay provided a chance for the last couple of friends left from 57 to linger in the Malogne House room.

For Bobby, the future was no clearer than the past. He still faced major doubts about his legs, not to mention a job and a home of his own. For the time being, he'd live with his "three moms" in the outskirts of Roxboro, North Carolina, a small rural town. When I asked how he planned to spend his days, he shrugged. Pat interjected that he'd need at least a month to fix up his bedroom. Bobby groaned and made a face.

Pat finally found her keys in a pair of jeans she had packed in a suitcase and carried out the last bags. Her brother, Porch, brought his pickup truck to carry Bobby's wheelchairs, canes, crutches, and various souvenirs of his long stay. Bobby packed only his memories.

★

The winter before he left for the Persian Gulf, Pete Damon had a morning ritual. On his way to work in Brockton, he bought a cup of coffee for a homeless man who slept in the frigid doorway of a Chinese restaurant. A friend who saw Pete care for the vagrant made a prediction: "It's going to come back on you tenfold one day."

On December 19, Pete's kindness was redeemed in full. He broke ground on a two-acre plot of land in Middleboro, Massachusetts, donated to him by Homes for Our Troops. Nearly 120 people from every phase of Pete's life assembled for a ceremony on a piney terrace, where a special-needs house would be built. Heavy construction equipment had already arrived for the excavation. But the event would dig up more than frozen earth for Pete, who'd taken leave of Walter Reed and his anxiety for the weekend.

He looked out at the crowd before him and thought of the distance he'd traveled. Not long ago, he would have been lucky to be wiring up a house on a plot this size for someone else. The last place Pete lived before joining the National Guard was the second floor of a ramshackle wood-frame house near the seedy bars of Lithuanian Village. The older brother of a friend suggested they set up a bachelor's pad. Before long, the roommate had moved his ex-wife and her brother and son into the one-bedroom apartment. Another ten people drifted in over time, leaving Pete a bed and a closet in which to lock up his few possessions.

Exactly a year earlier, John Gonsalves had told Jenn Damon that he wanted to build them a home. He had nothing in the bank but an idea to raise funds for disabled veterans of the Iraq war. Now the organization was raking in $25,000 a month, contributions ranging from $2 from the elderly widow of a World War II veteran to $10,000 from singer Billy Joel. In November, Gonsalves put down $200,000 of it for the first property acquisition: Pete's spread in Middleboro.

Jenn drove Pete to the site fifteen miles south of Brockton. The landmarks they passed highlighted the contrast to their hometown, a biracial, working-class city where after-hours life revolved around taverns, crack houses, and the Polish White Eagles Club. Middleboro was lily-white and largely free of violent crime, a haven of one-lane roads dotted by New England–style cedar-shingle houses, a country store, a clapboard church, and an immaculate cemetery with gravestones dating back to the 1720s. Instead of boarded-up shoe factories, it boasted cranberry farms and antiques shops. Even with $3,600 a month in disability payments that he'd receive when the military retired him, Pete could never have afforded a piece of this prime real estate.

Pete had always wanted to be recognized as special. How ironic that it took the loss of his means of livelihood and defense to achieve the goal. All these VIPs honoring him now had come from established institutions: the governor's office, military, labor unions, and local firms. If he had not gone to Iraq, Pete would have lived a lot like the neighborhood guys who packed his mother's small house in Brockton for a party that I attended the night before the groundbreaking. They were blue-collar workers who scratched out a living in the building trades and lived with their families or in rented apartments. The get-together brought back old times, with mountains of Italian food—Jenn delivered platters of calzone, lasagna, mushrooms stuffed with crabmeat, meatballs, Caesar salad, and tiramisu—and rivers of booze. Someone broke out a jug of glug, a homemade concoction of wine, spiced fruit, and vodka. The men filled cups and repaired to the backyard porch, where they smoked stogies and traded stories about past drinking bouts and brawls. Pete wore a new black prosthesis adorned with shooting red flames. He huddled with his buddies and boasted of Jenn's cooking. His rapid-fire laughter ricocheted off the walls.

I found myself fitting in easily with Pete's old crowd. They reminded me of guys I had grown up with on Chicago's South Side. Once I moved away, I discovered I could never really go home. So it seemed with Pete. He had no airs about him, no dropping names of politicians and celebrities he'd met or places he'd been. But he appeared more confident and worldly than his cronies. He had experienced more in eighteen months, from the adrenaline of war to the agony of amputation, than they would see in a lifetime. Along the way he had discovered a new meaning of manhood and a new measure of strength. His pals acted as if they noticed a difference. They deferred to Pete, proud to be known as his friend. Pete *was* bigger now. He had outgrown Brockton.

The next day's events reflected the changes in Pete's life. He had become a patriotic symbol, flanked by a flagpole waving Old Glory and brass from the Massachusetts National Guard. The ceremony opened with the national anthem and a flyover by a single Black Hawk helicopter. The bird hovered just above the treetops. "It took a little work, but we got one flyable for you," cracked an officer in dress uniform.

Every speaker noted Pete's sacrifice. Gonsalves, decked out in a black suit and white shirt, recalled their first meeting at Walter Reed. "There's nothing like going to Ward 57," he said, choking up. "If the American people could see what I saw there, we'd be building a lot of houses." Pete's best friend from the hospital, Alabama National Guard Staff Sergeant Larry Gill, stood nearby in dress uniform and fought back tears.

Pete and Jenn sat on folding chairs off the podium. He rose to hug or bump shoulders with each speaker. Finally, the honoree moved to the lectern. He was dressed like a hip-hopper in jeans, Boston Red Sox World Series jacket, and black running shoes. But he proceeded to address the crowd as poised as a Ph.D. candidate on dissertation day.

Pete spoke of his injury, Walter Reed's wounded, and HFOT's hope to ease the plight of homeless vets. He devoted a long section to someone who had dominated his recent thoughts: Paul Bueche. "I definitely got the better of the deal," Pete said, looking down. "I thank God every day for sparing my life and allowing me to be able to have a better life with my wife and children. I also pray that Paul is in a better place, free of war, death, and tragedy. I pray for the Bueche family to find the strength to overcome the immense loss of Paul."

With his days at Walter Reed dwindling, Pete was increasingly focused on the Bueches' mission to assign responsibility for that loss. "I know they're trying to do great things of their own in getting to the bottom of what happened that day," he said. "And I hope they succeed in all their efforts."

After Jenn recounted her family's struggles and thanked Gonsalves, she and Pete grabbed a shovel. Pete clamped his hook on the handle, next to her hand, and stomped on the top.

Before ending the ceremony, Gonsalves invited a minister to give the benediction. Reverend Ivan S. Fleischman, who had married the Damons a year earlier, stepped forward in a gray suit. He was carrying four flowers, wrapped in yellow ribbons as a reminder of Pete's sacrifice. He handed one rose each to Pete, Jenn, and their children to place at the site of their future home.

On the next day, Pete and Jenn marked their first wedding anniversary. He gave her a special gift: a pencil sketch of her favorite stuffed animal, a dog. He had spent ten hours on it— the drawing was finely detailed and shaded. To have drawn it with a natural hand would have suggested talent. For Pete to have done it with a hook on his nondominant arm was extraordinary. It was the first thing he considered good enough to present since he had returned to his childhood hobby in March. Now he realized he might be good enough to earn a living at it someday—handless art. He decided that once he got out of Walter Reed, he'd take some courses.

For now, his drawing grounded him. His life was moving so fast, he longed to capture the familiar. The objects had a light and form he had never appreciated before. Maybe he was looking within. Stretching out on his mother's kitchen counter after the groundbreaking, Pete sketched a Chinook helicopter, then an old tennis shoe and a walnut. He was leading up to a major piece that he wanted to present to Gonsalves when he handed over the keys to a new house. The subject: a combat soldier.

11.
THE UNCONSCIOUS MIND

Lieutenant Colonel Mary Miles was completing paperwork in her office at the Brooke Army Medical Center on the afternoon of January 13, 2005, when the phone rang. A familiar voice left her breathless: "This is Sergeant Luis Rodriguez."

"Holy cow, I'll be down there in a minute," said Miles, who hadn't seen Rod since he was airlifted from her field hospital in Mosul fourteen months earlier. Now he was in San Antonio, Texas, to give a speech and had heard that Miles had been re-posted there. He sought out the woman who appeared in his most poignant memories of combat medicine: the tearful night he brought in Specialist Derick Hurt with a mangled leg; the early morning delivery of the grisly remains of Specialist

Ryan Travis Baker and ten other soldiers in body bags; and his own arrival on a gurney.

At 3:30 P.M., the elevator doors opened in the cavernous lobby of the medical complex. Miles, in dress uniform, spotted Rod, sprinted toward him, and engulfed him in her arms. The rank-conscious, gender-sensitive army wasn't accustomed to such scenes: a forty-one-year-old female officer weeping on the shoulder of a male sergeant in camouflage. They embraced for a long moment.

In Iraq, Miles sweated to keep soldiers alive, and then sent them off on medevacs, never to see them again or know if they survived. As she hugged Rod, she kept repeating to herself: "Thank God he's alive."

For Rod, the embrace ended a chapter. Only people like Miles who had seen him at his best could appreciate how far he had fallen and what it had taken to crawl back. He had been a one-man army in Iraq, commanding a platoon, engaging in firefights, salving the wounded, and consoling them in hospital beds. After hitting rock bottom, he was back on top, so respected he was invited to San Antonio to address graduates of the army medics school at Fort Sam Houston. With his C-leg planted firmly on the ground, Rod threw his arms around his past and present.

The emotions released by that embrace left an imprint. Rod had always thought of his loss as singularly personal. The fact that his mere presence could bring an officer to tears raised his self-awareness. He began to understand his importance to others, even if he could no longer provide cover in a firefight or teach his daughters how to dance. Just being Sergeant Rod—a medic's medic, family man, teacher, and survivor who had made the most of his losses—was good enough.

Rod seized the moment to demonstrate his new sense of humility. Holding Miles's hands, he thanked her. It was an expression of gratitude that extended to all of the lifesavers she represented—medics, nurses, doctors, rehab therapists, and prosthetists—who had helped him do what he couldn't manage by himself: walk again in bigger shoes. He asked her to spread the word to Combat Surgical Hospital alumni that "Sergeant Rod is okay."

The lieutenant colonel pulled out a video camera, giving Rod a chance to speak for himself. She pointed it at him as they stood in the busy lobby. He spoke to the camera for a few minutes, thanking everyone for keeping him alive. "Without you, I wouldn't be here today," he said softly.

★

It seemed the applause would never stop for Pete Damon. A month after the groundbreaking of his house, Governor Mitt Romney invited him to his State of the State address in Boston. Pete first had a private meeting with Romney, who handed him a gold ticket and a signed copy of his book on his management of the 2002 Salt Lake City Olympics, *Turnaround*. Pete and Jenn sat in the balcony of the state legislature with the governor's wife and another member of the National Guard who had served in Iraq. Romney said he was "humbled by the sacrifice and inspired by the courage." A standing ovation lasted several minutes and literally shook the rafters of the historic building. A huge lightbulb fell from the ceiling and banged loudly on a state representative's desk.

No one was hurt; the glass was so thick it didn't break. But it was prophetic. Pete's fortunes were beginning to fall.

He returned to Washington in mid-January to cut through the red tape tangling his release from the National Guard and Walter Reed. Pete had lived on the hospital grounds for fifteen months and had already gone before the army's medical board to prove he wasn't fit for duty. But he couldn't get straight answers from the Medical Hold Company, which had authority over wounded soldiers awaiting their papers. One official warned Pete he wouldn't be able to leave until late March, after he took a course on reentering society—which seemed silly for a guardsman who had left society only for a brief stop in the Persian Gulf. Then he was told that the issue of discharge eligibility would be addressed by the unit's commander at a formation on Monday, January 24. He was instructed to appear at 9 A.M.

Pete lined up as ordered, even though he was sick with the flu. He asked for permission to fall out, but his platoon sergeant refused on grounds that the commander would be coming to examine Pete's personal documents. He was told to get them ready. That was the last straw. Pete had shuffled his papers from one office to another for months and wasn't about to let another high muck-a-muck chew over them. This was starting to feel like harassment, the kind of treatment prison inmates faced. Pete walked out of formation. He returned to his Malogne House room and decided to flex his new political muscle.

To Pete, politics was just another street fight. Winners knew how to go straight for the jugular. In the military it was congressional support, and Pete had a way of attacking it.

Senator Ted Kennedy, an outspoken critic of the war, had befriended his constituent as soon as he arrived at Walter Reed, telling Pete to call if he needed anything. Pete figured the mere threat of contacting the Massachusetts Democrat might ring some bells. He dialed up his National Guard unit on Cape Cod. "I'm so fed up with this fucking place," Pete told the sergeant. "You guys have an hour before I get on the phone with Senator Kennedy's office. I've got two phone numbers for him. I can talk to him directly today if I want to."

Ninety minutes later, a colonel who served as the National Guard liaison at Walter Reed called Pete to ask if she could help. "I want out of here," Pete replied. When he told her he had left the formation because he was sick, the colonel insisted he go to the hospital, and when Pete refused, she called the next day and threatened to send someone to his room. Pete blew up: "I'm thirty-two years old. I'm not a goddamn baby. Ma'am, I don't give a fuck who you are, what your fucking rank is, if you send someone over here, I'm going to flip him."

Pete conferenced Jenn in and kept telling her in a stage whisper, "Call Kennedy, call Kennedy." Then, he laid out his demand: "You're going to get me out of here this week." The colonel agreed to get the paperwork ready.

More than military bureaucracy was roiling Pete. After reading a copy of the army's accident report that I had sent him, he felt unfairly blamed for an explosion that wouldn't have happened if he had had the proper equipment. "That kid didn't have to die," Pete told me. "I didn't have to get my fucking arms blown off. I'm getting more pissed about it the more I think about it."

The frustration accumulated and started to overwhelm him. After his blowup at the colonel, he called Jenn and asked her to drive down from Brockton to help him pack. While talking to her, he started to feel tipsy. The symptoms he had before Thanksgiving—pins and needles and racing heart—had returned. He assumed the worst again, a stroke or a heart attack. Trying to settle himself down, he took long deep breaths. After a few minutes, it worked. At least he knew it wasn't a physical problem. He'd never be able to talk himself out of clogged arteries. But he couldn't stop the attacks either, apparently.

The night after Jenn had arrived, the couple was lounging in his room at about ten o'clock. Pete was thinking about how happy he was to have her there. It had been so frightening to go through one of those episodes alone. Suddenly, he went numb and fell into a dreamlike state. He started to hallucinate: he wasn't going home; Jenn wasn't really there. He tried to anchor himself by talking to her and looking at pictures of his kids. But he felt no connection to any of them, as if they were strangers. Everything slowed down and became distorted. He got scared. Maybe he had died. It felt as if he had no soul left, no emotion. "Am I going crazy?" he asked himself. More thoughts of death filtered in: maybe he was someone else who was imagining he was Pete.

Jenn had never seen her husband like this before. She rubbed his back. "It's all right, baby."

Gradually, Pete could feel himself come out of it, but a storm was gathering force inside of him. Then the clouds burst. He started to cry, deep, heaving sobs. For the first time in fifteen months, he let go of all the crutches: the anger,

resilience, intestinal fortitude, happy-to-be-alive talk, and de-
fensiveness that he had needed to keep him going. The tears
poured out. Dominating his thoughts was Paul Bueche. He was
a good kid who didn't deserve to die. Pete couldn't stop thinking of death, its suddenness and finality. He had come close
enough to shake its hand.

The sobbing lasted a full hour. He'd stop for a few minutes, then think of Paul and break down again. Pete didn't
know what had come over him. But when it ended, he felt un-
burdened, as if the tears had washed away his anxiety. He was
worried about his mental state, though, and wondered if he
was having a nervous breakdown or suffering from some kind
of disorder. Psychiatry had never appealed to him—he was
tough enough to work out problems by himself. But he knew
he needed help and could no longer afford to think that way.
He'd do anything to avoid another attack.

Early the next morning, Pete went to the psychiatry department at Walter Reed. He sat down with one of Hal
Wain's therapists in a small office and started to describe his
symptoms. Suddenly, as if conjured by his own words, they
reappeared: the sweating, the pins and needles, the crying.
The doctor walked him through some relaxation exercises
and explained that Pete was suffering from panic attacks. He
handed him a textbook on the syndrome, listing all the signs
and symptoms. When Pete detailed his fears of death, the
doctor pointed to a paragraph in the book that Pete could
have written himself. The therapist assured Pete that it was
a common malady, and that most people who had it thought
something more serious was going on. "The next time you
have one when your wife is present, just tell her to hit you

across the face with a two-by-four," he said, getting a laugh from the patient. "The good thing is you're not going to die." He prescribed Ativan, an antianxiety drug, to take when Pete felt an attack coming, and sent him on his way.

The therapy session helped Pete identify one of the reasons for his panic: leaving Walter Reed. The fact that medical care was just a few steps away was reassuring. At home, no one would know his medical history or what he had gone through. Pete carried the feelings of many Ward 57 alumni, desperate to leave the hospital and the military's Mickey Mouse rules, but terrified of the alternative.

Pete took a deep breath, and opted for the alternative. A few nights later, he and Jenn would head home to Brockton and an uncertain future.

★

The guard station of Walter Reed was like a time machine. Whenever I passed it, my mind took me back to the days as a patient. A year after my discharge, little had changed, except for the faces of young soldiers maimed in Iraq—and the numbers of them. By January 2005, the toll had risen to 214 amputees, 2 percent of the 10,400 soldiers wounded in action. The percentage had tapered off since I had been injured, but continued at a historically high clip. Transport planes had been disgorging an average of fourteen amputees per month since April, twice the rate of the previous nine months. Insurgent attacks during the four-month countdown to the first Iraqi elections on January 30 alone blew the arms or legs off sixty-nine U.S. troops; the increasing sophistication and firepower of the urban guerrillas were leading to more multiple-limb amputations. The first female soldiers who lost limbs in combat had arrived in the spring of 2004. More marines were also coming home without limbs and joining the army preserve of Walter Reed.

Ward 57 operated at full tilt, the same jarring scene of patients writhing in pain, nurses scurrying about, and families leaning against the wailing wall. The Dungeon had been expanded and remodeled. So had the physical therapy room.

I recognized only a few of the patients when I returned for weekly adjustments to my prosthesis. My class from Ward 57 had graduated long ago and returned to their families. Only Pete Damon remained, but not for long. I went to Malogne House to bid him good-bye on February 3.

Pete was unusually serene. He told me about his seizures and the shrink's diagnosis. He linked the panic attacks to questions of responsibility for his accident and was now fully committed to answering them. The experience had unlocked something in him. "I definitely have to bring this thing to an end," he told me. As a start, he wanted to meet face-to-face with the person who had the biggest concerns: his dead partner's mother, Maria Bueche. "She doesn't need to be wondering what the hell happened," he said. "I was the last person with her son. I need to tell her everything I know. She deserves my help." Pete shared Maria's feeling that something even more important than apportioning blame was at stake. "I don't want this happening to someone else," he said.

His openness was contagious. I had never before divulged my self-interest in his struggle. The time was ripe. The last inquiries I had made into my own injury had yielded ambiguous results. Pete might provide some clarity.

I explained the central dilemma: my motivation for grabbing the grenade.

Pete must have recognized the torment in my eyes. He listened carefully before commenting, "Sometimes your brain automatically kicks in, man, and you do shit that you wouldn't normally think of doing."

I said I didn't recall if I knew what I was picking up.

"Well, you knew it was something dangerous," he replied. He had zeroed in on the crux of it.

I ran my rock theory by him.

"You're not in the practice of picking up rocks," he said. "One way or the other, something came in and you picked it up. You realized the thing was hot, and you were trying to get rid of it, get it away from everybody. But it doesn't matter if you meant to do it or not. You still did it. If that thing had blown up inside, it could have killed people. Hey, Mike, you want to ask me? I think you're a fucking hero for saving people's lives. If you didn't pick that thing up, you wouldn't be here right now."

Pete reflected for a moment. "You gotta confront this in your own mind," he said. "I think it's like me. I'm still not sure if I'm the one who fucking caused this accident or not. Did I kill this kid even though I didn't mean to?"

In both of our cases, I noted, it came down to a matter of seconds and inches. If Pete had moved a little closer to the front of the tire, he may not have survived.

"I would have been just like Paul," he said. "But for some frigging godforsaken reason, it didn't happen. Hey man, why didn't I die? By all logical standards, I should be fucking dead right now."

Everyone and everything in the bustling foyer of Malogne House fell away as Pete and I spoke for ninety minutes about religious faith, fatalism, hooks, phantom pain, Democrats, psychiatry, and the recent Iraqi elections. It was the most intimate connection with a fellow amputee I had experienced since my injury. At the end of the cathartic session, we hugged and parted.

Driving home, I recalled something Pete had said—that I was unaccustomed to picking up rocks. It sparked a flashback from the bed of the Humvee: wisps of smoke coming from a foreign object. I had first seen it in a dream on Ward 57 and dismissed it as self-delusion. But I was more resourceful now, and more desperate for resolution. I figured the best place to find it was a munitions expert.

The U.S. Central Command hooked me up with Lieutenant Colonel David Ruff, who had spent time in Iraq. Ruff said that virtually all homemade devices, like the one I had described, emitted smoke from the ignition of gunpowder fuses. "Anything that burns will smoke." More than a year after I'd had a vision of a smoldering object, an army specialist in Iraqi explosives confirmed its likelihood. There probably had been a sign of danger after all. Rocks don't smoke. My intent was becoming clearer. But even if I had known that I had grabbed a weapon, I must have ignobly dropped it. The gaping hole in the wooden bench suggested that the grenade had detonated on top of it.

Ruff raised doubts, however, that the weapon had actually exploded on the bench. He explained that flat surfaces act as springboards for grenades, giving lift to an explosion in a cone-shaped pattern. If the device tossed into my Humvee

242 ★ ★ BLOOD BROTHERS

had blown up on the seat, the destructive force would not have moved down through the wooden plank. The bench would have served "as a means to direct the blast upward" because it would have created "resistance to the blast," the expert explained by e-mail. Deployed in midair, however, grenades usually spray blast and shrapnel in all directions, Ruff said. Enough of it could have slammed down into the bench to have ripped it open. In other words, the grenade must have gone off in the air.

If the explosion was airborne, the only question remaining was whether the grenade had blown up in my hand. Ruff doubted it because a hand would have absorbed much of the blast, reducing the force of shrapnel and making it less likely to have cored the bench. More likely, I had completed my throwing motion and released the weapon before it blew.

I recalled something Private Orion Jenks had said that helped me determine the point of detonation. He recalled the explosion leaving three thin red lines on his left cheek, the side facing me. The superficial burns had been separated by spaces the width of a finger, memorializing the last action of my right hand. I must have raised the grenade to the level of Jenks's head before releasing it. My fingers had blocked the blast, except for the gaps between them. "Your losing your hand saved my face," the private told me.

The evidence was in. I must have sensed danger in the object and tried to toss it from the Humvee, presumably to limit its damage. Mystery solved.

And yet I had a sense of peace, not of pride. I still didn't see my actions as courageous. Even if I knowingly seized and tossed a weapon, I didn't deliberately do it to save lives. My pantheon of heroes from Audie Murphy to Mahatma Gandhi had consciously chosen a path of self-sacrifice for a larger good. In the split second I had to act, I didn't weigh risks and consequences of picking up the object. My reflexes took over, not altruism. I had reacted without thought.

The self-evaluation was getting me nowhere. I was digging myself in deeper. I figured a shrink might hand me a shovel. I had stonewalled therapists on Ward 57, insisting I had no regrets, no second thoughts. I wasn't ready for help then. I was now. I followed Pete Damon's path to the psychology department.

On February 25, I entered Hal Wain's lair. I'd spoken to him before about his staff's work with amputees and briefly about my own progress, but never in a formal session. Wain was a stocky man who sported a salt-and-pepper pompadour and a borscht belt sense of humor. His office was adorned by an unframed portrait of Jean-Martin Charcot, a Parisian neurologist under whom Freud studied, and a tossed salad of papers and books amassed during his long stint at the hospital. Within seconds of exchanging pleasantries, he got down to business, commenting on my choice of prosthesis, my beard, and the tiny gold pins a military acupuncturist had placed in my ears to ease my phantom limb pain. "It draws attention to you, which is the nature of who you are," Wain said. "Look at the goatee. Even the fact that you walk around with gold earrings. Anyone who knows medicine would recognize the acupuncture treatment, but people who don't know it think you are a hippie. In the process you stand out. It lets you continually talk about what you gave up. You've been injured. It draws attention to that. These are indications of your personality.

244 ★★ BLOOD BROTHERS

Your comment is, 'I'm not ashamed of what happened—just
the contrary. Hey, I want you to know what happened. I want
you to know what I've been through, who I am.' That gives
you distinction."

Not bad for openers, I thought. But if I was so cocky, how
did he explain my self-doubt? "What you are doing now is trying to understand what you did and why," he said. "If you
know who you are, it gives you power." Wain said the last
time we met, he noticed the "incongruence" between the
way I carried myself and the way I thought of myself. "I had
difficulty understanding why you weren't more accepting of
yourself being a hero," he explained. "You were beating yourself up because you got some accolades. You didn't have the
sense that you did something heroic. But you did."

What if I hadn't consciously planned it? I asked. The psychologist took it as an opening to lecture me on instinctive
behavior.

"It was your unconscious thinking or your instincts
speaking when you went down and threw that grenade out. A
lot of us operate beyond a level of awareness—of what we see
in front of us. You sensed you were in a danger zone. You
were around enough mortar fire, enough stuff going on that,
instinctually, you knew you had to get rid of it."

I had one overriding objective, he said: self-preservation.
"That's what all heroes are made of. I have learned from guys
coming back that the instinct to survive, the instinct to take
care of oneself or others is incredibly potent. I really don't
care if you did it for your needs or for others; you did it. The
end result would have been the same—the fact that you saved
people's lives."

Wain defined heroism as quick response to a changing environment, like a driver who swerves into another lane for the purpose of avoiding an oncoming car and, in the process, saves the life of his passenger. "That wasn't his intent," he said. "But being flexible and shifting is a higher level of intelligence. The people who can't change die." According to Wain, I possessed this gift of flexibility but was too wrapped up in self-analysis and perfectionism to recognize it.

I did realize one thing, however, as the session drew to a close. In fifty minutes, he put the issue of conscious choice to rest. I hadn't reacted to the threat in the Humvee by accident; weeks of operating in theater had conditioned me to act reflexively in the face of danger. Ruff's forensics had indicated that my instincts had been true; the psychologist argued that they were just as worthy as premeditated action. But whether or not I had deliberately acted to save lives was irrelevant. The only thing important was the outcome, and it would have been the same.

Before seeing me out, Wain tried hypnosis to break my psychological logjam. He put me under using breathing techniques, and then directed me to "use that mind of yours that's so good at asking questions to discipline yourself." Suggesting that I was undergoing an "intense change, a survivability change," he commanded me to "recognize that you are ready to become whole." That felt like a tall order, but as the door shut behind me, it occurred to me that I was getting closer.

12.
THE PRIZE

When Pete and Jenn Damon pulled into their driveway shortly after midnight on February 6, 2005, they were too tired to boot up the computer. Not long before they completed their car trip home from Walter Reed, a soldier in Pete's Iraq unit had sent him an e-mail. The message from Sergeant Randy Cox surprised Pete when he retrieved it the next day. He wasn't that close to the Alabama National Guardsman. Pete hadn't heard from him since the accident. But the note conveyed a tone of urgency.

Cox had been an eyewitness to the accident, though he had divulged little to investigators in two sworn statements. After "struggling" with it, he wrote Pete, he was ready to break his silence, and had just gotten off the phone with

Maria Bueche. Cox blamed the October 21 accident on their supervisor, Sergeant Jason Roten, for improperly ordering the use of a faulty inflation system without a fail-safe device. Roten wanted to "feather his cap" with a "quick turnaround" of the Black Hawks that had just come in for maintenance. In Cox's opinion, "everything falls in his lap."

Pete forwarded a copy of the e-mail to me a few days later. He said he planned to reply. But I didn't have the impression he was in a hurry. Although he was eager to find out what had caused the accident, details seemed to throw him off balance. Without recall of the event, he didn't know how to weigh the information. Pete was signaling me to take the lead; I figured I owed him one.

It took me a couple of weeks to track down Cox by phone. When I did, he was eager to talk and possessed a detailed memory of the moments leading up to the accident, which he had observed from a few yards away on the other side of the Black Hawk. A highly specialized paper mill mechanic based in central Alabama, Cox at forty-one was older than most soldiers in the unit and more established.

His account poked holes in the official reports of the accident, which had been largely based on a sworn statement by Roten that asserted he had approached Pete in the hangar as he was servicing a Black Hawk tire with a nitrogen cart and asked him if he had operated one before; according to Roten's statement, Pete had responded in the affirmative.

Based on Cox's telling, army investigators—and possibly Roten—had missed a key part of that dialogue: Pete didn't know he was being asked about a defective unit. Having arrived in Iraq fifteen days earlier, he was working with an unfamiliar team and had never received formal training in nitrogen carts. Nor had he—contrary to *Flightfax*'s report—been alerted to the fact that the cart's regulated low-pressure tank was missing hoses and couldn't be used. Cox believed the journal had confused him with Pete. It was actually Cox who had tipped off Roten to the equipment problem and the absence of a fail-safe device.

Indeed, Pete may never have known about the broken tank until it was too late. He apparently did not hear Cox make the disclosure to Roten. When Cox returned to his nearby post, he assumed the NCO in charge would fetch replacements from a neighboring hangar. Instead, Roten walked over to Pete's side of the helicopter and, according to Cox, ordered a makeshift procedure: "Bump it on the high side," shorthand for quickly turning on and off the gas from the volatile high-pressure tank. Pete unwittingly complied.

Black Hawk mechanics are supposed to use nitrogen sources regulated for small helicopter tires; the tanks shut off as capacity is reached. As a safety backup, their hoses are run through yellow boxes to vent excess gas. With no fail-safe, Pete hooked up the hose directly to a tire—not standard practice, but not too risky as long as the controlled nitrogen source is in place. Roten never informed him that it wasn't working before his order to manipulate the high-pressure side. "I don't think Pete knew what he meant," Cox maintained. He didn't know he was unleashing a forceful and ungoverned source of the gas.

The question of who actually turned on the nitrogen remains a mystery, even to Cox. It wasn't Roten, who had moved to the aircraft's other side. It probably wasn't Pete, who was kneeling next to the wheel about ten feet from the tank. It may have been Paul Bueche, who was walking toward the tire when it blew up. Whoever had manned the controls apparently didn't turn off the gas quickly enough, though it wouldn't have taken long to overfill the tire and blow the steel wheel into deadly pieces.

At a capacity of 2,500 pounds per square inch, the high-pressure tank blasted enough nitrogen to overinflate the car-sized tire in a matter of seconds. Its capacity was 140 psi.

The Cox revelations amounted to a bombshell. The army investigation had cited Pete for failing to question an "improper directive," for using an unregulated tank, and for inflating the tire beyond capacity. But if Pete had not known the equipment was broken and that he was being asked to perform an unorthodox procedure, how could he have known that the order was improper or that he was overinflating the tire? "Pete had no responsibility in this accident," Cox insisted.

Roten had returned to Alabama after his guard unit left Iraq and worked as a civilian technician maintaining Black Hawk helicopters at an army facility in Mobile. When I had checked in with him by phone before speaking to Cox, he told me Pete had impressed him with his experience and seemed like a safe bet to operate the cart. He couldn't recall much of his preaccident discussion with Pete, including whether he had informed him of the equipment trouble before asking if he had ever used a cart. After interviewing Cox, I called back. Roten allowed that Pete may not have known of the malfunction.

With Roten's memory's spotty and Pete's blank, it's impossible to know exactly what happened. At the least, there was a tragic breakdown in communication. Pete probably had professed experience with nitrogen carts—Cox said he had heard him lay such claim. But he must have been referring to *functional* units. Roten may have assumed Pete knew about the malfunction and was referring to carts in *any* condition. The worst Pete could be accused of was failing to stress his limited capability. Roten, however, had given him no reason to think that kind of disclaimer was necessary. Less than eighteen months later, he was ready to take responsibility. "I should have stepped up and said we are not going to do this until we get the right equipment," he told me.

When I reported my findings to Pete, he was alternately relieved to be vindicated and furious at the army for making him the fall guy. But he couldn't feel exonerated without the blessings of Paul Bueche's parents. He hoped to visit them in Alabama on Memorial Day. He didn't know how welcome he'd be. But Pete was ready to try. If they wouldn't see him, "I'll just go to Paul's grave," he told me.

In late March, the Bueches brought their twin daughters to Washington for a special Iraq war memorial event. They stopped by the *Time* office for coffee and we talked about Paul and the army's disappointing investigation. I had told Pete they were coming, and he asked me to test the waters for a visit in late May. When I did, Maria lit up. "We'd love to meet him," she said. Memorial Day would work well for them. Maria even invited me to join Pete on the trip.

★

Home had become another hospital room for Bobby Isaacs. He was as cooped up as he'd ever been in his twelve months at Walter Reed. Bobby had blown out of the Washington facility in mid-December, eager to get back to the rolling hills of North Carolina. But his family's double-wide in the periphery of Roxboro, population nine thousand, wasn't ideally suited for a twenty-three-year-old man without legs. Lacking prostheses or a car with hand-controlled brakes, he had only a wheelchair for transportation, not the best vehicle for a five-mile trip to the nearest retail hub. Even getting a little fresh air was hard in a place without sidewalks. His only social outlet was offered by the services and Bible study at the Liberty Baptist Church in Durham. Twice a week, Pat piled him and his wheelchair, grandmother, and aunt into her Explorer and drove the twenty-eight miles directly south.

Moving back home required a major adjustment. Bobby had left for the army two years earlier, a religious boy from a small town who took a big bite of the world. He loved the freedom and comradeship of soldiers. Even Walter Reed, with its crisp, regimented ways and soldiers who shared Bobby's values and interests, had a military flavor. Now he was living under a roof he had outgrown. His old high school friends seemed immature to a man who had traveled so far. He had to rely completely on the women who had raised him, a sometimes frustrating dependency. Deciding to start a workout program, he asked Pat to buy him a set of dumbbells. But she was busy catching up on things that had gone wanting for a year, and Bobby had to wait a full month for her to get to the store. He had little more than TV and video games as distractions.

When he departed Walter Reed, he had only a prosthesis for his left stump. He donned it just to make himself feel complete, but he couldn't stand up on it. His left knee was too rickety; he needed something on the right side to balance him. His right stump had been reshaped by bone spur surgery before he left Washington and had to be refitted for a fake leg. After Christmas, Pat drove him to the VA hospital in Durham to start the process, and they were told he needed a doctor's referral before he could see a prosthetist. The first doctor's appointment available was six weeks away.

Bobby responded like a starving man who stumbled into a café and was told that lunch was no longer being served. He demanded to see a doctor right away, refusing to leave until he did. All he needed was two minutes to obtain a referral. When the nurse wouldn't budge, Bobby told her, "I met a whole bunch of people in Washington, and I'm going home and call on them if I have to." He headed down to the ER for help but couldn't find anyone to speed up the date for an appointment. Only after Pat intervened with a social worker did the VA agree to see him earlier.

The prosthesis for his right leg arrived January 18. Bobby brought the new leg home and sunk both stumps into hard plastic sockets, standing on two feet for the first time since his short-lived breakthrough at Walter Reed four months earlier. He walked without crutches from his bedroom to the den, then to the kitchen, staying upright for fifteen minutes. When he sat down for a break, his left knee froze. He pulled himself up, but the knee hurt too much to walk on.

After several adjustments to his left prosthesis in February, an orthopedist informed Bobby that the knee might have to go. Before they cut, prosthetists offered a few ideas for relieving the pressure. They rigged up a strap from his belt to the prosthesis to keep the knee straight; it also left it stiff. Next came a leather corset that laced from knee to groin and was designed to shift his weight to the thigh; it allowed him to walk but didn't stop the pain and natural stiffening of the knee.

Come April, it would be a year since Bobby had promised Liberty Baptist Church that he would be walking again. Pastor Jack Cox was waiting for the day when Bobby would stride onstage and realize his prediction. So was Pat, who wanted her fellow worshippers to see the living miracle that had resulted from their prayers. She relied heavily on her faith and attributed Bobby's survival and recovery directly to it. In January, she had planned to give witness at a prayer meeting, something she had never done in her fifteen years at the church. Her testimony would have been simple: "Thank God that last year is over." But the morning of the meeting, Pat lost her nerve. Bobby would give witness for her when he walked to the pulpit himself.

Bobby was quiet about his religion. He was raised to read the Bible and love God and not to lord it over others. Yes, he strayed from a Christian lifestyle during his army days. Yes, he avoided church then. No, he wasn't proud of it. He knew right from wrong. He had just put *right* on hold. Bobby took it off hold after his near-death experience. "When God did that, I had all those people praying for me," he told me over the phone in early spring. "I know those prayers helped me through it. If those people were willing to do that and pray for me . . ." He was about to say that the least he could do was rededicate himself to God. But Bobby stopped for a reason. He believed their prayers and his brushes with mortality could only have led him in that direction. For a full commitment to his faith, he'd have to make an affirmative decision himself.

For starters, he would answer the prayers of many by walking into Liberty Baptist. By early March, Bobby realized he wouldn't be able to move comfortably on artificial limbs for a long time and probably would need more surgery. But pressure to walk into church on two legs had built each time he wheeled himself into a service and sat in the back of the sanctuary. So he decided to get it over with and picked the first Sunday in April as the day he would reach his pew on foot.

I flew to Durham for the big event, arriving on Saturday, April 2. Bobby had invited me to his home, a drive down country roads that ended at a rural mailbox marked by patriotic colors and the words, "We won't forget." He greeted me in his wheelchair and introduced his aunt and grandmother, who were sitting with Pat in a den furnished in comfortable chairs and collections of antique dishes, old coke bottles, and military coins. We chatted for a while and left for a steak dinner at a local restaurant, where we ran into church friends who prattled about the "big day."

Bobby was subdued on the eve of his comeback. He seemed to feel more obliged than honored. I realized why as he climbed into his prostheses before dinner. When he bent his left knee, it crackled like the sound of dry twigs snapping. A skin graft on his left stump, rubbed raw by the hard plastic shell, oozed bloody fluid. Yes, Bobby could walk on two legs, but not without crutches and painkillers. He would be celebrating a hollow victory the next day. Bobby didn't like pretense. But the show had to go on and he'd be there on time. He had prayers to answer.

The morning service began at eleven o'clock. Liberty Baptist looked a lot like it did the previous April, with patriotic bunting skirting the pulpit and little American flags sprouting from planters. Bobby's grandmother, decked out in a red, white, and blue sweater and shawl, anchored the third-row pew reserved for the family. Pat, her sister, and one of their brothers joined her in the large modern chapel. The place was packed with young families and elderly men dressed in suits and medal-laden blue American Legion hats. Expectations for Bobby's appearance ran high. "It will signal the beginning of the rest of his lifetime," Renée Cox told me. "He's saying to us and everybody else, 'Hey, I'm back.'"

Bobby was waiting offstage. He had spent the morning getting ready to play the leading man. Slipping into his prostheses, he had tightly secured his left stump to prevent it from sliding. He spent a good deal of time combing his strawberry-blond curls over his forehead. He fussed about the tailoring of his new charcoal-gray suit, which he smartly set off with a powder-blue shirt and dark blue polka-dot tie. Before getting into Pat's Explorer, he had gobbled down a fistful of Percocets to ease his pain.

The church choir started out the service with a few patriotic songs, followed by a reprise of the short documentary on Bobby and a news clip of Doc Perez proclaiming, "It's a miracle he's alive." As the lights came back on, Pastor Cox emerged from the choir door. Clasping his hands, he recalled Bobby's prediction at the church a year earlier.

"I want us to welcome Bob Isaacs," said Cox. "He's walking today."

Bobby entered from left of the preacher. He slowly planted

THE PRIZE ★ ★ 257

one black oxford after another, leaning on crutches for balance. It took him ten seconds to complete the ten-foot walk to the podium. The congregation was on its feet and applauding each of Bobby's steps. Finally, he laid down his crutches on a chair and stood unassisted next to Cox.

The two-minute standing ovation moved Bobby. This was his church family. He had not only survived; with the help of medical science, he had returned whole. For a brief moment, as he gazed on hundreds of faces, Bobby forgot that he had ever left home, that he had strayed from the church's strict moral teachings, that he jumped into the jaws of war and only narrowly escaped.

A bolt of pain from his left knee brought Bobby back to the here and now. He remembered where he'd been and where he was—in the temple of God, a witness to his own amazing survival. Bobby broke into one of his choirboy smiles, dimpled and innocent. Then his composure changed, just as suddenly, and he brushed away a tear.

After the clapping subsided, Cox noted the extra height Bobby had gained from his prostheses. "I've got to look up to him," he joked. "When Bob left here, I said he's still a boy and he will come back a man. He is a man today. He served our country with just tremendous honor and pride."

The preacher asked his witness about life at Walter Reed and his generally upbeat moods in the face of continuous disappointment. "If there's any bitterness in this guy, I have never seen it," said Cox.

Bobby replied that whenever he got down, he reminded himself of "a lot of guys that were a lot worse off than me, other guys who didn't come home." He looked down at his legs and got a bit flustered. "I want to say thank you to everybody that has helped me and my family out." Then the young veteran walked offstage, moving even more slowly than when he entered. His pain was obvious to me. Bobby looked exhausted when he reached the pew and slid in next to his mother.

"I knew that one day you'd walk again," said the preacher. "God bless you, buddy." Cox gave a brief patriotic sermon and asked Bobby to come forward to greet worshippers after the service. Bobby moved on crutches to the foot of the pulpit. Hundreds of people stood in line to shake his hand or pose for a photo. When he got tired and sat down, he was handed Bibles to autograph.

Bobby warmed to the crowd. It was the first I'd seen him relax that weekend. Maybe he was just happy to have the spotlight dimmed a little. But I thought something else had happened, too. He had pulled up his roots two years earlier for a soldier's life. Faced with a soldier's death, the religious virtues he had left behind had "saved" him. On April 3, 2005, Bobby had come full circle, a man who embodied both worlds. He had found the right mixture of church and barracks. The pious boy who went to war was now decorated for both. It felt good to be home.

★

Luis Rodriguez kept a flip chart detailing the military toll of the Iraq war. He placed it at the entrance of his advanced school for medics. Every Monday, he drew a line through the previous week's number of dead and wounded and recorded the new tally. He hoped to bring a dose of hard reality home to his Fort Campbell trainees. The morbid count also reflected

THE PRIZE ★★ 259

the reality of Sergeant Rod's life eighteen months after that roadside bomb ended his career in the field: every day was Memorial Day.

Most Iraq war amputees retired from the military after recovery and picked up monthly disability payments. Sergeant Rod suited up and returned to the only place he could fight: the classroom. In truth, he never really left combat. His school was plastered with pictures of blown-up Humvees and bloodied soldiers. He relived his own dismemberment on the first day of each class.

Still, Rod was teaching, not fighting, an adjustment that didn't come easily. At the worst moments, when he questioned his worth, he recalled something his old commander had told him: "Other than dying, you've paid the ultimate sacrifice." But that didn't stop him from longing for action. He could still shoot a gun and dope out a battle plan. Why shouldn't he be out there? Breathing life into the wounded, carrying them to safety? That was his job, more importantly his goal, ever since he could remember. Rod felt guilty for failing to bear his share of the danger.

He tried to keep those feelings bottled up, even on the actual day of remembrance, May 30, 2005. At noon, he got into his red Nissan pickup and drove seven minutes to a new war memorial at the Fort Campbell headquarters of his beloved 502nd Infantry Regiment. The granite block topped by a black heart symbol of the "5-0-Deuce" was dedicated to its members killed in Iraq. Rod studied the little bronze plaques dedicated to three close comrades. He stood by himself for a couple minutes and recalled each man, then drove off in his truck and pushed it to the back of his mind.

He was cried out from the special service that his Church of God had held the day before. When Rod had seen Specialist Baker's face for the first time in the newspaper the previous April, he broke down. Seeing it again now, enlarged on a screen, served as an emotional trip wire. In Mosul, he had been the combat medic of his dreams. And almost as soon as it was realized, the dream was taken away. The pictures that conjured his moment of greatest triumph also brought back his most profound loss.

Along with his flinty independence, he had forsaken his sense of omnipotence. When he was lying in a Humvee soaked in his own blood, he didn't pray for the chance to dodge another bullet or rescue another soldier. He asked to see his daughters again. Rod now had faith in more than his own power. He believed in the strength of relationships, the ties to family, students, friends—and memories.

They were his destiny now.

★

Bobby Isaacs was becoming a minor celebrity in the world of fundamentalist Baptists. It started after Bobby walked to the pulpit of his Durham church on two prosthetic legs. Soon, preachers from as far away as Tampa, Florida, were calling and asking him to give testimony to their congregations.

The demand put Bobby in a bind. He believed that nothing less than the hand of God reached into his Humvee in Iraq and saved him. How else did he stay alive after he stopped breathing three times and needed to have his entire blood volume replaced twice? "No such thing as luck," he once told me. But Bobby felt no need to broadcast his blessing, no calling to go door-to-door for Jesus. The day he walked into his own church, he hadn't even mentioned God. When his pastor had given him an opening by asking how he stayed so upbeat, Bobby kept his response secular.

He had the time to travel for speaking gigs. Eighteen months after returning from Iraq, his left knee was so painful he scheduled a thirty-ninth operation in June to amputate it. Until he was fully recovered and could walk easily, he would put off efforts to find a college program or a job. He had enough money—$3,000 a month in military pension—to live comfortably in the meantime.

For every request to speak publicly Bobby asked himself a simple question: Will it help soldiers and their families? The answer came back "yes" to an invitation from a church in Asheboro, North Carolina, a mill town about eighty-five miles west of home. Bobby was asked to participate in a Memorial Day service on Sunday, May 29, a chance to wave the flag for troops in Iraq.

Bobby drove there in a new Dodge Ram he had bought in March. He could accelerate and brake the truck with the prosthesis on his right stump, so he didn't need hand controls. He did need crutches to take the pressure off his left knee as he walked into Bailey's Grove Baptist Church and met Pastor Jon Shook. Shook had booked Bobby for two services—the church was undergoing construction and couldn't accommodate in one seating the heavy turnout expected for a VIP like Bobby.

The services followed a format similar to Liberty Baptist, opening with the short biographical film. Bobby approached the pulpit on crutches, laying them against the podium as he faced Shook. The preacher drew out Bobby's testimony in an interview format, but couldn't help interjecting at one point that the woman hugged in the film by President George W. Bush at Walter Reed hospital was Bobby's mother. Shook was as solicitous of his twenty-four-year-old guest as a Little League coach hosting a Major League player at a team practice.

Bobby didn't have a swelled head. He was humble and laconic as always. His story rolled out easily, punctuated by occasional flashes of humor. Explaining how doctors had given him seventy-two hours to live and had medically retired him to increase his family's benefits, he chuckled. "I fooled 'em."

"Yes sir, God fooled us all, didn't he?" Shook declared. "God had a different plan, didn't he? Praise the Lord."

Bobby didn't go out of his way to credit divine grace, even when he was reciting the quirks of fate that saved him. If he had been sitting down, as his staff sergeant in front of him had been, he would have been killed. If Doc Perez had been riding in Bobby's Humvee that day, as he usually did, the medic would have been wounded and unable to practice his extraordinary lifesaving techniques on Bobby. For some reason, Doc had jumped into another vehicle. Only once did Bobby mention a higher being: "God took care of me and got me to the hospital and got me back home."

The preacher gave him a plaque, a $300 check, and tearful thanks. Bobby saluted the church "for caring, not so much about me, but there are a lot of guys out there who do deserve it." He was treated like a rock star after each service, surrounded by hundreds of worshippers who wanted to shake his hand, exchange a few words, snap a photo, or get him to auto-graph their Bibles.

Bobby's injury had contributed more than a couple of inches of height; he had grown in stature. He had become a revered figure in his community who had an audience and a story to tell. He got there through sacrifice, the cornerstone of his faith and patriotism. But in Bobby's world, heroes do more than take a hit. They do something for others. He talked about going to school to become a physician's assistant, a job where he could return the biggest favor of all: a life.

★

A little voice kept telling Pete Damon he was walking into a trap. I kept reassuring him that Maria Bueche's invitation to the Memorial Day gathering was completely sincere. But as the date neared, Pete began to worry he was being lured there so she could interrogate him about the accident. As a ser-geant, he outranked her son, Paul. As an aviation mechanic, he had more experience. Pete could imagine leading ques-tions about his responsibility for Paul's death.

Pete and Jenn made the nine-hundred-mile leg from Brockton to Savannah, Georgia, in sixteen hours. Feeling in-creasingly anxious, Pete decided to spend the night there, rather than traveling on as originally planned to the Bueches' home in Daphne, Alabama. Was he really ready to do a few rounds with his ghosts? He was still recovering from the acci-dent himself, still living at his mother's house while the con-struction of his own was hitting snags, still figuring out how to earn a living with no hands, still relying on larger and larger doses of methadone to deal with the crushing pain in his phantom hands. But he had come this far to ease his psyche. No turning back now.

The Damons rolled into Daphne on May 29. I had agreed to play chaperone and was waiting at a local motel. We drove a few miles through the pretty, affluent town on the eastern shore of Mobile Bay, reaching the Bueches' rancher just after six o'clock. We were greeted by Maria and her husband, also named Paul—at home their son had gone by the nickname P.J., he told us. He was a genial, burly man with a mane of gray hair who earned his living as a buyer for Saks, Inc.

As Paul led us into a sitting room for drinks, Pete's discomfort was palpable. He was stretching the muscles in his neck and shoulders to relieve the tension, like a prizefighter loosens up in the ring before the fight. His right stub, sheathed in the short sleeve of a red plaid shirt, stabbed the air for emphasis as he tried to make small talk. He held a beer awkwardly in his left hook.

Maria, a petite, gracious woman, broke the ice with a tour of her exotically landscaped backyard garden. It was the right place to reminisce about P.J., who had apparently loved the outdoors and saved wild creatures, including a noisy dove named Tweety that flew over to Maria's shoulder as if on cue. Maria pointed out a place where Paul had once built a fort. Pete allowed how he had built one himself at the same age. Before long, everyone was sharing Paul stories and relaxing. Pete recalled how Paul was a smoking buddy, a happy-go-lucky kid who was so irrepressible that one day a couple of the guys held him down while others wrapped his arms and legs in duct tape and taped his mouth shut. The Bueches wanted to know if P.J. had received their packages or talked about his pet snake Elvis. They proudly walked us through photo albums of the lanky, bushy-browed P.J. as a young boy, his high school athletic trophies, medals, and even a few pieces of shrapnel that he had collected in Iraq and were sent home with his personal possessions.

P.J. had led a privileged life of private schools, resort membership, and cotillion dance classes in a genteel southern town. Pete's Brockton occupied a different social latitude. But tragedy breeds its own soul mates. The Bueches were channeling P.J. through a man who had stood next to him in the last moments of his life. Pete yearned to shed the guilt of not doing more to keep him alive.

We were halfway through a dinner of filet mignon, two kinds of potatoes, and tomato salad when Pete broached the subject we had been tiptoeing around. He mentioned that someone had given him the *Flightfax* article in which he was quoted. "I want you to know, I would never have said that," Pete stated in a quivering voice, looking Paul in the eye. It had always been his cardinal rule to put safety above everything else. The mere suggestion that he might not have been prudent in Balad was so troubling, he told the Bueches, "this is on my head all the time."

Paul barely gave Pete a chance to finish. "We want you to know, we don't blame you for anything," he said. "You just go on with your life. We pretty much have come to terms with the whole situation. We got down to as much detail as we could." The senior Bueche said his family had pinpointed two reasons for the accident: lack of proper equipment and lack of supervision from commanding officers, who, he said, threw safety to the wind and sped up the overhaul of helicopters to "make a name for themselves."

Pete, his head bent, listened carefully from the other end of the table.

Maria noted her disgust with the accident investigators, whom she now believed had framed Pete to cover up the army's lapses in command and equipment. Pete had been in no position in Ward 57 to defend himself against the misleading findings of a closely held report. The truth had come out only after Randy Cox had the courage to stand up and disclose those lapses. Maria recalled how the colonel who delivered the report the previous July had the nerve to blame P.J. for obeying improper orders.

"We know it wasn't your fault, and hopefully you can put it behind you," interjected Paul, getting teary.

"Oh, I appreciate that," Pete replied, nodding his head.

"You have a beautiful lady to live with and two kids," said Paul, looking down the table at Jenn, who had barely spoken since arriving. "I want you to live for the day."

"Thank you, I appreciate it," Pete repeated. The room went silent for a few seconds as Pete shifted his gaze from Paul to Maria.

The verdict Pete had longed to hear had been delivered, yet despite his relief, he couldn't get past the awkwardness of the situation. Here he was eating steak with the family of the young man who had died a few feet from him. Part of Pete still believed he should have been the one who died, not his partner.

Maria served up cake, coffee, and more P.J. stories until

ten o'clock, when we left. The next morning, Paul would pick us up early for a trip to Mobile National Cemetery on the other side of the bay.

The Civil War–era graveyard was nearly empty when we entered through the tall white stucco columns just before nine o'clock. A soft spring rain was falling as Paul steered his gray Toyota sedan to the southern end of the cemetery and parked. He guided us to P.J.'s plot at the end of a row of simple headstones. As soon as we arrived, Pete berated himself for forgetting to bring something personal to leave.

"You brought yourself," said Paul. "That's enough." He and Maria lingered for a moment, then walked away to leave us alone.

Pete was churning emotionally as he faced the source of nineteen months of anguish and guilt. Breathing heavily, he rocked back and forth on the balls of his feet and folded his left hook across his chest. Grimacing, he stared at the engraved milestones of a short life: "Paul Joseph Bueche, Specialist, U.S. Army, Iraq, November 8, 1983–October 21, 2003, and beloved son and brother." Pete exhaled loudly and bowed his head. His knees buckled into a crouch. He closed his eyes and uttered the most important words of his life in silence. "I'm trying to remember what happened that day, Paul, but I just can't. Remember the frigging laughs we had before? You were the funniest guy there. You were the happiest guy there. I really liked you and respected you. I don't know why it had to be you, man."

Five minutes passed. Pete rose slowly. He moved a step back and stood next to Jenn, who had been holding an umbrella over him. Pete laid his short right stump on her shoulder and spoke plaintively. "He didn't have to die. Someone's stupid, careless mistake. I wish I could go back to that day."

Pete kept talking to no one in particular. "He was walking by the tire when this happened. A split second. If he just stayed a split second longer in that spot, wherever he went— just tied his shoes or whatever—he'd probably be here. I wish I knew what happened. I don't remember. All I got to go on is these reports and what people say."

His voice got harsher, his face angrier. "It really sucks that the army can't just say, 'Sorry, we made a terrible mistake. It shouldn't have happened.' And then I hear they were going out and saying Paul didn't have to do that; as if he could have refused to do that. Fuck those guys. He trusted them. Then, when something happens, they blame it on him? That's just terrible. When that colonel came around, I would have kicked him in the head. They would have thrown me in jail. That's just terrible."

Pete left Alabama feeling nearer to closure. He believed Paul had heard his silent graveside communion and understood his lingering distress. The Bueches had given him a measure of absolution.

The only one left to grant him clemency, he now realized, was himself. He had to stop the self-flagellation and second-guessing. The events nineteen months earlier were tragic, but over. For whatever reason, he had survived his partner. It was time to take the advice of Paul's father to count his blessings and move on.

A couple of weeks after the Memorial Day trip, Pete finally sounded ready to begin the process. "People look at us and say, 'Boy, you got it rough,' " he told me by phone in early June. "But we don't have it half as rough as the people who lost their lives. I'd much rather be here with no arms than be dead in a coffin right now. I don't know what my kids would do without me. It's better to lose a limb than to lose a life."

I had heard Pete say those words before—the first time I set eyes on him at Walter Reed, in fact. How brave I had thought he was to express that idea. But it took even more guts to live it—a job he'd just begun.

★

Early that summer I began a ritual. Once a week, I took Skyler and Olivia to breakfast at the Whole Foods coffee shop on the way to day camp. Over hot chocolate and muffins, my daughter chattered about her upcoming ballet recital and horseback riding, my son about Little League home runs and the Medal of Honor video game. Like most kids, they asked a lot of questions about what I had been like at their age, prompting me one morning to bring along a dog-eared copy of a favorite poem from my childhood, Rudyard Kipling's "If." My mother had introduced it after my father died, and it became a beacon for me. Simplifying the language, I walked them through two lines at a time and did my best to decode the symbolic language. One verse got their attention more than others: "If you can bear . . . to watch the things you gave your life to, broken, and stoop and build 'em up with worn-out tools." I had plenty of illustrations from my own life to share.

I was steadily settling into a rhythm at home as well. Rebekah was happily ensconced, picking up singing gigs and setting up a new studio under a skylight in the family room. Her son, Daniel, had adjusted to a new school and made friends easily. My priorities were shifting. When Michael Duffy asked me to cover a trip to Iraq by Deputy Defense Secretary Paul Wolfowitz, I honored my pledge to stay out of war zones and declined an assignment for the first time in my career. I was still recovering from my last military tour, though nerve-pain pills and electro-stimulation devices lessened my phantom pain. With a big assist from technology, I could pop the cork of a wine bottle, write on a word processor using verbal commands, and swim laps with a waterproof prosthesis. I was amazed by what I could do with one hand.

★

The seeds of understanding planted in Hal Wain's office back in February were taking a little longer to sink in. On July 3, Rebekah and I flew to Rancho Mirage, California, to celebrate my stepfather's ninetieth birthday. My mother hosted a party in the main ballroom of a swank hotel, The Lodge, for over sixty family members and friends, who dined on filet mignon and sautéed whitefish, danced to a saxophone and piano duo, and toasted the spry nonagenarian until nearly midnight. Inevitably, when the subject of my accident came up and led to admiring comments, I felt a familiar twinge of guilt and embarrassment. I still couldn't embrace the notion of my so-called heroism.

Lying awake that night, I was reminded of one of Wain's comments. I had been expressing my frustration about the fact that such a major ordeal had seemed to have so little effect on me—I was still the same impatient, competitive, and self-critical person I'd always been. If I had acted so nobly, why didn't I feel more content? Wain's response at the time struck me as somewhat facile: rather than bring about change, he said, the good deed had left me angry at myself. "You're thinking you could have done the same thing and didn't have to lose the hand. You love a perfect win, and didn't get that perfect victory that you wanted and maybe deserved."

As I tossed and turned in the early hours of Independence Day, the simple truth of the psychologist's words hit me. It was true: I was mad at myself for failing to pull off a clean sweep. And it was that anger that was preventing me from savoring the achievement of a lifetime: saving my own skin and that of three others. My failure to get rid of the grenade before it exploded was only the first in a long list of wrongs I would have to pardon before I could finally put the ordeal behind me.

I had gone to Iraq for adventure and glory, discounting the interests of family and friends.

I had blithely ridden into danger with little to gain journalistically.

I had focused more on the loss of my hand than on the higher importance of preserving life.

The shortcomings were tough to swallow. But I was resolved to begin the process, keeping in mind Hal Wain's definition of heroism: self-preservation. By that standard, I had scored a perfect win after all. As had Pete, Bobby, and Luiz.

The prize was the rest of our lives.

NOTES

This exploration of human loss and redemption is based principally on interviews with three men who experienced both: Pete Damon, Luis Rodriguez, and Bobby Isaacs. I spent dozens of hours speaking to each of them in the eighteen months after my arrival at Walter Reed. The book's depiction of their thought processes and perceptions arises directly from those conversations. I drew on a wealth of material to corroborate and fill out their accounts, gathering the recollections of family, friends, and caretakers and pursuing a documentary trail left by hospital records, diaries, e-mails, and calendar entries. As the book's fourth subject, I learned firsthand the pitfalls of memories strained by narcotics and pain. I attempted to report my own story as rigorously, using the same tools to gain clarity. In all, I interviewed more than one hundred people for the book, those

who provided insight into the struggles of wartime amputees
and their own battles as supporting characters.

Prologue

The account of Corporal Bobby Isaacs at the Bailey's Grove Baptist Church is based on interviews with him and Pastor Jon
Shook and a tape recording of his remarks.
Details of Sergeant First Class Luis Rodriguez at his church are
from him.

I. Toy Soldier

The description of events in the Humvee is based on interviews
with Jim Nachtwey, Pfc. Jim Beverly, Private Orion Jenks, and
Specialist Billie Grimes.
The account of the Gunner Palace aid station and drive to the
helipad is from Nachtwey, Beverly, and Grimes.
The description of medical treatment of Nachtwey, Beverly, and
Jenks is theirs. The dialogue between me and the nurse was
re-created from interviews with the nurse, Major Donna
Lehman, a Massachusetts reservist.
The conversation with Captain Nina McCoy was re-created
from interviews with McCoy and *Time* magazine news direc-
tor Howard Chua-Eoan.
The identification of Sergeant Pete Damon as the soldier in Mc-
Coy's story was arrived at by the process of elimination. Mc-
Coy refused to divulge the name to protect the confidentiality
of the soldier. Pete has a vague memory of such a conversation; he isn't absolutely sure because he was heavily sedated.
But according to U.S. Army databases and word of mouth,
two double-arm amputees other than Pete preceded me at
Landstuhl. One was already married; the other was single and
had no plans for marriage. A third soldier had lost one hand

and the thumb and index finger from his other hand. He also was married before going to Iraq.

The search for Dr. Andrew Friedman was described to me by my sister, Leslie Flesch, and the doctor she consulted, Gary Gitnick, of the University of California.

The conversation between Leslie and Friedman is from Leslie's notes as confirmed by Friedman.

The behind-the-scenes campaign to get me into Walter Reed was described by *Time*'s Michael Duffy and Mark Thompson.

The call to Congresswoman Eleanor Holmes Norton from WTOP radio political analyst Mark Plotkin was described to me by Plotkin. Norton and Acting Army Secretary Les Brownlee confirmed the call from Norton to Brownlee.

The description of me as the first reporter wounded in war to receive treatment at Walter Reed came from the Walter Reed public affairs office; the hospital's unofficial historian, John Pierce, who is writing a book on the institution, knew of none other; nor did Vietnam War patient Jack Farley. A search of newspapers and magazines by the *Time* library staff found nothing to contradict them.

The account of Corporal Bobby Isaacs's injury and rescue is from Isaacs and medics Dorian "Doc" Perez and Neil Mulvaney.

The information about Bobby's seventy-two-hour death watch is from his medical records and two of his surgeons, Lt. Col. Dennis Eastman and Major Yong Choi.

The description of Bobby on the C-141 aircraft flight to Washington is from Bobby and Howard Chua-Eoan.

2. Ward 57

The description of the challenges to Ward 57 nurses is from Major Tammy LaFrançois.

The Walter Reed history was provided by Dr. John Pierce, a

pediatrician and retired colonel in the U.S. Army Medical Corps who worked at Walter Reed for fifteen years.

The Vietnam War years at Walter Reed were described by Jack Farley, U.S. Army captain, who lost his right leg above the knee in January 1969 and recovered at the hospital.

The Bush visit controversy was re-created with the help of LaFrançois and Major General Kevin Kiley, then commander of Walter Reed.

Statistics on amputees and their percentage among the wounded are from military databases, including the Defense Department's Directorate for Information Operations and Reports and the U.S. Army Medical Department's Medical Evacuation Statistics, compiled by the Office of the Army Surgeon General, and Amputee Care Program Database, compiled by Colonel Chuck Scoville, retired, program manager for U.S. Army Amputee Care Program.

The historical comparisons are from John Greenwood, the U.S. Army's medical historian.

Details on Sergeant First Class Luis Rodriguez as a platoon sergeant are from Rodriguez and two of his platoon members, Specialist Nicholas Cutcher and Staff Sergeant Neil Mulvaney.

The account of Rodriguez as a patient in the 21st Combat Support Hospital is from Lt. Col. Mary R. Miles.

The descriptions of Rodriguez's injury are from Rodriguez, Doc Perez, and Captain Daniel Morgan, Rodriguez's commander.

Background on Corporal Bobby Isaacs is from Bobby and his mother, Pat Isaacs.

Bobby Isaacs's role in the April 2003 battle of Karbala was described by Bobby's platoon leader, Lt. Mark Austin.

A description of Bobby in Mosul was provided by his platoon buddy Specialist Tim McKinnis.

The McKinnis words at Bobby's bedside are from McKinnis.

The personal and National Guard background on Sergeant Pete Damon is from Damon.

The description of Pete Damon's accident came from the Department of the Army's "Investigation Concerning the Death of Specialist Paul J. Bueche" and members of Damon's unit in Iraq: Sergeants Jason Roten and Dominic Alvini and then-Specialist Randy Cox.

The account of Pete in the Humvee is from Pete and Alvini, who accompanied him.

The explanation of the high survival rate in Iraq and statistics are from John Greenwood and Colonel Paul Cordts, director of health policy and services, Office of the Army Surgeon General.

The description of Sergeant Luis Rodriguez's battlefield actions, including his Bronze Star heroics, is based on a written commendation from his superiors.

The account of Rodriguez's rescue is from Rodriguez and his medic Doc Perez.

The rescue of Bobby Isaacs was described by Perez.

"Get the surgeon," was said by a 21st CSH nurse, Lt. Heidi Miller.

The Bobby Isaacs operation was described by two of the surgeons at the 21st CSH, Lt. Col. Dennis Eastman and Major Yong Choi.

The description of the blood drive to transfuse Bobby is from Captain Lisa Moore, a medical technologist who headed the blood bank and general lab at the 21st CSH; Lt. Col. Mary R. Miles, head of the emergency room; Major Linda Lapointe, head nurse of the ICU; Major Pat Fortner, head nurse of the operating room; and Staff Sergeant Sharon Vinston, a lab technician. Dr. Francis M. Chiricosta, medical director of blood services at Walter Reed Army Medical Center, provided general background on blood and transfusions.

The actions and thoughts of the surgeon are those of Dr. Yong Choi, who conducted the all-night vigil.

3. Cutting Time

The exchanges between me and Dr. Andrew Friedman and John Zenie were refreshed by interviews with them.

The description of the surgery was provided by Dr. Friedman.

The *Today Show* statement by Jim Nachtwey is from the program transcript.

The description of Rodriguez's December 8 operation is from Walter Reed records.

The account of Rodriguez's workouts, brief celebration, anger at the bad news, and reaction to the December 24 operation is from him.

The portrayal of Jim Mayer is based on an interview with Mayer and several Ward 57 alumni.

The account of "Mr. Nick" is from Mr. Nick, James Melvin Nicholas.

The description of difficulties encountered by Ward 57 nurses is from Major Tammy LaFrançois and nurse Tami Barr.

The LaFrançois reaction to a two-handed amputee is from LaFrançois.

The description of coping mechanisms of Mr. Nick and Barr is from each of them.

Captain Katie Yancosek's strategy for coping and her dealings with Heath Calhoun are hers, with details on Calhoun confirmed in an interview with Calhoun.

The description of a diagnosis and treatment of my pulmonary embolism is from Dr. Robert Browning, a pulmonary critical care fellow and lieutenant commander in the U.S. Navy, who cared for me at Walter Reed.

4. Hooks and Hearts

The description of Pete Damon's initial problems, gradual independence, and progress on his trip to Brockton is from Pete.

The personal background of Jenn Damon is from Jenn.

The description of Pete and Jenn's wedding is from them and their minister, Reverend Ivan S. Fleischman.

The exchanges between David Maraniss and Thomas Hinger is from Maraniss.

Details of exchanges with Marje Hoban were refreshed by an interview with Marje.

The description of psychologist Hal Wain's training tool and his staff's activities is from Wain.

The term "Cripples' Cavalcade" was coined by Staff Sergeant Andy McCaffrey, who told me about the meetings.

The description of Bobby Isaacs as an infant and as a patient having a nightmare is from Pat Isaacs's diary, supplemented by interviews; the same for Bobby's "Butt out" statement.

The way Pat Isaacs monitored Bobby's battalion in Iraq and learned of his injury is from Pat.

Pastor Jack Cox's remarks to his congregation on December 10 were described by Cox in an interview.

The description of Pat's first sight of her injured son and of her reaction to Bobby's desensitization is from Pat's diary and interviews.

The account of Katrina Fair's first reaction to her injured husband, her care of him, and her difficulties in convincing him of his lost hands and her description of his moods are from Katrina.

The description of Staff Sergeant Maurice Craft's wife, her activities, and his reaction to them is from Maurice. I could not find Andrea Craft to comment on Maurice's account.

5. Hornbook for the Handicapped

The description of how a myoelectric hand works is from prosthetist John Miguelez; description of phantom pain from various doctors and medical journals. Among the leading researchers into phantom limb pain whose work informed me are V. S. Ramachandran, head of the Brain Perception

Laboratory in the Department of Psychology at the University of California, and Ronald Melzack of McGill University.

The number and hours of Bobby Isaacs's operations came from Pat Isaacs's diary and Walter Reed records.

The descriptions of Bobby's wounds, the January 6 amputation of his right leg, and the three options for his left leg are from one of his surgeons, Captain Leon Nesti.

The description of peripheral nerve blocks is from Geselle Mc-Knight, research coordinator of the U.S. Army Regional Anesthesia and Pain Management Initiative at Walter Reed.

The reunion and conversations of Sergeant First Class Luis Rodriguez and Sergeant Derick Hurt were described by them in interviews.

6. New Muscles

National statistics on amputees are from prosthetist John Miguelez.

The hiring of Joe Miller and his impact on Walter Reed's policy toward prostheses was described by Miller.

Miguelez's plan for upper-extremity prostheses was described by him; the costs were provided by Walter Reed.

The descriptions of Staff Sergeant Andy McCaffrey's efforts to return to active duty and his training with a prosthesis are his.

The repartee between physical therapist Justin Laferrier and Sergeant First Class Luis Rodriguez was described by both men.

The description of Bobby Isaacs's work with therapist Isatta Jackson is hers.

The account of the initial call from John Gonsalves to Jenn Damon, and Pete's reaction to it, came from all three.

Details on Gonsalves's first view of Pete on NBC *Nightly News* and the impact of Pete's image are from Pete and Gonsalves.

The description of the interview with Mike Barnicle and subsequent call to his live radio show is from Pete and Gonsalves.

7. A Hero's Welcome

The description of how a prosthetic glove is made is Mike Curtin's. The cost of the Curtin glove was disclosed by Walter Reed.

The account of Brian Bennett's efforts to play Rebekah's song in Baghdad is from Brian.

The description and their cost of how C-legs work and their cost are from prosthetist Joe Miller.

Rodriguez's moodiness was reported by his wife, Lilliam Rodriguez.

The description of Rodriguez's April 18 reunion is from him, Lilliam, his former commander Captain Daniel Morgan, and one of his platoon members, Specialist Nicholas Cutcher.

The account of "Bobby Isaacs Sunday" at Liberty Baptist Church is based on a videotape of the event. Bobby and Pat provided details of his tearful reunion with Jordan Caldwell.

8. "Look Back, But Don't Stare"

The April 3 ceremony at Otis Air Force Base at which Pete Damon saluted with his hook was described in the *Brockton Enterprise*.

The description of the January 15 interview of Pete Damon by an army investigator is based on a transcript of the session.

The U.S. Army's promise to Maria Bueche to send a report on her son's death in about three months was disclosed by Maria.

The disclosure that the author of the *Flightfax* article, Major Ray Jenkins, had participated in the investigation of Specialist Paul J. Bueche's death came from *Flightfax*'s managing editor, Paula Allman. She referred all questions about the article to Jenkins, who did not respond to efforts to reach him.

Maria Bueche's May 1 barbecue was described by her.

The May 10 e-mail to Maria from one of her son's coworkers citing "faulty" tire-inflating equipment and the command's failure to fix it was made available to me by Maria.

The description of Colonel Ernest T. Erickson's July 5 visit to the Bueche residence and the exchange between Maria Bueche and Erickson is based on interviews with both parties.

9. Standing Up

Although Pete Damon said he had never seen Senator John F. Kerry at Walter Reed, the 2004 Democratic presidential nominee had in fact visited there on May 1, 2004.

The reactions of Ibrahim Kabbah and Isatta Jackson to Bobby Isaacs's first steps onto prostheses were described by each of them.

The scene in the Toys "R" Us store was described by Pete and Jenn Damon. The Damons retained a lawyer to pursue the complaint that Pete had first described to me in 2004. Before going to press in March 2006, I called the corporate headquarters in New Jersey to discuss the incident. Kelly Cullen, a senior public relations manager, said company policy prohibited employees, including the night manager in question, from speaking publicly about store business. After checking with the legal department, she said that "any grievances" that Pete had were "resolved to his satisfaction." When I asked if that meant a legal settlement had been reached, she declined to comment. Pete didn't want to discuss the case further when I reached him.

The incident with Southwest Airlines was reported by Pete and Jenn Damon.

The analysis of Pete Damon's role in *Fahrenheit 9/11* is based on a review of the NBC News interview of October 31, 2003, and Michael Moore's film. NBC's licensing policy was explained by a company spokesman in an August 9, 2004, article in the *Army Times.*

The fund-raising success of Homes for Our Troops after Pete signed on was described by its founder, John Gonsalves.

10. Anniversary

The safety lapses involved in the death of Sergeant Henry Ybarra III were revealed in the army's accident report of January 25, 2004.

11. The Unconscious Mind

The description of Luis Rodriguez's call to Lt. Col. Mary R. Miles and their meeting is from both of them.

Governor Mitt Romney's remarks are from news accounts of his State of the State message.

Descriptions of Pete's seizures and the session with the mental health professional are from Pete.

My dialogue with Pete at Malogne House was tape-recorded.

Remarks by Bobby Isaacs and Pastor Jon Shook of the Bailey's Grove Baptist Church were tape-recorded and provided to me by Shook.

Statistics on amputees and their percentage among the wounded are from military databases, including the Defense Department's Directorate for Information Operations and Reports and the U.S. Army Medical Department's Medical Evacuation Statistics, compiled by the Office of the Army Surgeon General, and Amputee Care Program Database, compiled by Colonel Chuck Scoville, retired, program manager for U.S. Army Amputee Care Program.

My session with psychologist Hal Wain was tape-recorded.

12. The Prize

The account of Corporal Bobby Isaacs at the Bailey's Grove Baptist Church is based on interviews with him and Pastor Jon Shook and a tape recording of his remarks.

Details of Sergeant First Class Luis Rodriguez at his church are from him and his wife.

ACKNOWLEDGMENTS

There would never have been a *Blood Brothers* if I had spilled more blood. Thanks to the skill of medic Billie Grimes, the surgery of Major Gregory Hill, and the nursing care of Majors Donna Lehman and Sonia Neumeier, I left Baghdad missing only a hand. My guardian angel, Brian Bennett, kept me as comfortable and sane as any new amputee could be and got me on the plane out. Bill Kalis helped to ease me on the long ride from the army field hospital to the Baghdad airport.

My hospitalization at Walter Reed was a privilege that I owe to the love and adeptness of my sister, Leslie Flesch, and the political sensibility of my childhood pal Mark Plotkin. Eleanor Holmes Norton was everything a congresswoman could be and Acting Secretary of the Army Les Brownlee was generous to open the doors of a great medical center. I was very lucky to have landed in the golden hands of Dr. Andrew Friedman and Dr. Al Seyfer. Lt. Col. Chester C. Buckenmaier III and his anesthesiology crew limited my pain with their peripheral nerve block. My doctors, including Lt. Col. Jeff Gambel and Lt. Commander Robert Browning, got me home. Hal Wain gave me the tools to move on.

Much of the material for *Blood Brothers* came from my three-week stint on Ward 57 and seventeen months as an active outpatient. Major Tammy LaFrançois indeed ran the Ritz-Carlton of hospital wards. Nurse Tami Barr was every patient's dream. Jim Mayer and Marje Hoban were rightfully known as "angels." No one helped me more than Captain Katie Yancosek, her boss, Colonel William Howard, and her band of "OTs," including Oren Ganz, Ibrahim Kabbah, and Harvey Naranjo. Thanks to Lt. Justin ("Muscle-ini") Laferrier, I fit into a thirty-two-inch waist. Prosthetist John Miguelez's assistants—Dan Conyers, John Zenie, Chuck Barnett, Rebecca DeLeon, Kristi Wolfgram, and Kristin Gulick—were skillful arms merchants. Mike Curtin's team showed how art can really change people's lives.

Not long after arriving at Walter Reed, I received a visit from *Washington Post* editor Bob Kaiser, who had almost died of a heart ailment earlier that year and welcomed me to the "near-miss club." He led a long list of friends and colleagues who cushioned my return home, including Demetra Lambros, Jim Warren, Larry Meyer, Michael Browning, David Cohen, Wayne Berman, Arne Christensen, Maralee Schwartz, Scott Reed, Karen Tumulty, Viveca Novak, Mark Thompson, Terry

McAuliffe, Peter O'Keefe, Mark Neuman, Mark Paoletta, Scott Pastrick, Bill Hamilton, Louis Berney, Arthur Earl Jones, Donald and Gay Kimelman, Mark Corallo, Susan Schmidt, Mary Martin, Massimo Calabresi and Guy Gugliotta, Matt Cooper, Babak and Muffy Razzaghi, Peter Frias, and David Mayers. Thanks also to my lawyer, David Schloss.

The idea of a book emerged after I left 57 and discovered that other war amputees were the only ones who really understood what I was going through. I hoped that a book would expand the universe. But I needed collaborators to tell the full story. I couldn't have asked for three better ones than Pete Damon, Luis Rodriguez, and Bobby Isaacs. They opened their hearts and minds to lead me through dark moments of suffering and shining breakthroughs of recovery. Equally generous were their family members, including Pat Isaacs, Lilliam Rodriguez, and Jenn and Janet Damon, and a cast of their medical caretakers: Specialist Dorian "Doc" Perez, Staff Sergeant Neil Mulvaney, Lt. Col. Dennis Eastman, Major Yong Choi, Major Don Gajewski, Captain Leon Nesti, Bart Vitelly, Isatta Jackson, Major Pat Fortner, Lt. Col. Mary R. Miles, Captain Lisa Moore, Major Linda Lapointe, Staff Sergeant Sharon Vinston. I learned about their backgrounds from close associates, such as Pastor Jack and Renée Cox, and their army buddies, including Captain Dan Morgan, Lt. Mark Austin, Staff Sergeant Joey Gaskin, Specialist Tim McKinnis, Specialist Derick Hurt, and Specialist Nicholas Cutcher. Maria Bueche was always brave and gracious on a difficult subject. Sergeant Randy Cox provided a conceptual breakthrough and Colonel Ernest Erickson and Sergeant Jason Roten patiently answered my questions.

Because of my days at Walter Reed as a patient, I had extraordinary access as a writer. Among those who smoothed the way were public affairs chief Lyn Kukral and her assistant Bill Swisher. Steve Springer did a wonderful job of tracking Ward 57 alumni and putting me in touch with them. Joe Miller taught me everything I needed to know about C-legs. Chuck Scoville kept me abreast of the latest statistics on Iraq war amputees. John Greenwood provided a historical perspective on the war and its casualties. John Pierce gave me colorful anecdotes of Walter Reed's past.

Thanks to my fellow passengers Jim Nachtwey, Jim Beverly, Orion Jenks for helping me re-create what happened in the Humvee the night of December 10.

My family at *Time*, led by managing editor Jim Kelly, aided every phase of my recovery and reentry. Michael Duffy pulled strings to get me out of Iraq and cared for me like a brother once I returned. I'd travel anywhere with Howard Chua-Eoan. Judith Stoler did everything to ease my hospital stay and my return home. Kelly gave me the time and encouragement to write this book. Camille Sanabria helped me stay solvent. I received other support from Jay Carney, Lisa Beyer, Romesh Ratnesar, Michele Stephenson, Brooks Kraft, Sheila Charney, and Sharon Roberts.

Blood Brothers is an odd mixture of memoir and biography, a concept inspired by my treasured agent, Joni Evans, and Henry Holt editor in chief Jennifer Barth. Jennifer kept me honest and focused on the trajectory of three protagonists, an effort that deserves a silver star for editing prowess. Joni retired as I completed my manuscript, leaving Suzanne Gluck to push me past the goalpost.

The importance of friends and family highlighted my recovery, as it did the production of this book. My first and
toughest editor, Marci Stillerman, aided everything from
word choice to streamlining. David Maraniss provided sound
advice and smart changes to the manuscript, as did Valerie
Straus. Michael Flesch helped me excavate what I had done in
the Humvee. Judith Katz encouraged the book along with
every phase of my recovery. My kids, Skyler and Olivia, kept
a close eye on their role and kept my heart filled with love,
along with my stepson, Daniel Edminster, in-laws, David and
Elizabeth Edminster, and stepfather, Jack Stillerman.

Rebekah touched every part of this book, as she had my
life. The kind Ivan S. Fleischman, who married the Damons,
did the same for us in October 2005. As *Blood Brothers* went
to press, Rebekah gave birth to a baby girl, Mari Isabella,
whose right hand is a miniature replica of my own.

INDEX

ABOUT THE AUTHOR

A senior correspondent for *Time* magazine,
Michael Weisskopf is coauthor of *Truth at Any
Cost* (with Susan Schmidt) and *Tell Newt to
Shut up* (with David Maraniss), a Pulitzer Prize
finalist, and winner of the George Polk Award,
Goldsmith Award for Investigative Reporting,
National Headliners Award, Daniel Pearl Award
for Courage and Integrity in Journalism, and
Everett McKinley Dirksen Award for Distin-
guished Reporting of Congress. Weisskopf lives
in Washington, D.C.